Globetrotting

SPORT AND SOCIETY

Series Editors
Randy Roberts
Aram Goudsouzian

Founding Editors
Benjamin G. Rader
Randy Roberts

*A list of books in the series appears
at the end of this book.*

Globetrotting

*African American Athletes
and Cold War Politics*

DAMION L. THOMAS

UNIVERSITY OF ILLINOIS PRESS
Urbana, Chicago, and Springfield

First Illinois paperback, 2017
© 2012 by the Board of Trustees
of the University of Illinois
All rights reserved
1 2 3 4 5 C P 5 4 3 2 1
♾ This book is printed on acid-free paper.

The Library of Congress cataloged the cloth edition as follows:
Thomas, Damion L.
Globetrotting : African American athletes and
Cold war politics / Damion L. Thomas.
p.   cm.—(Sport and society)
Includes bibliographical references and index.
ISBN 978-0-252-03717-7 (hardcover : alk. paper)—
ISBN 978-0-252-09429-3 (e-book)
1. African Americans—Sports—History.
2. Sports—United States—History.
3. African American athletes—Social conditions.
4. Racism in sports—United States.
5. Discrimination in sports—United States.
6. Cold War—Influence.
7. United States—Politics and government—1945–1989.
I. Title.
GV583.T53   2012
796.08996073—dc23   2012009672

Paperback ISBN 978-0-252-08263-4

To Johnnie Pearl Knox,
who through the sheer force of her willpower
raised me to be the man that I am today

Contents

Acknowledgments

This book would not have been possible without the support of a number of scholars, teachers, friends, and family members. As hard as it is to do so, there are three who are deserving of the highest thanks: Andrew Knox, Jaime Goodreau, and Robert Hill. Andrew Knox is my grandfather, and my role model. I don't really know if he knows all of the things that I learned by watching him. He had a love of reading. When I was a boy he would read two newspapers every night, and he helped me develop a love of reading. Jamie Goodreau was my high school history teacher. Her ability to connect the past to the present, as well as her passion for the subject, has had a lifelong impact on me. She was the first teacher to inspire me, and for that I am truly grateful. When I started my undergraduate education at UCLA, I wanted to be a sports executive. However, Professor Robert Hill's Introduction to African American History class changed my life. I decided that I wanted to have the same impact on my students as he had on me. He taught me how to read critically and gave me a language through which I could explain the African American experience.

During the decade that I spent at UCLA, I met a number of people who have had a lasting impact on me, and I want to make sure that I acknowledge their contribution: Tsekani Browne, Keidra Morris, Sydney Reece, La'Tonya Reese Miles, Valerie Smith, Sidney Lemelle, Mark Sawyer, Jessica Millward, Brandi Brimmer, Rochelle Watson, Henry Yu, Mark Sawyer, Ellen DuBois, Jessica Wang, Sheila Patel, Barbara Bernstein, Brenda Stevenson, J. Arch Getty, Jan Reiff, Joan Waugh, Erika Blum, Fernando Barbosa, Darnell Hunt, Michelle Talley, Nhlanhla Thwala, Dan O'Neill, Daniel Negash, Sean Anglon, Hamid Qasim, Ayana Herbert, Shani O'Neal,

Scot Brown, Shantina Jackson, Ebony Utley, Mary Dudziak, Richard Lap-chick, Jeffrey Sammons, Laura Belmonte, Martha Biondi, Robert Edelman, Susan Brownell, Douglas Hartmann, Michael Krenn, Maureen Smith, Jules Tygiel, Penny Von Eschen, Mark Scoggins, Michelle Peace, Mieko Davis, Deckard Hodge, Samuel Steinberg, Holicynth Bryan, John Alston, Douglas Daniels, Claudine Michel, Fredrik Logevall, Reginald Sims, Althea Sims, Aaron Howard, Michael Walker, Darron Walker, Malinda Williams, Doris Sims, Maliaka Howard, Althea Howard, Melvin Sims, Tamara Benefield, Calvin Madlock, Lawrence Williams, Bonnie Williams, Ranell Holmes, Kenneth Osgood, as well as the staff at Magic Johnson's Starbucks.

Similarly, I want to thank all of the people I met while I was employed by the University of Illinois at Urbana-Champaign. You have all helped me reach my goals: C. L. Cole, Sundiata Cha-Jua, Fanon Che Wilkins, Bar-rington Edwards, Monica White, Karen Flynn, Mark Perry, Clarence Lang, Helen Neville, Adrian Burgos, David Roediger, Brendesha Tynes, Wojtek Chodzko-Zajko, Synthia Sydnor, Tom Weissinger, Barbara Keys, Nicole Robinson, Porsche Montgomery, Edwin Wilson, Kira Barber, Chrystalyn LaGarde, James Anderson, Christopher Spann, Antoinette Burton, Kristin Hoganson, Erik McDuffie, Linda West, Tina Candler, Corean Elam, Ker-suze Simeon, Mark Dyreson, Leonard Moore, C. Keith Harrison, David K. Wiggins, Carol Anderson, Michael Lomax, James Coates, Othello Harris, Stephanie Lang, Yvonne Smith, Tricia Vanderkooy, Akilah Carter, Emmitt Gill, Rueben Buford May, Jeffrey Ogbar, and John Singer.

Last, I would like to thanks the many friends, colleagues, and cowork-ers who have helped shape me as a scholar and person since I have been a faculty member at the University of Maryland–College Park: David Andrews, Jaime Schultz, Michael Silk, Shannon Jette, Jane Clark, Brad Hatfield, TaMira Peterson, Debbie Jones, Gniesha Dinwiddie, Jaslean La Taillade, Jeffrey McCune, Elsa Barkley Brown, Johanna McCants, Kevin Blackistone, Nicole Isaac, Sharon Harley, Dana Brooks, Odis Johnson, Kris Marsh, Dave Zirin, Ronald Smith, Kevin Witherspoon, Thomas Hunt, Ericka Ligon, Erika Van Buren, Fareed Nassor Hayat, Norrinda Brown, Tanya Ellis, Anitra Grisales, Derek Musgrove, Patrice Ford, Doris Corbett, the staff at Busboys and Poets, and my colleagues and the support staff at the University of Maryland–College Park.

To the editors and support staff at the University of Illinois Press, espe-cially Bill Regier and Dick Wentworth, thanks for believing in this project and putting in the hard work that was necessary to bring it to publication.

Finally, to my family in Los Angeles, especially Kimberly and April, I love you and I miss you.

Globetrotting

Introduction

In 1959 the United States State Department asked the six-foot-ten African American professional basketball player Bill Russell to take a goodwill tour of Libya, Liberia, the Ivory Coast, Sudan, and Ethiopia. Russell was an intriguing choice for a goodwill ambassadorship because he had a self-acknowledged reputation for being grouchy, opinionated, and ungrateful to the White Establishment. Described as one of the "most cantankerous figures ever to have walked across the American sports page," Russell did not try to curry favor with the public, especially if that meant being silent on racial abuses.[1]

Russell's "grouchiness" was sparked immediately upon his arrival in Africa: "The State Department representatives who greeted me were seedy, alcoholic types who started calling me 'boy' before I reached the last step of the exit ramp from the plane, and they spoke of their African hosts with contempt," Russell stated. "One after another they seemed to be arrogant louts, almost competitively eager to be racist. I was stunned."[2] Despite his experience with the American representatives, the energetic atmosphere, the pervasive air of expectation, and "the fever for independence" were invigorating.

"Why are you here?" was the initial question posed during a large press conference at Russell's first stop in Tripoli. The American State Department had warned him to be careful because communist writers would try to embarrass the United States through his visit. "I am here to play basketball and to show the people of Tripoli something about a sport which I love because I believe they will love it, too," Russell stated. This response revealed a truth that Russell would later admit: he was uninformed about international politics and unaware of the political undercurrents of his trip.[3]

Ostensibly, Russell traveled throughout Northern Africa conducting basketball clinics. He opened his presentations by explaining the sport with the aid of an interpreter. Thereafter, he would motion for the kids to stand. Singling out one of the young participants, he would playfully toss the ball in his or her direction. Basic passing and dribbling drills followed. Russell closed the clinics by holding his long arms in a huge circle so that the children could practice shooting baskets. The kids would be laughing, crawling all over him, and bubbling with energy when the clinic finally ended.

Bill Russell was energized by his experiences teaching basketball to the African youth: "I felt renewed by the notion that I could go out under the sky in a foreign land, with nothing but a hundred words and a basketball, and communicate so well with kids that within a half hour I'd see the same looks of joy that I'd felt with my first high leap. The experience made me feel like a magician."[4] The excitement, joy, and fun that accompanied the play activities did not require the aid of a translator. Russell's experiences testify to the powerful communicative potential of athletics across linguistic and cultural barriers.

Toward the end of his trip, during a question-answer period held in a schoolroom in the upcountry section of Liberia, a young black child asked Russell a now familiar question: "Why are you here?" Unlike his earlier response, Russell, noted for his unemotional disposition on the basketball court, became choked with emotion: "I came here because I believe that somewhere in Africa is my ancestral home. I came here because I am drawn here, like any man, drawn to seek the land of his ancestors." With those two brief sentences, he "poured forth a deep, inner feeling" that he had never recognized. The feeling was so strong that it moved him to tears and ended the question-answer segment. Russell's comments caused the Liberian children to rise to their feet in a standing tribute to the passion, sincerity, and fraternal nature of his pronouncement.[5]

Why was Russell sent on a goodwill tour to teach basketball in Africa? The basketball champion initially suggested that his trip was motivated by a shared altruistic desire between him and the State Department to help promote the international growth of the American sport. His later explanation that his trip had helped him come to grips with his ancestry was certainly not the purpose of his State Department–sponsored tour. In fact, Russell's co-optation of the tour for his own personal growth and sense of identity had not been the desired outcome that the government had anticipated. Unsatisfied with both of Russell's explanations, I am venturing to provide a more nuanced, complex, and politically grounded answer to questions surrounding the State Department's use of African American athletes, including Russell and other middle-class black folks, as goodwill ambassadors.

Russell's trip and similar athletic tours provide ideal spaces to explore the deceptive use of popular culture as a manipulative tool of U.S. foreign policy. During the early days of the Cold War, international condemnation of U.S. domestic race relations was a major hindrance to American foreign policy objectives. Consequently, the State Department began to send prosperous African Americans on overseas goodwill tours to showcase African Americans as the preeminent citizens of the African Diaspora, rather than as victims of racism. These tours were designed to undermine anti-Americanism as a foundation for racial and political identity formation throughout the African Diaspora. Because sports were, arguably, the most publicly visible American institutions to integrate, athletes were prominently featured in the State Department campaigns.

The athletes themselves were, at times, victims of manipulation. Russell was such a victim. He was one of the most politically astute athletes of his generation; nonetheless, Russell still found himself caught in the midst of the government's propaganda offensive. The State Department was often able to hide its involvement in the tours by partnering with private organizations that had been awarded international jurisdiction over amateur athletics. For example, in the case of basketball and track and field, the two most popular sports in the State Department program, the government agency worked in collaboration with the Amateur Athletic Union. Typically, when the State Department decided to send a sports team abroad, it developed the team's itinerary but let the sport's governing organization choose the specific players who would be involved. Hence, many of the touring athletes were unaware of the State Department's sponsorship of their visits and the nonathletic aims of their goodwill tours abroad. However, as the tours became more extensive and controversial in the 1960s, African American athletes began to provide counternarratives to State Department claims about American exceptionalism—most notably during the 1968 Mexico City Olympic protest. Hence, sports became highly contested sites for competing interpretations of American race relations.

Globetrotting: African American Athletes and Cold War Politics uses the expansion of opportunities for African American athletes after World War II as a means to investigate the cultural politics of the Cold War as they related to the State Department's attempt to influence the African

Diaspora. Prior to the beginning of the Cold War, African Americans had been depicted as symbols of American democracy, but these efforts had been sporadic and uncoordinated and lacked significant government involvement. For example, Jesse Owens's success at the 1936 Nazi Olympic Games and Joe Louis's two fights with German boxer Max Schmeling had placed African Americans in the international arenas as symbols of the American way of life. However, during the Cold War, U.S. government officials consciously attempted to systematically promote African American athletes as examples of American willingness to incorporate people of color into the American social system. This project attempts to answer several questions: Why did the U.S. government use athletes as political agents? Why did American race relations become a crucial international issue during the Cold War? Why were athletes willing to accept their status as Cold Warriors? Why did athletes revolt against their role as political agents during the mid-1960s?

The unpunished lynching of African Americans, segregated schooling, and rampant obstruction of black voting rights were increasingly becoming problematic for American efforts to assume a leading role in world affairs after the onset of the Cold War. By the late 1940s, reports from diplomatic posts made it clear to the U.S. government that segregation was having a negative impact on its foreign policy. One diplomat in Ceylon (present-day Sri Lanka) wrote that racial segregation in the United States attracted more attention than any other subject. Another report said that local papers in Accra, Ghana, had little interest in international news, with the exception of racial discrimination in the United States. Furthermore, prominent American figures such as Walter White, Richard Nixon, A. Philip Randolph, Paul Robeson, Eleanor Roosevelt, and Secretary of State Dean Rusk publicly stated that the single biggest burden that the United States carried in its foreign policy was its domestic policy of racial discrimination. U.S. ambassador to the United Nations Henry Cabot Lodge accurately described American race relations as its "international Achilles heel" because nations of color saw the treatment of African Americans as reflective of the nation's attitude toward all people of color.[6]

In the late 1940s, State Department officials estimated that almost one-half of Soviet anti-American propaganda focused on American racial discrimination.[7] By drawing connections between imperialism and the exploitation of people of color and between capitalism and racial discrimination, the Soviet Union made effective use of American segregation as a valuable means to undermine American foreign policy throughout the African Diaspora. Only South Africa, an American ally, received greater criticism than the United States for its policies of racial discrimination in the immediate years after World War II. As the United States assumed responsibility for protecting the security and social system of the West during the Cold War, it drew attention to itself and unintentionally to its policies of racial discrimination. When people looked at the United States, they saw the achievements of democracy, but also saw a society deeply divided by its systematic racism—de jure and de facto.[8]

Chester Bowles, the U.S. ambassador to India, maintained that questions about race were the most frequently asked about American life. "A year, a month or even an week in Asia is enough to convince any perceptive American that the colored peoples of Asia and Africa, who total two-thirds of the world's population, seldom think about the United States without considering the limitations under which our 13 million Negroes are living," Bowles said before an audience at Yale University. The racially based denial of rights gave American claims to world leadership "a distinctly hollow ring." Bowles asked rhetorically, "How can the colored peoples of Asia be sure we are sincere in our interest in them if we do not respect the equality of our colored people at home?" On another occasion, the ambassador acknowledged that it was impossible to exaggerate the impact that achieving racial harmony in America would have upon America's foreign interests. Similarly, Dean Rusk wrote to Walter White of the NAACP that the "greatest burden we Americans have to bear in working out satisfactory relations with the peoples of Asia is our minority problems in the United States."[9]

Incidents such as the lynching of Robert Mallard were the basis of the criticisms leveled against U.S. race relations. As Carol Anderson notes, on November 20, 1948, black businessman Robert Mallard, his wife, and three other family members drove toward his thirty-two-acre farm in Toombs County, Georgia. Cruising in their new automobile, they were ambushed by three other cars filled with unmasked white men wearing white robes. Mallard was killed when a shot fired from one of the cars struck him in his chest. Police officers interrupted Mallard's funeral and arrested his grieving wife during the ceremony and charged her with his murder as an act of intimidation and expression of local white political power. Nine hours later, the charges were dropped, and she was released into the custody of her attorney.[10]

Mrs. Mallard provided the name of two men whom she recognized as participants in the ambush—William L. Howell and Roderick Clifton. Both men were arrested and charged with the murder of Robert Mallard. As the case became the subject of national inquiry, Georgia's governor, Herman Talmadge, derided the case as part of a "campaign to destroy states' rights . . . through the civil rights campaign." Talmadge's invocation of states' rights as an issue is significant because Mallard was murdered because he voted in the November 1948 election, in which President Truman was elected based upon his appeal to the black vote. Just four months before the lynching of Mallard, President Truman had issued two executive orders—one desegregating the military and the other outlawing discrimination in the federal government.[11] Both orders were seen as a threat to the "southern way of life." Therefore, many southerners remained determined to stifle the economic and political advancement that Robert Mallard's successful farm and civic engagement represented.

At the trial of the two defendants, T. Ross Sharpe, the defense attorney, called two jurors as character witnesses. Under Georgia law, anyone in a courtroom, except a trial judge, could be called as a character witness. Both jurors testified on behalf of the defendants by asserting that the testimony of Mrs. Mallard, a schoolteacher, should not be believed, based upon her "bad reputation." Immediately following their testimony, they returned to their seats in the jurors' box. After deliberating for twenty-six minutes, the jury (including the two character witnesses) returned with a not guilty verdict. Frustrated by southern justice, NAACP legal counsel Thurgood Marshall said that the trial illustrated "the incapacity of local authorities to deal with the crime of lynching." He called the arrest, indictment, and trial of the men "perfunctory motions" for the sole purpose of preventing federal intervention.[12] This case provides an illustration of the corruption of the southern justice system where white men who were known to be guilty of murdering African Americans went unpunished. High-profile incidents focused international attention on the racial abuse that African Americans faced even as the United States tried to position itself as the leader of the free world and principal protector of the rights of mankind worldwide.

Similar instances of "justice" had captured the attention of the President's Committee on Civil Rights, which had been organized in 1946 by President Truman. The committee argued that rather than focusing on the Soviets as prime sources for the critique of the nation's racial problem, the United States needed to concentrate on bridging the gap between its inclusive rhetoric and its divided reality. The committee's report, *To Secure These Rights,* reflected President Truman's support for civil rights reform. The committee recommended that if the United States could "establish the fact that our darker skinned citizens are truly first class citizens, it will create a reservoir of sympathy for us among all the dark skinned peoples of the world." Acting secretary of state Dean Acheson's letter to the chairman of the Fair Employment Practices Commission captured the mounting frustration many government officials felt regarding the growing influence of American segregation on America's moral leadership. Acheson exasperatedly noted, "Frequently we find it next to impossible to formulate a satisfactory answer to our critics in other countries."[13]

Dean Rusk, an assistant secretary of state, received two letters from the President's Committee on Civil Rights concerning the impact of race relations on U.S. foreign policy. Specifically, the committee wanted to know: "Do you feel that the formulation and conduct of a sound and desirable foreign policy is handicapped by our bad domestic record in the civil rights area? If the answer is in any sense in the affirmative, does this mean that American security is in fact endangered by this condition?" Rusk responded, "There is no question . . . the moral influence of the United States is weakened to the extent that the civil rights proclaimed by our Constitution are not fully observed in practice." He continued, "Our failure to maintain the highest standards of performance in this field creates embarrassment out of proportion to the actual instances of violation." Rusk was willing to acknowledge that "on a small scale" African Americans were affected by racial discrimination, but his judgment that foreign press coverage of racial oppression was more important than the prevalence of racial discrimination in the United States was crucial. Although Rusk's suggestion was contrary to the recommendations of the President's Committee, his strategy became the primary response to dealing with international condemnation of American racism during the Truman and Eisenhower administrations. Because southern segregationist congressmen were unwilling to support civil rights legislation, President Truman used Rusk's analysis to justify focusing on altering international perceptions of the nation's race relations rather than removing the legal impediments to African American advancement.[14]

President Truman and his successor, President Eisenhower, defined the protests of African Americans as a threat to the nation's security. Hence, as the Cold War intensified, the U.S. government began a campaign of silencing dissenting black voices. W. E. B. DuBois and Paul Robeson, both harsh critics of American racism, had their passports revoked because of their ability to attract large international audiences. Silencing DuBois, Robeson, and other dissenting voices was crucial to the State Department's attempt to manipulate foreign perceptions of race relations in the United States.[15] Consequently, rather than providing immediate, substantive changes to the social landscape, the U.S. government moved to redefine and recontextualize the slow and unsteady advancement of African Americans into the American mainstream as a narrative of progress and as an example of American democracy.

After working to marginalize prominent African Americans who were critical of American race relations, the State Department recruited prosperous African Americans who projected middle-class American values to participate in goodwill tours abroad. With this goal in mind, African American athletes, along with jazz musicians and other artists, were sent abroad as cultural ambassadors and "rebuttal witnesses."[16] By overemphasizing the extent to which social mobility was achievable for African Americans, the State Department sought to influence diasporic political alignments during the Cold War. The U.S. government tried to show that American policies were supportive of the liberation and rise of all people of color worldwide, and the touring athletes were depicted as symbols of America's commitment. Hence, sports were at the forefront of American propaganda efforts.

Henry Luce, one of the most important media figures of the twentieth century and a principal shaper of the post–World War II world, advocated for a more concerted and directed effort to utilize the appeal of popular culture as a political medium in his überinfluential text, *The American Century*. One of the most poignant of Luce's observations was his recognition of the leading role that American popular culture would play in the "American Century." "Once we cease to distract ourselves with lifeless arguments about isolationism," Luce charged, "we shall be amazed to discover that there is already an immense American internationalism. American jazz, Hollywood movies, American slang, American machines and patented products, are in fact the only things that every community in the world, from Zanzibar to Hamburg, recognizes in common." Heretofore, Luce maintained that the internationalism of American popular culture was "blind, unintentional, and trivial."[17] One of the most overlooked arguments that his book pushed was the notion that America needed to develop a systematic approach to exporting the unique aspects of American culture. *The American Century* suggested that the United States needed to turn to seemingly insignificant aspects of American society, such as sports, as effective means to answer questions about American values and social customs.

President Eisenhower's 1959 Committee on Information Activities Abroad, otherwise known as the Sprague Committee, affirmed Luce's notion that popular cultural was a valuable means to export the "American way of life." The committee's report asked, "Why are we so confident that what we stand for is in line with the aspirations of other peoples?" The committee concluded that the interests of the United States were consistent with the aspirations of peoples in Europe, Africa, Asia, South America, and the Middle East because all human nature, regardless of cultural, national, and social background, shared the same inherent desires. Although that perspective is difficult to prove, by defining American conceptions of freedom, justice, individuality, property ownership, and religion as universal, the Sprague Committee reinforced the notion that the United States had a responsibility to remake the world in its image, or at least defend the world against Soviet disregard for "fundamental human desires."[18] Notwithstanding this America-centric notion, the pervasiveness of racial discrimination was one of the most scrutinized aspects of American society, and for America to assume a leadership position it had to convince the world that its racial problems were being solved. Consequently, the success of African American athletes was marshaled as a means to answer international charges.

The Sprague Committee clearly expressed the purpose of goodwill tours involving African Americans: "to *define* and *influence* the African Diaspora."[19] The tours were a crucial aspect of the State Department's three-pronged approach to transforming international understandings of American racial dynamics: subversion of the rhetoric and organizational affiliations established in the prewar period that linked the African American struggle for equal rights with African and Asian struggles against colonialism; reconfiguration and reinterpretation of the battle to end American racial segregation within the contours of the American democratic tradition of progress, rather than as a facet of the global anticolonial movement; and portrayal of the "advancement" of African Americans as evidence of American commitment to creating a world where race was not a basis for oppression.

There were varied reasons sport was prominently featured in the complex State Department efforts. First, after Jackie Robinson integrated baseball, the swiftness with which sports integrated far outdistanced all other American institutions, thus giving sports a privileged space in the discussion of U.S. race relations. Second, foreign audiences were less likely to see sport tours as politically motivated. Consequently, the mistaken yet widespread notion that sport was nonideological minimized athletics' vulnerability to the charge of cultural imperialism that plagued other American propaganda efforts. Third, the Cold War contest between the United States and the Soviet Union elevated the significance of sport in the international arena because it was one of the few places where the two nations competed head-to-head after the Soviet Union reentered the Olympic Games in 1952. Finally, sport appealed to children, teenagers, and other "high-value" audiences that officials hoped to reach before they developed hostile, anti-American attitudes.

Given the rising international significance of U.S. race relations in the post–World War II period, when Jackie Robinson integrated baseball he was taking part in shaping the political and social destiny of this country. For an African American man to play in the national pastime had ramifications that extended far beyond the playing field. It is not too strong to assert that Jackie Robinson became a symbol of the Cold War; in particular, Robinson symbolized the accessibility of the "American Dream" to African Americans. As the symbol of Cold War integration, his success was advanced to support the notion that aligning with the United States as the "leader of the free world" held forth a realistic chance that people everywhere would be able to live the American Dream.

When Robinson integrated Major League Baseball in 1947, the National Football League had just reintegrated the year before, and the National Basketball Association integrated three years later. However, by 1968 one-fourth of the professional baseball league, one-third of the NFL, and one-half of the players in the NBA would be African American. Given the growth of the popularity of all of the leagues in the postwar period due to television, an improved travel infrastructure, and postwar prosperity, this development was astonishing. The rapidity of the advancement of the black athlete served as a reference point for those who were calling for widespread integration. For a generation of African Americans, the exploits of Robinson, Joe Louis, and others confirmed their belief that if provided a fair chance, African Americans would show that they were capable of performing at the highest levels in all professions.

Initially, most African Americans were supportive of the tours because integration of the athletic arena was thought to be a foreshadowing of widespread integration. However, the symbol of the black athlete became contested terrain during the mid-1960s. The articulation of African American athletic success as a positive, progressive racial force became contestable because the success of black athletes did not translate into widespread access to better housing, education, or other high-prestige employment.

One of the unintended consequences of the State Department goodwill tours was that they helped politicize athletes and former athletes such as Tommie Smith, John Carlos, and Harry Edwards. Edwards, the organizer of the Olympic Project for Human Rights (OPHR) that helped produce the lasting symbols of the athletic revolution[20]—the raised fists of John

Carlos and Tommie Smith at the 1968 Mexico City Olympics—became determined to produce a counternarrative to the State Department's story of progress. Rather than celebrating the suggestion that sports were at the forefront of racial advance, the athletes increasingly came to assert that sports were tied to a racist, oppressive system.

In essence, this manuscript explores the geopolitical significance of the integration of sport during the early days of the Cold War, 1947–68. Chapter 1 examines the implications of Jackie Robinson's historic testimony before the House Un-American Activities Committee (HUAC) as Cold War–era repression defined the politically acceptable parameters of African American dissent during the battle between the United States and Soviet Union for influence worldwide. Chapter 2 focuses on the Harlem Globetrotters as Cold Warriors between 1947 and 1954. This is an important moment because prior to the passage of the 1954 *Brown v. Board of Education* decision, the State Department was in the unenviable position of trying to defend segregation while stressing racial progress. Chapter 3 highlights the formalization of U.S. Cold War sport foreign policy. As the Soviet Union reentered the Olympic movement in 1952, sport took on heightened meaning, and this chapter highlights how the two superpowers fought for athletic supremacy. Chapter 4 examines the Eisenhower and Kennedy administrations' attempts to utilize sport to overcome hostile, international responses to the violent repression of the civil rights movement. Chapter 5 investigates the shifting political landscape after the passage of the 1964 Civil Rights Act as African American athletes increasingly began to use sport to challenge continued oppression rather than celebrate racial progress.

1. The Showcase African American

*Paul Robeson, Jackie Robinson,
and the Politics of Cold War
Prosperity and Repression*

Commissioner Kennesaw Mountain Landis convened a historic meeting at the Hotel Roosevelt on December 3, 1943, between the Major League Baseball club owners and the publishers of eight leading African American newspapers. Heretofore, African American newspapers had waged an unsuccessful campaign to force Major League Baseball to allow African Americans to compete for positions on Major League teams. One of the newspapers' most ardent protesters, Sam Lacy of the *Pittsburgh Courier,* convinced the commissioner to grant the African American press an extensive audience after years of being rebuffed.

Why did Commissioner Landis agree to the meeting? There is no evidence that Landis supported integration in the intervening two decades after he was appointed baseball's first commissioner in 1920. A well-respected attorney who had been appointed to a federal judgeship in 1905 by President Theodore Roosevelt, Landis's acceptance of the commissioner's post served as "a symbol that reassured the [white] public of baseball's honesty and integrity" after the Black Sox scandal of 1919. Through his power to mediate disputes, interpret rules, and police "conduct detrimental to baseball," Landis gained the respect of Major League fans. However, African Americans distrusted Landis because he was the judge that presided over the dubious conviction of Jack Johnson, the first African American heavyweight champion, who was considered a public pariah because of his penchant for marrying white women. After several failed attempts, Johnson was convicted of violating the Mann Act, which forbade the interstate transportation of women for immoral purposes. The law had been intended to stop prostitution: Johnson was convicted for traveling with his wife. Given the political nature of Johnson's conviction, Landis did not appear to be a "friend" to African Americans.[1]

Commissioner Landis's wide authority, coupled with the perception of him as a supporter of the color line, made him a favorite target for African Americans who opposed segregation in baseball. Landis's opening comments at the 1943 meeting portended an ominous outcome. Landis began by repeating an oft-stated argument, "I want it clearly understood that there is no rule, nor to my knowledge has there even been, formal or informal, or any understanding, written or unwritten . . . against the hiring of Negroes in the Major Leagues!" By denying the existence of collusion among the owners to prevent American Americans from competing for playing positions in the Major Leagues, Landis's opening statement attempted to preemptively undermine the arguments that would be put forward by the press officials.[2]

Undeterred by Landis's denial, the three representatives of the African American press who were chosen to address the owners made impassioned pleas for greater access for black ballplayers. John Sengstacke of the *Chicago Defender* appealed to the owners' patriotism. "The forces of hate, at home and abroad, are hard at work," Sengstacke argued. "But we do not believe they will ever sell racism to Americans who have purchased democracy and their right to be free men through blood, sweat, and tears." The thrust of Sengstacke's remarks echoed the powerful "Double V" rhetoric that many African American activists employed during World War II: African Americans soldiers were fighting against German racism abroad and American racism at home. Consequently, Sengstacke's sentiments pressed the point that African Americans had earned an opportunity for full equality based on their wartime sacrifices. Next, Ira F. Lewis of the *Pittsburgh Courier* appealed to the financial interest of the owners. Lewis argued that the public had already accepted African Americans as athletes by pointing to the large crowds at integrated football and baseball games. His presentation was followed by the *Baltimore Afro-American*'s Howard Murphy's recitation of the publishers' recommendations: First, baseball officials should take "immediate" steps to accept African Americans into the Major Leagues. Additionally, African Americans should not be restricted from competing in the minor league system or barred from entering the high school draft and other spaces from which Major League players were scouted. Last, Major League Baseball was asked to release a public statement saying African Americans were eligible for trials and permanent places on Major League teams.[3]

One of the peculiarities of the meeting was Landis's decision to invite another African American to address the owners: Paul Robeson. Certainly, Robeson was the most famous of all the African Americans who were in attendance. Robeson's stature was so immense, at the time he was the only African American who could make a reasonable claim to be as well known globally and domestically as Joe Louis, the heavyweight boxing champion. The famed actor and singer had maintained a prolonged public profile dating back to his selection as an All-America football player in 1917 and 1918 as a student-athlete at Rutgers University. His success on the field caused one sportswriter to label him a "football genius." Walter Camp, the legendary coach at Yale University, referred to him as a "veritable superman" when he made him the first Rutgers player to appear on his All-America team. Robeson, who attended Rutgers on an academic scholarship, proved himself equally adept in the classroom: he was elected into the prestigious Phi Beta Kappa Society for his academic achievement, and he was the class valedictorian.[4]

While making a living as a professional football player, Robeson completed his law degree at Columbia University, but was refused admittance to the American Bar Association. Turning his attention to acting and singing, Robeson became an international star. Among his most memorable performances was as the lead character in a Broadway run of Shakespeare's *Othello*. After receiving rave reviews during his twelve years in London, Robeson became the first black actor to reprise the role on Broadway. As a singer, Robeson was noted for his command of Negro spirituals. His exceptional talents caused many white Americans to assert that "the system worked," despite the steep racial barriers African Americans faced. Robeson symbolized the idea that ambitious and talented African Americans could overcome racial restrictions no matter how daunting. Some people referred to his success as validation of the American social order, despite the prevalence of segregation.[5]

Landis invoked Robeson's great career when he explained to the baseball officials why he had personally invited the stage star and former athlete to address them. "I brought Paul here because you all know him," Landis explained. "You all know that he is a great man in public life, a great American." Explaining that he accepted Commissioner Landis's invitation because he was "deeply" committed to fighting racial injustice, Robeson offered a personal account of his experiences as the first African American to play varsity football at Rutgers University, as a professional football player, and as the foremost African American stage actor of his generation. Robeson asked the assembled delegates to ignore the fear of financial repercussions. Alluding to the threats of cancellations and disturbances that accompanied his participation on Rutgers's football team, the skilled orator noted that the "games were played and nothing happened." Describing the owners' fear of racial violence as "groundless," Robeson beseeched the owners to look at his success and the lack of accompanying violence on the football field and in high-class theaters as evidence of the American public's willingness to accept integrated competition. The essence of Robeson's message was that the "social" side of integrated sports had been settled. His speech was met with a rousing ovation.[6]

As the unprecedented meeting drew to a close, Commissioner Landis asked the owners if they had any questions. His plea was met with an unsettling silence. Had the patriotic and financial arguments as well as Robeson's personal narrative been convincing? Immediately after, Commissioner Landis held a two-hour closed-door conference with the owners. As baseball's decision makers discussed the merits of the arguments presented, the African American press officials and other sympathetic press members waited for an official response to the meeting. With an air of expectation, the assembled newspapermen listened carefully as Landis emerged from the owners' private meeting. Anticipating a momentum-shifting statement, they were disappointed as Landis began: "Each club is entirely free to employ Negro players to any and all extent it pleases. . . . The matter is solely for each club's decision, without restriction whatsoever."[7] Rather than a groundbreaking condemnation of the unwritten rule, coupled with a plan of action, the awaiting press officials were presented with a statement that echoed earlier denials.

There were a number of frustrated responses to Landis's timid declaration. Alvin Moses, a columnist for the *Atlanta Daily World,* dismissively referred to the entire affair as "window dressing." The *Cleveland Call and Post*'s Bob Williams accused Landis of inaction by noting that Landis had "adroitly sidestepped any actual facing of the issue." Williams's sentiments were echoed by Joel W. Smith of the *Atlanta Daily World.* Smith castigated Landis's statement as "typical," by which Smith argued Landis sought the "easiest way out" by placing the blame elsewhere. Indeed, Landis's words did not commit the commissioner's office to a course of action. Nonetheless, Landis's words also engendered hope among many in the African American community.[8]

Some press accounts noted that Landis's statement suggested that he would not be an obstacle to the successful integration of Major League

Baseball. African American columnist Wendell Smith referred to Landis's words as an "official bombshell." Smith, who had attended the meeting, reported in the *Pittsburgh Courier* that he told the commissioner that he had made friends in black America because of his "uncompromising stand on Negro ball players." Smith reported that Landis replied, "I am glad to know that. Perhaps something will develop. I don't know." Landis's statement placed the burden of action upon the owners. One unidentified publisher who attended the meeting said that the meeting helped them clarify their target. This was a decisive moment because the agitators now knew that they could "localize" their fight for integration. Robeson told the *New Guide and Journal*: "Pressure in each town must be brought upon the team to hire Negroes." Robeson's support of the new strategy suggests that he thought the meeting and the new targeted campaign held potential.[9]

It is debatable whether this meeting had a profound effect on the effort to integrate baseball. However, there are some important elements that dovetail with subsequent developments. Branch Rickey was in attendance at the meeting. However, Rickey did not stress the 1943 meeting as a stimulant for his plan to integrate baseball. Localized campaigning was a tactical tool in Boston and New York, where several high-profile attempts to integrate baseball were unsuccessful between the 1943 meeting and the signing of Jackie Robinson. For example, in Boston it was illegal to play baseball on Sundays. However, the Boston Braves and Boston Red Sox had been granted waivers to the law, which allowed them to schedule games during lucrative weekend dates. In 1945 city councilman Isadore Muchnick threatened to block the waiver if African Americans were not allowed to try out for the teams. Based on Muchnick's resolve, three African American players—including Jackie Robinson—were allowed to display their skill in a tryout for the Boston Red Sox. Subsequent accounts of the move stressed that the athletes did not have a realistic opportunity to compete for roster positions. The tryout did not lead to integration, but it did support the idea that local pressure was an important weapon.[10]

Nonetheless, it is indisputable that Robeson was firmly committed to lending his fame and personal narrative to the efforts to desegregate baseball. As an ardent supporter of the oppressed, Robeson had a track record of speaking out against injustice. In many ways, Robeson's hatred of segregation and injustice was matched by the man who integrated baseball in 1947, Jackie Robinson. One of the ironies of both of their lives is that they would eventually end up pitted against each other by U.S. government officials before the House Un-American Activities Committee in

1949. Robeson, whom the HUAC sought to chastise for "anti-American" comments abroad, was both praised and condemned by Jackie Robinson during his moving testimony.

"The Showcase African American: Paul Robeson, Jackie Robinson, and the Politics of Cold War Prosperity and Repression" explains both the Cold War context and the costs associated with Jackie Robinson's integration of Major League Baseball. Traditional narratives about the integration of baseball tend to look back to World War II or ahead to the civil rights movement. By placing the integration of sport between these two monumental events, sports are depicted as a moment on a continuum of racial evolution that highlights progress. However, if we examine Jackie Robinson's integration of baseball as an aspect of the Cold War, we see that integration and Cold War repression are closely aligned. This chapter argues that the integration of baseball had a direct relationship with a core American foreign policy objective: manipulating international perception of American race relations. Hence, it explores the relationship between Cold War repression and racial integration after the articulation of the Truman Doctrine. By examining the historical context of Jackie Robinson's testimony before the House Un-American Activities Committee, this chapter examines the processes through which the U.S. government resolved to alter international opinions of American race relations rather than provide substantive changes to the segregated racial order in the early days of the Cold War, as well as the transformations in American political thought that allowed for those changes.

The Ideological Underpinnings of Cold War America

Allied wartime egalitarian rhetoric had suggested that post–World War II access to the "American Dream" would expand for African Americans. To that end, immediately after World War II, athletics were at the center of the effort to construct a more inclusive American society. Happy Chandler, who was named commissioner of Major League Baseball in April 1945, said that if African Americans could die fighting for freedom in foreign lands, they should be able to enjoy it in their homeland. "I am for the Four Freedoms," Chandler stated, "and if a black boy can make it at Okinawa and go to Guadalcanal, he can make it in baseball."[11] Branch Rickey, the general manager of the Dodgers, saw Chandler's openness as an opportunity to improve his baseball team by signing African American players.

Branch Rickey was a complex and innovative man: pious, moralistic, yet sensitive to the delicate balance one often had to navigate between one's faith and one's financial opportunities. Rickey frequently claimed that he had spent forty years thinking about how to integrate baseball. Yet he rejected confrontation as a tactical approach. To that end, he was furious when Benjamin Davis, a Georgia-born, Harvard-educated, communist city councilmen in New York, published a pamphlet that depicted a dead African American soldier on the cover with the caption: "Good enough to die for his country but not good enough to play baseball." The fiercely anticommunist Rickey acknowledged that "I am for your cause [the integration of baseball] more than anybody else I know . . . but you are making a mistake using force . . . dictating in this matter. . . . It will fail because it is a matter of evolution, not revolution."[12]

Described by *Time* as a mixture of P. T. Barnum and Billy Sunday, Rickey correctly gauged that postwar America would be willing to experiment with the notion of racially mixed baseball teams. Nonetheless, he moved very cautiously and calculatedly with his plans to integrate. After extensive planning, Rickey chose Jackie Robinson to be the "lone standard bearer, upon whose success or failure the fate of the entire venture would be determined."[13]

Rickey's choice of Jackie Robinson was shocking. Robinson certainly was not the best player in the Negro Leagues: Satchel Paige and Josh Gibson had far better baseball credentials. However, Rickey had developed six criteria: the man chosen would have to be "right off the field," he had to be "right on the field," he had to be liked by black America, the press reaction had to be favorable, a roster position had to be readily available, and the reaction of his potential teammates had to be encouraging. Rickey knew that the man he chose had to be more than a baseball player; he had to be a man who possessed incredible self-control and unwavering confidence. Furthermore, the Dodgers' general manager sought an athlete in the mold of Joe Louis, the heavyweight champion, who offered only mild criticism of U.S. race relations and consequently was considered a "credit to his race." Rickey was impressed by Jackie Robinson's baseball skills and the fact that Robinson did not smoke, drink, or womanize. Furthermore, Robinson was articulate, college educated, and poised.[14]

Rickey made sure that Robinson understood that his major objective was to be a great baseball player rather than a social reformer. During their initial meeting, Rickey lectured Robinson on the difficulties that he would face. The Dodgers' general manager had consulted with leading experts in the field of race relations and read the work of historians and sociologists. According to historian Jules Tygiel, Rickey was heavily influenced by the research of Columbia University professor Frank Tannenbaum. Tannenbaum's work contrasted racial attitudes in Latin America and the United States. He found that the United States had erected strict racial barriers, whereas Latin cultures allowed blacks to intermarry, mix socially, and become citizens. The thrust of the Tannenbaum thesis, although later disputed by historians, suggested that "greater 'proximity' of blacks and whites encouraged more amicable relations." Rickey used the Tannenbaum thesis to reach the conclusion that the pursuit of common goals would help individuals overcome their racial prejudices.[15] By suggesting that Jackie Robinson could help the Dodgers win a pennant, Rickey was attempting to define his relationship to the team based upon factors and considerations that did not revolve around social pioneering in race relations.

Among the first people that Branch Rickey took aside before he signed Jackie Robinson was radio announcer Red Barber, whose popularity with the Brooklyn fans was equal to that of the most beloved Dodger players. Barber had been raised in the South and still held many of the racial assumptions that he had been taught. Rickey's plan to have an African American join the Dodgers caused Barber to examine his beliefs about race and his own values. Rickey had anticipated that Barber would agonize over the decision, but would decide to be fair and just toward African American players.

Reflecting upon his meeting with Rickey at Joe's Restaurant in Brooklyn, Barber said that when Rickey informed him of the plan to desegregate, "I gave him back no support. I gave him back 100 percent silence, because he had shaken me. He had shaken me to my heels." That night, Barber went home and told his wife, "I'm going to quit, I don't think I want—I don't know whether I can—I'm going to quit." At his wife's urging, he delayed announcing his decision. "The thing was gnawing on me. . . . It tortured me," Barber acknowledged. "I set out to do a deep self-examination. I attempted to find out who I was." Ultimately, rather than quitting, Barber decided to stay and battle the legacy of his southern upbringing. Admitting that it was at times hard, Red Barber later said, "I thank Jackie Robinson. He did far more for me than I did for him."[16] The success of Rickey's desegregation plan hinged on whites undertaking the same painstaking reappraisal of their racial beliefs as Barber had.

Jackie Robinson made his first appearance as a member of the Brooklyn Dodgers on April 15, 1947, before a home crowd at Ebbets Field. As the first African American Major League Baseball player in the twentieth century, Jackie Robinson assumed the oft-passed mantle as "a savior, a Moses leading his people out of the wilderness." After a successful rookie campaign in which he batted .297, while finishing first in the league in stolen bases and second in runs scored and leading his team in home runs, he was named Rookie of the Year. In the process, Robinson had become the game's biggest drawing card since Babe Ruth, and like Ruth, his success had ramifications that transcended the world of sports. As Tygiel suggested, "Robinson's entry into organized baseball . . . created a national drama, emotionally involving millions of Americans, both black and white."[17] For many African Americans, Jackie Robinson's success personified their optimistic embrace of the "American dilemma."

An American Dilemma was the result of the Carnegie Foundation's in-depth study of African Americans. Picking a lead scholar had been a tricky undertaking: the Carnegie Foundation knew that African Americans and Yankees would not be acceptable to southerners, and the foundation believed that all Americans harbored too many preconceived notions to write an objective and insightful study. Therefore, the foundation turned to Swedish economist Gunnar Myrdal to head the project.[18] Myrdal, described by European colleagues as an "inventive and productive" scholar, was an attractive lead investigator because he was unfamiliar with U.S. race relations, had never visited the American South, and had had limited contact with African Americans. The Swedish scholar was surprised by the Carnegie Foundation's offer and initially turned it down based on the very factors that made him attractive to the Carnegie group. However, the Carnegie Corporation impressed upon him that they were looking for someone whose life experience suggested that he would be impartial. As a result, Myrdal changed his mind and accepted the challenge.[19]

Myrdal's study, *An American Dilemma,* appeared in 1944 and became arguably the most important book published on race relations since Harriet Beecher Stowe's *Uncle Tom's Cabin.* In a *Saturday Review* critique of the book, Robert S. Lynd, the noted writer, called Myrdal's work "the most penetrating and important book on contemporary American civilization that has ever been written." More pointedly, Ralph Ellison declared that the work destroyed the respectability of racism. Twenty years after the book's publication, the editors of the *Saturday Review* asked twenty-seven esteemed men and women of letters, "What books published during the past four decades most significantly altered the direction of our society?" Only one, John Maynard Keynes's book *The General Theory of Employment, Interest, and Money,* was mentioned more frequently. Harry McPherson, an adviser to President Lyndon B. Johnson, said that Myrdal's ideas supplied "a kind of background music for the civil rights effort." Undoubtedly, the moral- suasion perspective employed in *An American Dilemma* reflected the nonviolent, direct-action tactics of the civil rights movement. Charles Thompson, the dean of the Howard University faculty and collaborator with Myrdal on the study, said that whether *An American Dilemma*'s thesis was right or wrong, it supplied the rationale for civil rights organizations to adopt offensive strategies rather than defensive postures.[20]

Myrdal's work argued that the inconsistencies between democratic ideals and racial prejudice bothered Americans greatly. As Nikhal Pal Singh has argued, Myrdal's work identified a "national theory" that supported freedom and equality for all, even though it was not the reality in segregated America. Certainly, Myrdal was expressing American support for two core Enlightenment ideals—liberty and equality—as Singh suggests. However, the most significant idea that Myrdal's work underscores is the notion of progress. As the defining trend in American history, progress became the central Cold War–sanctioned mantra regarding the "American dilemma."[21] The belief that the United States was progressing toward a society devoid of racism and that the American capitalist, democratic system contained the mechanisms to achieve this desired social order established the parameters of acceptable Cold War–era discourse regarding American race relations.

An American Dilemma predicted that America's treatment of people of color would affect its prestige, power, and sense of security worldwide. Myrdal argued that "all concessions to Negro rights in this phase of the history of the world will repay the nation many times, while any and all injustices inflicted upon them will be extremely costly."[22] The full realization of the American Century mandated that America illustrate to the world that African Americans could be successfully integrated, that American democracy was not synonymous with white supremacy.

Predicting that the Soviets would exploit any attempt by the West to preserve white supremacy, Myrdal asserted that domestic and international forces would force civil rights reform in the United States. Nonetheless, he remained adamant that white America's sincere desire to live up to democratic and Christian principles would be the preeminent force driving reform. The Swedish economist had faith that the United States would make the right decision when he issued his oft-quoted challenge: "America is free to choose whether the Negro shall remain her liability or become her opportunity."[23] The successful integration of baseball the year after the release of *An American Dilemma* suggests that Myrdal's thesis held merit.

Before 1947 baseball reflected the values of American segregation. However, after the emergence of Jackie Robinson, African Americans and white Americans suggested that the successful integration of professional baseball represented the movement toward a society devoid of racial prejudice, a major concern during the early days of the Cold War. The notion that America was moving toward a social order where African Americans would be fully accepted in the United States was strengthened when one poll labeled Robinson the second most popular man in the United States behind only Bing Crosby. As one of the first and most visible institutions to accept African Americans on relative terms of equality, baseball became viewed as a model for the nation and would help provide a blueprint for future widespread integration.

The HUAC Hearings and Their Aftermath

Many African Americans accepted Myrdal's premise; however, several leading black thinkers, including Robeson and Oliver Cox, denied that African American subordination was a question of morality. In *Caste, Class, and Race,* Cox denied that the "dilemma" to which Myrdal referred was "peculiarly American." Rather than accepting Myrdal's idea that racial oppression in the United States was a moral issue, Cox argued that class interests were closely aligned with racist ideology. Thus, Cox questioned Myrdal's inability to provide a class interpretation for racial abuse. He maintained, "If the 'race problem' in the United States is pre-eminently a moral question, it must naturally be resolved by moral means, and this conclusion is precisely the social illusion which the ruling political class has consistently sought to produce." Thus, for Cox, Myrdal's analysis failed to provide a solution to the race problem, except to rely upon "time as the great corrector of all evil." Given the social climate, Myrdal had made a tactical decision to avoid including an economic analysis, which may have tainted his manuscript as "communist inspired."[24]

Throughout the 1920s and 1930s, Robeson was among the many African Americans who ascribed to the notion of the "talented tenth." The theory suggested that the achievements of the African American elite would lead to greater freedoms and rights for the masses. Hence, he believed that he could make his most important contribution to racial progress by improving his reputation as an artist. Initially, Robeson rejected direct political engagement because he did not want his artistic contributions compromised by political entanglements. Trips to the Soviet Union in 1934 and Spain in 1938 forced him to reassess his political hesitancy.

After his experiences abroad, Robeson evolved "from an artist with a conscience to an artist committed to political action." Thereafter, he committed himself to direct political confrontation with racial injustice and rejected the "talented tenth" theory.[25] Undoubtedly, the most important expression of Robeson's political disavowal of racial segregation was his 1949 speech in Paris.

Paul Robeson addressed two thousand delegates from fifty nations at the Paris World Peace Congress in April 1949, where he and W. E. B. DuBois led the American delegation. The Associated Press (AP) reported that Robeson said, "It is unthinkable that American Negroes would go to war on behalf of those who have oppressed us for generations against [the Soviet Union] which in one generation has raised our people to the full dignity of mankind." Martin Duberman, the author of the most comprehensive biography of Robeson, argued that Robeson was misquoted. Duberman maintained that Robeson stated, "We shall not put up with any hysterical raving that urges us to make war on anyone. Our will to fight for peace is strong. We shall not make war on anyone. We shall not make war on the Soviet Union." After the AP's misreporting of his words, Robeson maintained that his message had been "garbled." However, as scrutiny intensified, Robeson embraced a defiant posture by declaring that he was not afraid of communists. Moreover, when he returned to the United States, he embraced the alleged misquotation at his homecoming rally in New York. By making derogatory statements about the United States on foreign soil, he had violated a crucial unwritten rule of U.S. foreign policy for American citizens: criticism of the United States is acceptable only when made at home. Stern denunciations followed: the white press portrayed his as a traitor; black leaders were quick to deny that he spoke for the black community.[26] Robeson had been making similar charges since the United States entered World War II. However, the onset of the Cold War meant the political landscape had shifted by 1949.

President Harry S. Truman articulated what has become known as "the Truman Doctrine" before a joint session of Congress on March 12, 1947. This speech defined the rationale for U.S. involvement in the Cold War. The Truman Doctrine warned the nation of the communist threat, and it pledged U.S. support for nations struggling for freedom in a speech that became the dominant reference point for U.S. foreign policy for the next twenty-five years. "At the present moment in world history every nation must choose between alternative ways of life," Truman said. He characterized the "American way of life" with references to "free institutions, representative government, free elections, guarantees of individual liberty, freedom of speech and religion, and freedom from political oppression," whereas the "Soviet way of life" was depicted as relying upon "terror and oppression, a controlled press and radio, fixed elections, and the suppression of personal freedoms." The Truman Doctrine linked America's vision of itself as a nation with a purpose and destiny with the postwar battle against communism for worldwide supremacy. The anticommunist sentiments of Americans were fused with Luce's notion of the American Century to assert a vision of global responsibility. As John Fousek has argued, the Truman Doctrine did not create a new worldview, but it "encapsulated and reified ideological beliefs that were already widely shared, and it used them to mobilize support for the Truman administration's major foreign policy objectives."[27]

With the articulation of the Truman Doctrine, the Red Scare, which was launched in 1946, intensified. World War II had positioned the Soviet Union as a superpower and a threat to the "American way of life." Russian domination of Eastern Europe, the communist upsurge in Turkey and Greece, coupled with the trials of U.S. government officials on espionage charges empowered American anticommunism. In 1947 lawmakers proposed legislation that would have outlawed the Communist Party, forced the party and affiliated organizations to register with the attorney general, and compelled labor union officials to file noncommunist affidavits. Concurrently, President Truman established a federal loyalty program that was used to dismiss employees for being affiliated with any group "designated by the Attorney General as totalitarian, fascist, communist, or subversive."[28]

The increasingly repressive atmosphere led to a fundamental shift among black organizations, which had previously argued that African American struggles to end segregation were linked to anti-imperialist struggles throughout Asia and Africa. Cold War consensus meant that organizations such as the NAACP had to affirm their commitment to the democratic capitalist system in the United States by embracing the messianic vision of the Truman Doctrine. Hence, Walter White and other NAACP leaders began to assert that the United States was the legitimate leader of the "free world." As part of their reshaping of African American political and rhetorical strategies, White ceased his criticism of U.S. foreign policy. As Penny Von Eschen has argued, the subsequent privileging of African Americans as American citizens first "left no room for the claim of commonality with Africans and other oppressed peoples." Consequently, the promise of advancement for African Americans "came at the expense of muting their belief in the international character of white racial domination in the early Cold War." Thereafter, White attempted to convince the president that domestic discrimination had to be eradicated because international condemnation of American domestic racism was a hindrance to U.S. foreign policy.[29]

Walter White realized that criticism of U.S. foreign policy was becoming untenable, yet conformity helped open new opportunities to promote civil rights within the administration. Thus, White and others gambled that they could achieve their goals through an alliance with the president, rather than through working to create linkages between the domestic civil rights agenda and the global anticolonial movement. As David Levering Lewis argues, "The Negro civil rights establishment played out the hand dealt it by the national security state—uncritical patriotism in return for incremental race relations progress."[30]

A major impetus for the political alignment between Walter White and the president was the creation of President Truman's Committee on Civil Rights in 1946. *To Secure These Rights* was the title of the report that the committee released the following year. The report recommended that the federal government take responsibility for ensuring that the civil rights of African Americans were not violated. The committee advocated for antilynching legislation, an anti–poll tax measure, and an end to segregation in the military. When the president publicly embraced the report, Carl Rowan, an African American journalist, stated that Truman affirmed "unequivocally that the federal government has the primary responsibility to secure the basic civil rights of minority group citizens." *To Secure These Rights* established a national agenda that the civil rights movement mainstream pursued for the next twenty years.[31]

Walter White's embrace of Truman was reflected in the invitation that was extended to the president to address the NAACP. Three months after his Truman Doctrine speech, the president gave a historic speech at the NAACP annual meeting on June 29, 1947. Truman's remarks made him the first president to speak before the NAACP, and it marked the first time in modern history that an American president defined civil rights as "a crisis." President Truman addressed an immediate audience of ten thousand, a national radio audience (the four major radio networks carried the speech), and an international audience that tuned into the State Department's short-wave broadcast of the speech.[32] Arguably, the most significant aspect of Truman's remarks at the NAACP annual meeting, and in ensuing discussions of the race problem, was that he symbolically committed the office of the president to addressing civil rights concerns.[33]

Truman's speech in the shadow of the Lincoln Memorial stressed the notion that racial minorities should have their civil rights defended because American history, immediate domestic circumstances, and geopolitical considerations demanded it. Urgency was the dominant theme of the address. Truman argued that civil rights reform was an "immediate task," that the nation "must work as never before," and that America "can no longer afford the luxury of a leisurely attack." The speech acknowledged domestic civil rights violations in the context of international standards of human rights. The *Philadelphia Afro-American* praised Truman for conceding that "America's claim to world leadership is at stake each time a right is abridged or a privilege denied" to racial minorities. This was an important development because Congress's unwillingness to fight against racial discrimination in the late 1940s made civil rights advocates nearly totally reliant on the White House and the courts.[34]

The Democratic Party regained control of key congressional committees after the elections in 1948. This shift in power was important because it placed many southern, segregationist Dixiecrats in positions of influence as chairmen of committees that reviewed proposed civil rights legislation. Dixiecrat congressmen favored the doctrine of states' rights and were adamantly opposed to the increased role of the federal government in the arena of civil rights. Consequently, many of the recommendations that Truman's Committee on Civil Rights proposed were blocked and stalled in committee. Using his limited power, Truman issued executive orders to desegregate the federal bureaucracy and the military. Furthermore, he also had the Justice Department support several desegregation cases that were being contested in federal court. However, because Truman was not able to push through any substantial civil rights legislation, as the Cold War escalated, he also concentrated on attempting to alter international perceptions of American race relations.[35] This meant that in order for him to be the definitive voice on U.S. domestic race relations, Truman had to silence African Americans who disagreed with his optimistic and progressive depiction of American race relations. This shift was evident during the high-profile HUAC hearings regarding the loyalty of African Americans that were organized after Paul Robeson's controversial statements at the World Peace Conference in Paris in 1949.

In an attempt to forestall the inevitable Red Scare backlash after Robeson's pronouncements, African American leaders and the African American press issued a swift rebuke. Mary McLeod Bethune challenged Robeson's opening comment, "I bring you a message from the Negro people of America . . ." Bethune responded, "But when Mr. Robeson presumes to speak for me—and I believe the same would be true in the cases of millions and millions of other Negroes—in expressing disloyalty to our country, then I think he has missed his cue and entered the stage during the wrong scene." Bethune's snarky rebuttal clearly was a public rebuke of Robeson as an authoritative spokesperson on racial issues. Roy Wilkins of the NAACP agreed. "Mr. Robeson does not know his people," he concluded. Wilkins's claim was a snide remark directed at Robeson's international travels because of his attempt to keep the anticolonial, antiracism international alliances strong, which he saw as vital to the success of both movements. Conservative columnist George Schuyler lent his voice to this critique. Schuyler charged that Robeson has "never had any mandate to speak for colored Americans and never will have any."[36]

Robeson's remarks drew the ire of his close friend and former teammate Fritz Pollard. Pollard was the first African American to be named to Walter Camp's All-America football team as well as the coach and quarterback for the Akron Pros, for whom Robeson competed during the early 1920s. Pollard dismissed Robeson as a grandstanding thespian. Mockingly, Pollard said that Robeson "just likes to play Emperor Jones," a reference to the title character's establishment of himself as the ruler of an unnamed Caribbean island in the 1933 film adaptation of Eugene O'Neill's stage play. Robeson had been the lead actor in the film.

Arguably, the most scathing critique appeared in the NAACP's widely circulated magazine, the *Crisis*. The unattributed article questioned Robeson's authority to act as a representative of African Americans. Arguing that it was "pertinent to examine his record of service to his race," the *Crisis* asked, "How much has he done to help [African Americans] in their upward struggle?" The magazine acknowledged that he was an inspirational figure, but concluded that he had largely been missing from the trenches in the fight to overcome racial oppression. Hence, the criticism, which New York City councilman Ben Davis labeled a "gutter attack," argued that the great singer was unfit to be seen as a leader.[37]

Despite quick efforts by African American leaders to isolate Robeson, his comments reinvigorated abandoned attempts to investigate communist infiltration of the African American community. The initial 1948 hearings were tabled because of election-year political calculations, especially since African Americans were an essential component of the emerging Democratic coalition. Compounding these fears was the recurring ill health of the committee's chairman, J. Parnell Thomas, a Democrat from New Jersey. Furthermore, the committee's preliminary findings suggesting that the communists had made "surprisingly little progress in recruiting Negroes" caused the hearings to be postponed.[38] However, Robeson's comments, coupled with a change in committee chairmanship, made rescheduling the hearings a high priority.

HUAC was approved by Congress in 1938 to investigate extremism across the entire political spectrum. Southerner Martin Dies, a representative from Texas, was HUAC's first chairman. Fellow southerner John Rankin of Mississippi put together a coalition of conservative Republicans and southern Democrats to establish HUAC as a standing committee in the House of Representatives on the opening day of the Seventy-ninth Congress in 1945. Rankin saw HUAC as a valuable tool in the southern effort to impede efforts to improve civil rights. HUAC provided a forum through which many advocates for segregation tried to link the civil rights movement with communism. By arguing that the attempts to disrupt the racial status quo were communist inspired, southerners sought to show that there was a direct link between the two.[39] Suppressing efforts that challenged segregation remained a priority. Yet as the Cold War intensified, the committee's focus expanded, as HUAC positioned itself as a vital instrument and significant facet in the government's countersubversive, anticommunist efforts during the 1940s and 1950s. Indeed, as in the case of the 1949 hearings, there was an attempt to conflate these two efforts.

Alvin Stokes, an African American, was the lead HUAC investigator regarding communist infiltration of the African American community. Stokes, who had years of experience as an investigator for several state and local agencies in New Jersey, had joined HUAC one week after Jackie Robinson integrated the Major Leagues in 1947. He was the first witness to testify at the HUAC hearings. Stokes maintained that in the course of his investigation, he had interviewed hundreds of African American leaders "in every walk of life." Based on his interviews and committee records, he concluded that fewer than fourteen hundred African Americans, or one-tenth of 1 percent of the African American population in the United States, were members of the Communist Party. Despite being "the targets of constant and relentless Communist propaganda," black Americans did not view communism as the answer to solving the racial problems in the United States, Stokes argued. Nonetheless, his research indicated that many white Americans doubted the loyalty of African Americans. Stokes picked seven large American cities and assigned white investigators to conduct a thousand "man-in-the-street" interviews among white citizens. Stokes admitted that he was astounded that 52 percent of the interviewees believed that Robeson's alleged words were indicative of the

sentiments of the African American community. Therefore, one of the
purposes of the hearings was to alter white public opinion regarding the
loyalty of black citizens.[40]

The committee also invited several other prominent African Americans
who had served in the U.S. military to testify, including Charles Johnson,
Thomas Young, Lester Granger, and Jackie Robinson. Charles Johnson,
the president of Fisk University, a leading African American sociologist,
and former regimental sergeant-major during World War I, testified that it
was "absurd" to question the loyalty of African Americans. Thomas Young,
the editor of the influential black newspaper the *Journal and Guide,* declared that Paul Robeson had done "a great disservice to his race" and that
his words had "disqualified" him as a representative of black Americans.
Lester Granger, the executive director of the National Urban League, was
one of the first African American officers in World War I. Granger also
served as a special assistant to James Forrestal, the navy secretary during
World War II, traveling throughout the European Continent advising on
problems involving African American personnel. As a result of his service,
he was awarded the U.S. Navy's Distinguished Civilian Service Medal and
the President's Medal for Merit. Granger argued that the small defection
of African Americans to the Communist Party had more to do with the
United States' "failure to make good on our democratic professions" than
the appeal of communism. Consequently, he recommended "less worry
about Robeson and more concern for democracy."[41]

The final witness was Jackie Robinson, who read a prepared statement
before the committee on July 18, 1949. Why was Jackie Robinson chosen to speak before the HUAC hearings regarding the loyalty of African
Americans? Certainly, representatives from the black press, civil rights
organizations, and the black intelligentsia were appropriate choices for
such an important task. Alvin Stokes suggested that the committee chose
Robinson because they wanted to have someone whose popularity rivaled
Robeson's. Jackie Robinson was the obvious choice: he had recently been
the top vote getter in Major League Baseball's all-star balloting, and he
was leading the National League in batting, hits, runs batted in, and stolen bases. Perhaps only Joe Louis rivaled Robinson's popularity in both
black and white America. For Robinson's testimony, the committee waived
its strict rules against newspaper cameramen and photographers, which
meant that Robinson delivered his statement before a crowded room in
the Old House Building. Pictures of Robinson were featured in newspapers
across the country the following day.[42]

Robinson was asked to perform this important task because the integration of baseball was the most publicly discussed development in American race relations between the end of World War II and the *Brown v. Board of Education* decision. Yet it is hard to quantify the impact of Jackie Robinson's accomplishments upon African Americans. As Peter Golenbock has suggested, "So great was his effect that it is almost beyond measure." Early in his career, whenever Robinson played, thousands of African Americans came to the stadium to see him compete. The *Philadelphia Afro-American* reported that African Americans from as far away as Baltimore, Washington, D.C., and other cities along the eastern seaboard requested tickets for the first Dodgers-Phillies series in Philadelphia during the 1947 season. Later that year, a "Jackie Robinson Special" train ran from Norfolk, Virginia, to Cincinnati, Ohio, stopping to pick up African American fans willing to travel to see Robinson play in the Dodgers-Cincinnati series. Mike Royko, a white sports columnist, attended Robinson's first game at Wrigley Field in Chicago. A quarter century later, Royko described the scene: "In 1947, few blacks were seen in downtown Chicago, much less up on the North side at a Cub game. That day they came by the thousands, pouring off the north-bound ELS [elevated passenger train] and out of their cars. They didn't wear baseball-game clothes. They had on church clothes and funeral clothes—suits, white shirts, ties, gleaming shoes, and straw hats. . . . The whites tried to look as if nothing unusual was happening, while the blacks tried to look casual and dignified." When Robinson was at bat, Royko recalled that African Americans "applauded long, rolling applause. A tall middle-aged man stood next to me, a smile of almost painful joy on his face, beating his palms together so hard they must have hurt."[43]

Ever since Branch Rickey signed Jackie Robinson in 1946, historians and sportswriters have attempted to grasp the gravity of the development. Historian Martha Biondi rightly acknowledges that desegregating baseball, along with forming a permanent Fair Employment Practices Committee and ending segregation in the military, was among the top civil rights goals during the 1940s. Baz O'Meara, a reporter for the *Montreal Daily Star,* argued that Robinson's first game as a member of the Dodgers organization was in a way "another Emancipation Day for the Negro." African American sportswriter Sam Lacy wrote that by himself, Robinson "represents a weapon far more potent than the combined forces of all our liberal legislation." The implication of Lacy's claim is that Jackie Robinson had the hopes, aspirations, and ambitions of thirteen million black Americans on his shoulders. In essence, Robinson was viewed as if he was a "one man civil rights movement."[44] Many African Americans thought that Robinson's success proved that if given a fair chance, African Americans would be productive and responsible and exhibit a strong work ethic. Perhaps all-time home run champion and Hall of Famer Hank Aaron best captured the sentiments of black America when he said, "[Jackie Robinson] gave us our dreams."[45]

Robinson's careful and skilled negotiation of the highly politicized color line—as a baseball player—suggested that he would be the ideal person to assume Paul Robeson's leadership role in the African American community. Indeed, Robinson's testimony at the HUAC hearings suggested a changing of the guard. For many years, Robeson's success proved to white America that the American social order was just, that a "deserving black man could make it in the system." However, the Paris incident coupled with his other leftist activities meant that Robeson, the "showcase black American," had turned out not to be suitably representative after all—and it became imperative to isolate, discredit, and then replace him.[46]

After receiving an invitation to address HUAC, Jackie Robinson was hesitant to testify against Robeson because of Robeson's support in the fight to break baseball's color line. Hence, he sought the advice of his mentor, Branch Rickey. Noting that Robinson had not been subpoenaed, but invited, Rickey impressed upon his star player that it was an "honor to testify in the Congress of the United States." Wanting to produce a statement worthy of the moment, yet sensitive to the highly political environment, Rickey and Robinson decided to enlist the help of another public figure, Lester Granger, the head of the most conservative of the national African American organizations, the National Urban League. The year before, Rickey and Robinson were honored by the National Urban League for their contributions to racial progress. Working together, Granger and Robinson crafted a statement that reflected the "extremely delicate position" in which Robinson found himself.[47]

Once word leaked that Robinson would testify, there were several words of warning printed in the African American press. The *Philadelphia Tribune,* in a provocatively titled article, "Robinson versus Robeson," reminded Robinson and the other witnesses to avoid being "trapped into the position of declaring that they are satisfied" with racial progress in the United States because "Congressman Wood of Georgia and his fellow Dixiecrats would like nothing better than to have an array of Negroes testify that everything is ok." The paper reminded Robinson to stay away from making a comment that could be misinterpreted as an expression of contentment.[48]

In a much more aggressively worded article, "Drop That Gun, Jackie," the *Baltimore Afro-American* concluded that Robinson could not "fill Paul Robeson's shoes." Referring to Robeson as a "conscientious objector," the newspaper lauded Robeson's stand. Noting that the "bigots among the white race in the South are far more dangerous than the Russians," the paper advised Robinson to "put away his pop gun and put on his baseball uniform." Similar to the attacks leveled at the suitability of Robeson as a spokesperson for the race, the *Baltimore Afro-American* called Robinson's status into question. Acknowledging that Robinson was a "good American," the newspaper referred to Robeson as an equally "good American."[49]

Jackie Robinson began his testimony by asserting that a "sense of responsibility" led him to accept the committee's invitation to speak. He asserted that African Americans had legitimate concerns regarding racial oppression in the United States. He told committee members that it was a mistake to see African American agitation against racial discrimination as "a creation of Communist imagination." Maintaining that African Americans were "stirred up long before there was a Communist Party," Robinson said that communist denunciations of "injustices in the courts, police brutality, and lynching . . . [don't] change the truth of his charges." Nonetheless, he stressed that he had "too much invested in our country's welfare . . . to throw it away." Referring to Robeson's suggestions that African Americans would not fight against the Soviet Union, Robinson said, "It sounds silly to me." He then reaffirmed his faith in the U.S. democratic system by asserting that "we're going to fight [racial discrimination] all the harder because our stake in the future is so big. We can win our fight without the Communists and we don't want their help."[50]

Robinson's testimony was met with overwhelmingly positive reviews by white and black citizens, as well as several members of Congress. The *Boston Globe*'s headline read, "Jackie Robinson Brands Robeson's Talk Plain 'Silly.'" The *Globe* captured the general tenor of the mainstream press's coverage, which placed emphasis on Robinson's critique of Robeson's pronouncement as "silly." The *St. Louis Post-Dispatch* praised the speech for its "good sense and moderation." The *Post-Dispatch*'s patriotic headline simply read: "Jackie Robinson, American." Despite widespread adulation, it is noteworthy that many of the mainstream newspapers minimized the pro–civil rights sentiments in Robinson's remarks. Conversely, the African American press tended to focus on his claim that the United States needed to continue to work to eradicate racial discrimination. The *Baltimore Afro-American* placed the blame for African American flirtation with communism on the "country's failure to make the principle of

democracy a practical one." The *Philadelphia Tribune* acknowledged that
its staff had been "disturbed" by Robinson's invitation; however, the paper
gleefully reported that the baseball player "lambasted segregation and
discrimination with all of his strength."[51]

Representative Arthur G. Klein, a Democrat from New York, introduced
a resolution authorizing a half-million copies of Jackie Robinson's speech
for distribution. Klein defended his action by stating that Robinson's statement was "at once a dignified exposition of the just grievances of colored
Americans and a ringing declaration of the deep faith they have in the
American credo." Representative Bernard (Pat) Kearney, a Republican
from New York, recommended Robinson for the Veteran of Foreign Wars
Gold Medal for good citizenship based on his testimony.[52]

Paul Robeson was not invited to address HUAC. The committee feared
that he would use the occasion to sully the reputation of the United States,
while advocating for the virtues of communism, as he had done earlier
when he testified before the Joint Finding Committee on Un-American
Activities in the state of California in October 1946. In California, when
Robeson had been asked if he was a member of the Communist Party, he
provided a pointed and direct response, "If I wanted to join any party I
could just as conceivably join the Communist Party, more so today than I
could join the Republican or Democratic Party." The famed singer praised
the Communist Party for its stand against fascism; consequently, he had
"no reason to be inferring communism is evil." Giving a gifted orator like
Robeson a stage to respond to the HUAC charges was not an appealing
proposition to Chairman Wood.[53]

After Jackie Robinson's testimony, the press sought a response from
Robeson. The famed singer refused to denounce Robinson or respond to
his criticisms. Alternatively, Robeson proffered praise for Robinson. Aware
than Robinson was under enormous pressure and stress as he addressed
the charged racial situation in the United States Congress before a committee dominated by southern Dixiecrat legislators, Robeson applauded
Robinson as "having done more for his race than any colored man of
modern times" because of his success on the baseball field. Furthermore,
Robeson felt encouraged that Jackie "felt it his responsibility to be more
than just a ballplayer." Notwithstanding Robinson's personal critique of
Robeson, Robeson determined that he was not going to allow the issue
of racial injustice to be obscured. Consequently, he sought to defuse the
notion that it was a showdown between him and Robinson by vilifying
HUAC for its "ominous silence in the face of the lynchings" of African
American veterans and other noble citizens.[54]

What is interesting about the testimony of Jackie Robinson and the other African Americans who testified before the HUAC hearings was that they took as harsh a stance against Jim Crow as Paul Robeson had. However, what distinguished Robinson from Robeson was that he continued to identify the American capitalist, democratic system as the vehicle through which African Americans would achieve full equality. Jackie Robinson's highly publicized and heralded testimony demonstrated the new limitations that would be placed upon African American dissent. As Jackie Robinson's testimony exemplified, black folk would still be allowed to criticize the United States, but only if they expressed firm, resolute confidence and faith in the promise of "progress under the American capitalistic, democratic system." From here on, African American protest groups had to make it clear that their protests were designed not to challenge or undermine democracy, but rather to help the United States live up to its ideals. The politics of the Cold War limited African Americans' ability to offer a cynical and defeatist critique, as such criticism was deemed outside the bounds of acceptable Cold War protest.[55]

Jackie Robinson's testimony moved him—the national test case for integration—into the spotlight as a Cold Warrior. The linking of the Cold War and civil rights after the articulation of the Truman Doctrine led to the notion that if African Americans wanted civil rights reform, they would have to take a calculated risk and publicly testify to their "Myrdallian faith" in the American capitalist, democratic system to solve the racial problems in the United States.[56] For U.S. government officials, Robeson's pronouncement that African Americans would not fight against Russia suggested that African Americans had lost faith in the U.S. system to resolve its internal racial problems. If this were the case, it would have severely hindered U.S. efforts to incorporate emerging nations in Asia, Africa, and Latin America into the U.S. sphere of influence.

Prior to the Cold War emphasis on consensus, African Americans such as Walter White and the NAACP articulated links between the liberation movements in Asia and Africa with African American struggles for civil and economic rights in the United States. This was a continuation of the arguments made by African American anticolonialists during World War II who had argued that their struggles against Jim Crow racism were "inextricably bound to the struggles of African and Asian peoples for independence." In order to protect the civil rights movement, African American protest organizations were constrained to affirm their Americanism and to prove that their crusade was not Kremlin inspired. Consequently, many African American leaders abandoned criticism of the United States and adopted the position that the United States was the leader of the free world, while attempting to identify the struggle for African American equality with the anticommunist impulse.[57]

After the HUAC hearings, the State Department intensified its campaign of silencing dissenting black voices, which they deemed to be "legitimate security threats." Paul Robeson and W. E. B. DuBois, both harsh critics of American racism, had their passports revoked because of their ability to attract large international audiences. The seizure of Robeson's passport did not spark widespread protests on his behalf. Yet there were a few editorials that sought to defend him based on his fight against racism, not because of his communist sympathies. For example, an August 26, 1950, editorial in the *Baltimore Afro-American* mocked the State Department's claim that Robeson's comments were not in the "best interests of the United States." "There are many Americans whose express opinions are not in the best interest of our country. Some of them are in Congress. . . . [Robeson] holds no public office. He has stolen no valuable formulas or plans for the H or A bombs. He's been called a Communist and perhaps he is, but no one ever accused him of turning over our secrets to Russia. . . . [I]f his words ring of Communism, his heart is simply crying aloud against the oppression of his own people in the United States because of their color."[58]

Historically, the State Department had denied passports for limited reasons: the applicants lacked citizenship, to protect citizens from dangerous nations abroad, and to circumscribe the movements of suspected criminals. However, State Department censorship of Robeson and DuBois sought to effectively curtail their ability to publicly express discontent with American capitalistic democracy, thereby hindering America's ability to portray the plight of African Americans as a story of progress. The government's brief in the court of appeals case after Robeson's passport was revoked defended the State Department's actions: "The diplomatic embarrassment that could arise from the presence abroad of such a political meddler, traveling under the protection of an American passport, is easily imaginable." No prominent African American organization stepped forward to join the international outcry after Robeson and DuBois were denied their right to travel globally. By silencing Robeson, the government supported the contention that suppressing African American protests against racial segregation was a more immediate response to redressing international concern regarding domestic racial abuse than attacking the infrastructure of American segregation.[59] After silencing DuBois and Robeson, the department began a concerted campaign to manipulate African and Asian perceptions of race relations in the United States.

Reframing the "Negro Problem"

The discrediting of Robeson helped the State Department initiate a new aggressive approach toward answering international condemnation of American race relations. Rather than accepting the notion that racism was an "Achilles heel," the State Department pledged to show that race relations was one of the proud accomplishments of democracy. Instead of being ashamed of race relations, government officials sought to portray the history of African Americans as a story of redemption. The purpose became to acknowledge racial inequalities without tarnishing democracy and to illustrate how slow and steady progress would provide African Americans with the full measure of their rights.[60]

The 1950 publication *The Negro in American Life* illustrates the government's new approach to dealing with the race issue: the State Department had arrived at the conclusion that merely labeling international discussion of racial discrimination the product of "communist manipulations" was not effective. *The Negro in American Life* opened by acknowledging that the persistence of racial segregation in the United States was disconcerting to America's international allies and a valuable source of propaganda for communist enemies. Rather than concentrate on slums, segregation, and lynching as "dying vestige[s] of the post–Civil War . . . [that are] unequivocally condemned as any other criminal behavior, by both the government and by responsible citizens in every section of the country," the report argued that the most noteworthy aspect of American race relations was progress. The State Department realized that it was futile to deny that there was discrimination in the United States. Instead, it argued that the United States needed to place the facts into historical perspective.

The publication concluded that prejudice in the United States had deep historical roots, beginning with the nation's involvement in slavery. Slavery "troubled the conscience of Americans so much that they fought one of the bitterest civil wars of history in order to free the Negro. Freeing [African Americans] was easier than granting him full rights of citizenship." Numerous incidents and claims were employed in order to stress how the United States had tried to address the "Negro problem." Despite these difficulties, American representatives were encouraged to suggest that African Americans had made greater progress than any other comparable minority in the same period of time. The report concluded by claiming that the United States had a "record which should give encouragement to minorities everywhere." The argument of the report was a reflection of the widespread influence of Gunnar Myrdal's 1944 work, *An American Di-*

lemma: The Negro Problem and Modern Democracy. The Negro in American Life highlighted two of Myrdal's assertions: white Americans experienced inner turmoil because of the injustices heaped on African Americans, and the nation would take fundamental positive steps to amend oppressive, racist practices.[61]

The report suggested that the majority of Americans had fought against the institution of slavery since its inception. Arguing that the perpetuation of slavery had been a political compromise at the time of the founding of the Republic, the report asserted that America took immediate steps to contain the growth of slavery's geographical, economic, and political landscape. For example, in 1787 the nation adopted a resolution to prevent the importation of slaves after a twenty-year period, in 1804 New Jersey became the last northern state to abolish slavery, in 1808 the African slave trade was abolished, and in 1820 the importation of African slaves became a capital offense. By situating American slavery as the backdrop by which the plight of African Americans should be measured, *The Negro in American Life* sought to shift the focus from the nation's failure to live up to its egalitarian principles to the nation's racial progress.[62]

Admitting that prejudice and discrimination contradicted the principles of democracy, the report argued that the situation could not be wholly alleviated by legal means. By arguing that fundamental changes in human attitudes were essential to ending racial segregation, the article shifted the discussion from federal legal action to the responsibilities of black and white citizens. "Legal tools have helped solve the problem of race discrimination in America," the publication concluded, "but it remains essentially a question of evolving human relations." The phrase "evolving human relations" was a euphemism for the core concept that was repeatedly used in relationship to the American racial landscape: progress. Throughout the Truman and Eisenhower administrations, the ideology behind *The Negro in American Life* was a central component of U.S. government propaganda campaigns, as exemplified by the influence of John Silvera's work.

In June 1953, John Silvera wrote a widely circulated paper titled "Color— a Factor in U.S. Psychological Warfare" as a term paper for an officers course at the U.S. Army's Psychological Warfare School. Silvera, an army captain staff specialist, had served as a public relations consultant for issues surrounding African Americans for the National Citizens for Eisenhower-Nixon during the 1952 presidential campaign. According to Silvera, the Soviet propaganda campaigns successfully promoted several negative images associated with the treatment of African Americans:

African Americans were a despised group, universally hated by the rest of America; blacks were forced to work for slave wages and live in depressed neighborhoods and denied free access to public facilities; African American citizens were denied the right to trials by jury; additionally, the Soviets said that blacks were denied the opportunity to participate in the affairs of the United States. John Silvera acknowledged that there was a parcel of truth in the communist claims, which he described as "distorted" and "decontextualized."[63]

Race relations were crucial to the future of American society. The degree to which the United States could garner the friendship of Asia, the Near East, the Far East, as well as Africa and South America based on the principles of equality and brotherhood made racial issues paramount. Consequently, altering international perceptions of American race relations was essential to this endeavor. "We should envision the Negro as a primary weapon in attacking the Big Lie about what has become the Number One propaganda theme of the Communists," argued Silvera. Stressing the need for the United States to take the offensive on the race issue, he maintained that the story of African Americans, rather than undercutting professions of democracy, proved the worth and viability of the "American way of life"; indeed, he claimed, African Americans were to be pointed to with "pride as sources of inspiration and living examples of the success of the American social system." Moreover, Silvera believed that this approach needed to be adopted on a wide scale and would be decisive in the Cold War.[64]

Throughout his twenty-five-page paper, Silvera repeatedly stressed the need for America to emphasize the "Americanness" of black Americans. At various points he claimed, "the Negro is America's great opportunity," "the Negro can be the most potent weapon available to the free world," "the story of the Negro is indeed the saga of America," and "the history of mankind holds no parallel to the meteoric rise of the American Negro." These contentions were supported by myriad data. For example, figures from the Bureau of Census's report *Facts on the Economic and Social Status of Negroes, 1940–1950* buttressed his argument. African American home ownership grew 129 percent, while home ownership among the general population grew by only 81 percent. It also noted that school enrollment among African Americans rose by 17.2 percent, substantially higher than the 6.1 percent growth experienced by the general population. These figures hid the reality that African Americans were usually limited to inferior housing and educational institutions. These distorted and decontextualized figures suggested greater rights and privileges for

African Americans; however, African Americans still faced segregated living and working environments.

Despite the limitations and distortions of the arguments espoused by John Silvera, two influential African Americans—Dr. James C. Evans, a nationally renowned educator, and Lester Granger, the executive secretary of the National Urban League who had testified at the 1949 HUAC hearings—supported the increased involvement of African Americans in the Cold War battle to win the hearts and minds of the world's people of color. In a letter to C. D. Jackson, the head of the Cold War psychological warfare efforts during the Eisenhower administration, Lester Granger said John Silvera's conclusions were sound and practical. Granger was most adamant about the need for the United States to send more African Americans who were "firm in [their] faith regarding the power and vitality of true democracy" abroad as representatives of the American social system. Granger had spent almost two months in India consulting social welfare organizations, universities, and civic groups. That experience helped him see the depth of skepticism among Indian citizens about American democracy, particularly as it related to the treatment of African Americans. Granger shared Silvera's recommendation that America make deliberate, planned, and skillful use of African American spokesmen away from American shores.[65]

Conclusion

After Jackie Robinson integrated baseball, the swiftness with which sports integrated far outdistanced all other American private institutions, thus giving sports a privileged space in the discussion of U.S. race relations. The Cold War helped create a space in American society for the advancement of African Americans. However, as Robinson's HUAC testimony demonstrates, access meant that African Americans had to adhere to the politics of Cold War–era calls for national consensus. As the United States faced increasing condemnation for its racial policies, it turned to African American athletes as symbols of American racial progress. One of the first athletic teams to represent improved race relations in the United States during the Cold War was the Harlem Globetrotters. The next chapter looks at the origins of the team and analyzes their role as goodwill ambassadors for the United States.

2. "Spreading the Gospel of Basketball"

The Harlem Globetrotters, the State Department, and the Minstrel Tradition, 1945–54

James Michener, the noted Pulitzer Prize–winning author, was an acclaimed writer whose work reflected his conviction that writers should commit themselves to addressing social issues because they were the "conscience" of the nation. To that end, in his 1975 nonfiction work *Sports in America,* Michener revealed how a Harlem Globetrotters game forced him to reconsider his long-standing support for the notion that African American success in sports alleviated racial inequality. Michener began the chapter "Sports and Upward Escalation" by acknowledging that he had been taught and readily accepted the argument that sports were "the salvation of the black race . . . the highroad to upward escalation, the way he will escape from the ghetto." For Michener, the previous success of Jesse Owens, Jackie Robinson, Joe Louis, and others had proved two contentious points: in the sporting arena, African Americans thrived or failed solely based on their individual merit; and access to careers in athletics meant that social mobility was attainable for the masses of African Americans.

In *Sports in America,* Michener recounted a conversation with a colleague that challenged his understanding of sports as a viable vehicle through which to pursue the American Dream for African Americans. His unnamed counterpart, a sociologist, disagreed with Michener's perspective and countered Michener's arguments by saying, "All you're saying is that if a young Negro has superhuman capacities . . . he can win the normal decencies that the ordinary white man takes for granted. We'll have no social justice in this country until the day when an ordinary Negro with a ninth-grade education and no outstanding skills, has full equality." Michener momentarily pondered this position, but quickly dismissed the sociologist as a known troublemaker and potential communist.[1] Despite Michener's dismissive words, this encounter had a profound impact upon him.

Shortly after this exchange, James Michener attended a Harlem Globetrotters game in Hawaii. He laughed as the all-black team made fools of their white opponents and the white referee. Michener was amused by the trick basketball that contained a heavy weight inside the bladder, which caused the ball to bounce at unnatural angles. As he laughed and applauded, Michener noticed the troubling facial expressions of one of the Globetrotter players who sat on the bench. For the first time, he saw the face of a black man who seemed to find the team's antics unpleasant and distasteful. Immediately, he tried to understand the evening's game from the standpoint of that particular player. Michener began to see the Globetrotters' antics as validating widespread racist notions that African Americans were lazy, gangling, sly, and given to wild bursts of laughter. As he left the arena, he concluded that the team's racial message was "despicable."

Michener began the evening cheering, but by the end of the game, he supported the notion that the Harlem Globetrotters did more damage than good because they "deepened the stereotype of the lovable, irresponsible Negro," a notion that dominated the American minstrel tradition and had profound implications for the Globetrotters' comedy routines. Globetrotter players whose talents were, in many cases, equal to those of white professionals were reduced to earning a living by exhibiting derogatory stereotypes that had been propagated to disparage African Americans. Michener's insights are important because they highlight several meaningful interpretations of the Harlem Globetrotters during the 1950s. First, he demonstrates how the Globetrotters had to cater to dominate racist ideas regarding African Americans to maintain their financial viability. Second, Michener's account demonstrates the privileged role of sport in the national imaginary and discussions of race. Third, by beginning his account on the role of sport in race relations with a discussion of the Globetrotters, Michener acknowledged the importance of the Globetrotters in the larger discussions of race relations. Fourth, Michener's self-reflection is consistent with the reassessment that many whites experienced as they reexamined long-standing assumptions regarding African Americans as the civil rights movement dominated the American social and political landscape. And, finally, the facial expressions of the troubled Globetrotter and, by omission, the seemingly contented facial expressions of other members of the Globetrotters entourage hinted at the contentious debates regarding the Globetrotters' depiction of black humanity.

"'Spreading the Gospel of Basketball': The Harlem Globetrotters, the State Department, and the Minstrel Tradition, 1945–54" argues that the State Department actively attempted to develop a relationship with the Harlem Globetrotters in the years immediately preceding the 1954 *Brown v. Board of Education* decision. Prior to the 1954 Supreme Court ruling that outlawed segregation, the State Department sought to emphasize the idea that the "American Dream" was available to individual African Americans despite segregation. Additionally, State Department sponsorship could be interpreted as suggesting that the Globetrotters' cooning as well as their degrading caricatures of African Americans reflected the behavior, attitudes, and mind-set of most black Americans. Hence, State Department arguments simultaneously stressed racial progress, but also the notion that African Americans' "unsophisticated behavior" made them unfit or at least ill-prepared for full equality during the era of segregation.

The politics of symbolism associated with the Globetrotters' tours was designed to give legitimacy to existing racial inequalities in American society by stressing "progress" during the early Cold War era, despite the social, political, and legal barriers that hindered African American advancement. The symbol of the successful yet *segregated* athlete allowed the government to argue that segregation was not an impediment to the advancement of *individual* African Americans. Undoubtedly, international condemnation of U.S. race relations influenced the State Department's utilization of the Globetrotters as cultural ambassadors. The Globetrotter players' success symbolized before the world the accessibility of "the American Success Myth" for African Americans, thereby propagating the notion that talented and motivated African Americans could succeed in American society despite their minority status. Perplexingly, for American State Department representatives, the Globetrotters, a team formed because African Americans were excluded from white professional leagues, represented the "American Dream."

American Racism and International Politics

After working to marginalize prominent African Americans such as Paul Robeson and W. E. B. DuBois, who were critical of American race relations, the State Department sought to promote other prosperous African Americans as international spokesmen for American race relations. Not surprisingly, the U.S. government returned to HUAC's star witness, Jackie Robinson. In 1952 the State Department willingly offered financial support for a plan to send the Brooklyn Dodgers and the Cleveland Indians, the first two teams to integrate the National and American Leagues, on a worldwide goodwill tour. In accordance with President Truman's "Campaign of Truth," the State Department's Educational Exchange Service thought the tour would help further international goodwill and understanding. Perhaps more important, the symbolism associated with the first two teams to integrate would have served as a rebuttal to international criticism of racial segregation. Secretary of State Dean Acheson's letter to Walter O'Malley, the Dodgers' owner, revealed that racial concerns were crucial factors in the department's agenda. Acheson wrote, "Such outstanding American baseball teams as the Cleveland Indians and the Brooklyn Dodgers, representing perhaps the most typically American sport and comprised of participants of every nationality, creed and color, can do much to demonstrate the democratic principles upon which our government is based."[2] While supporting the goals of the program, O'Malley informed the State Department that the Dodgers would not be able to participate in the tour after he could not reach a satisfactory monetary agreement with State Department officials.

In addition to the financial challenges, a survey of American embassies worldwide suggested that baseball did not have broad international appeal. For example, the U.S. Embassy in Beirut listed the pros and cons of sending two baseball teams to Lebanon. There were several reasons supporting the tour: there was a general interest in sports in Lebanon, baseball was a useful demonstration of America's national pastime, there was potential for goodwill emerging from the players' personal contacts and public appearances, the game might serve as a diversion from local political preoccupations, and it would refute communist charges of U.S. racial discrimination. However, the challenges were daunting. Baseball was virtually unknown in Beirut; ready-made playing fields did not exist anywhere in the country. Arguably, the most important reason against the tour was that baseball did not have the "intrinsic . . . attraction of basketball and other continuous action sports."[3] Without the traditional American environment, atmosphere, and nostalgia surrounding the game, it was concluded that baseball might lose much of its appeal.

Despite the obstacles that derailed the attempt to send two integrated baseball teams abroad, the State Department experienced success helping facilitate the Harlem Globetrotters' tours. Given the Globetrotters' history, they were an interesting choice to be goodwill ambassadors. Arguably, the team was a better representative of U.S.-style segregation rather than American democracy because the team reflected many of the arguments that were expressed to explain why African Americans had not been granted full equality.

Reimagining the Harlem Globetrotters

Although the team had been referred to as "the Globetrotters" since the 1920s, the Chicago-based "Harlem" squad did not travel across the North Atlantic until their 1950 trip. Playing throughout Europe and northern Africa, the "self-styled missionaries spreading the gospel" of basketball were showered with superlatives: "fantastic," "incredible," "extraordinary," and "the greatest sports spectacle."[4] The team played seventy-three games in nine European and North African countries: Portugal, Switzerland, England, Belgium, France, Germany, Italy, Morocco, and Algeria. The Globetrotters and their white traveling companions, the "American All-Stars," played in Coimbra, Portugal, and Oporto, Portugal, in early May 1950. As was typical of their international trips, the Globetrotters and the American All-Stars played local amateur teams before playing each other. For example, in one game, the "American All-Stars" beat the Portuguese National Championship team, 79–9, before losing to the Globetrotters. In addition to playing games, the teams also conducted basketball clinics and taught basic skills. The success of the trip was evident in the American Consulate report that acknowledged the "unusually wide and deep impression of open friendliness both inter-racially and inter-nationally" suggested by the Globetrotters' and American All-Stars' good sportsmanship. It was common for the State Department to monitor the activities of Americans abroad during the early 1950s, but the accolades given to the Globetrotters were quite glowing.[5] The U.S. government realized that the success of the Globetrotters' tour attested to the power of sport to act as a cultural bridge across imposing racial, political, social, cultural, and linguistic barriers.

As goodwill ambassadors, the Globetrotters were enlisted to help the United States successfully persuade the world that the U.S. capitalist, democratic system was preferable to the Soviet communist government, even for minority groups. Their first official mission began on August 22, 1951, when they flew into Berlin, West Germany, for a contest against the Boston Whirlwinds before the largest crowd to attend a basketball game: seventy-five thousand people. Three days before the Berlin contest, the U.S. high commissioner in postwar Germany, John J. McCloy, watched the Globetrotters play in Frankfurt. At a meeting after the game, McCloy told Abe Saperstein that the Communists in East Berlin had effectively characterized the United States as a racist nation with their propaganda efforts. The Soviets had repeatedly lambasted the United States for preaching democracy but not practicing it. McCloy asked the Globetrotters to play a game in West Berlin because he thought the team's success was "a fine advertisement for American democracy." Initially, Saperstein was hesitant, because of the violence that had occurred a few months before at a Sugar Ray Robinson fight in West Berlin.[6] However, once Saperstein agreed to play the game, the high commissioner along with the State Department facilitated the contest. In fact, the American occupation authorities sponsored the free show for the Berlin public.

The impetus for the government's enlistment of the Globetrotters was the Communist-sponsored Third World Festival of Youth and Students scheduled for August 1951 in East Berlin. Two million youth from more than fifty nations were expected to convene for the two-week festival that principally featured Soviet-bloc dancers, musicians, and athletes. The theme of the festival was "For Peace and Friendship—against Nuclear Weapons." Fearful that the festival would contain rhetoric that denounced the United States as an imperialist power that sought to dominate all people of color, the State Department sought the assistance of the Globetrotters to present an alternative depiction of African American life. The game was part of democratic West Berlin's effort to mount its own counterfestival to attract and influence the many delegates who were expected to wander across the demarcation line into West Berlin.[7]

One of the biggest highlights of the contest was the halftime appearance of Jesse Owens. A U.S. Air Force helicopter circled the stadium three times before it landed during the halftime intermission. Owens, the African American sprinter who had won gold medals in the 100- and 200-meter dashes, the broad jump, and the 4 x 100 meter relay race at the 1936 Berlin Olympic Games, emerged from the helicopter wearing the same uniform that he had worn fifteen years prior. The crowd greeted Jesse Owens with a thunderous standing ovation that lasted five minutes. Initially, Owens stood at midfield, waving and bowing. Then he ran a lap around the stadium, which replicated the cheerful, easy strides of a victory lap. Hitler had declared that the 1936 Berlin Games would demonstrate the mastery of the Aryan race and on at least one occasion condescendingly referred to Owens and other African American athletes as "America's African Legion." However, Owens's success challenged Hitler's theory of Aryan supremacy, despite the fact that the Germans won the unofficial medal count.[8]

While Abe Saperstein depicted Jesse Owens as a symbol of African American advancement in Berlin, Saperstein's relationship with Owens was tainted with examples of exploitation. Jesse Owens had been employed by the Harlem Globetrotters periodically during the 1940s and 1950s as the traveling secretary, sports commentator, and halftime performer for one of the Globetrotters' farm teams. The former star track athlete and middle-aged man would run in circles, jumping over hurdles around the basketball court, during the degrading halftime performance. Saperstein also drew the ire of the black community when he preyed upon the financial troubles of Joe Louis and Jesse Owens by promoting a race between the two: Louis ran backward, and Owens crawled on his hands and knees. Nonetheless, upon returning to the United States after the basketball game in Berlin, Owens maintained, "We did a great job in selling America."[9] Apparently, the State Department agreed.

A December 22, 1951, State Department Circular Airgram from Secretary of State Dean Acheson recognized the potential value of the Globetrotters:

> The Department has been following the progress of the Harlem Globetrotters (Negro basketballers) and recognizes their value as ambassadors of goodwill, particularly in countries that are critical of U.S. treatment of Negroes. . . . Their itinerary is world-wide and has included all areas except Southeast Asia. . . . [T]heir attraction consists not only in superb skill but also showmanship and broad humor which is intelligible to all regardless of race, language or knowledge of basketball.
>
> *The Department feels that there are unlimited possibilities for racial understanding and good will in the visits of these teams* as already demonstrated in Latin America, North Africa, the Near East and Europe, which may provide an effective answer to Communist charges of racial prejudice in the U.S.A. The visit of these world-famous athletes might tie in with various physical education programs in prospect in nearly all Far Eastern countries such as the projected national fitness program in Burma.
>
> At present the Department is merely investigating the possibility of encouraging the Globetrotters to include Southeast Asian countries on their itinerary for 1953.[10]

What did Acheson mean by "racial understanding"? At the time of his statement, one of the principal reasons that the Globetrotters had become one of the best basketball teams in the world was because they had a near monopoly on African American basketball talent because of the exclusion of African Americans from white professional leagues.

Did the team's racially degrading humor suggest racial understanding by implicitly arguing that African Americans were not ready for full integration in American society? Indeed, the racist images and perceptions that they reinforced implicitly suggested that they were not the social equals of white Americans. The racially coded antics of the Globetrotters helped reinforce prevalent stereotypes of black men as infantile, shiftless, irresponsible, inept, "inadequate souls, who longed for the guidance of white men." Galloping on the court with high-stepping strides, bellowing out jungle shrieks, dancing feverishly, and grinning broadly, the Globetrotters reaffirmed widespread notions that African Americans were lazy, mischievous, and mentally inferior. Consequently, while emphasizing the notion that African Americans had opportunity in American society, the image that the Globetrotters portrayed suggested that African Americans were still capable of handling only limited tasks and responsibilities.[11]

In addition to offering an explanation for racial oppression in the United States, the Globetrotters' success also suggested that capitalism would help alleviate the racial oppression that blacks faced. The privately funded nature of Saperstein's team was important to the U.S. government because it highlighted the American capitalistic system and supported their notions about gradual progress. Most of the Globetrotter trips abroad were not funded by the State Department. However, the department acted as a facilitator and encourager of the Globetrotters' efforts. An airgram dated July 28, 1952, from Secretary of State Acheson claimed that the "Department is facilitating the Globetrotters' tour in every way possible, but has not subsidized their appearance at any place."[12] One of the principal reasons that the government did not provide direct support for these world tours was because the Harlem Globetrotters were a private organization, which allowed the government to make claims about the ability of capitalism to open doors for racial minorities in America society. Furthermore, the government was able to argue that the Harlem Globetrotters supported the claim that America's free-enterprise social system produced better athletes and sports teams than the Soviet state–sponsored system.[13]

On April 19, 1952, in Panama City, the Harlem Globetrotters initiated their first world basketball tour to celebrate their twenty-fifth anniversary. The tour spanned four continents—South America, Europe, Asia, and Australia. The team played in eighty-five cities and thirty-two countries. Recognizing the tremendous success that the Globetrotters had had on their excursion to Europe and North Africa the previous summer, the State Department sent the Globetrotters' itinerary for the world tour to American diplomatic and consular officers with the expressed demand that "all appropriate courtesies and assistance be extended to Mr. Saperstein and the Harlem Globetrotters."[14]

Dave Zinkoff, a noted Philadelphia sports announcer, who had accompanied the team on previous European tours, served as the team's general manager for the 1952 world tour. In addition to Zinkoff's official duties, Saperstein asked him to keep a diary of the trip, which Zinkoff eventually published in 1953 with the assistance of his coauthor, Edgar Williams. *Around the World with the Harlem Globetrotters* was a 218-page press release and propaganda piece that sanitized the team's racial history. The text contains many of the factual errors that continue to obscure the Globetrotters' past. Zinkoff relied on Abe Saperstein as his principal source of information. As Ben Green has suggested, Saperstein had "a chronic tendency to embellish, exaggerate, and sometimes lie," which makes it difficult to distinguish between myth and fact concerning the Globetrotters.[15]

Written on the heels of the wide-ranging NAACP boycott of the minstrel television show *Amos 'n' Andy,* which expressed the hostile attitude African Americans held toward the minstrel images the Globetrotters reflected, Zinkoff's text was an attempt to redefine the Globetrotters as Cold Warriors. By emphasizing the Globetrotters as symbols of racial progress in the United States, the team sought to create a relationship with the State Department that would help further the team's financial foundation, as well as provide the organization with valuable government allies if it encountered difficult situations while abroad by contributing to the State Department's efforts to win hearts and minds worldwide.[16]

In the foreword to Zinkoff's book, Abe Saperstein maintained that the Globetrotters "tried to sell America" wherever they traveled. As a complement to the Marshall Plan in Europe, the Globetrotters stressed the "Saperstein Plan." The team attempted to suggest before the world that the success of the African American players was indicative of the opportunities that were available to all African Americans in American society. Saperstein thought that the tour had been a great success, especially with "yellow, brown, and black peoples." Saperstein was most emphatic about his team's ability to counteract communist-inspired propaganda about American race relations: "The Communist argument is that the American Negro is exploited and held in bondage. The Globetrotters, without saying a word, refuted much of that by living at the best hotels and behaving in the manner of educated men." Similarly, David Zinkoff said that the world tour gave credence to the notion that "sports can be the broadest meeting ground in the world. . . . We erected basketball courts where there weren't any, made friends and, in our own way, tried to 'sell America' wherever we went. I think that we succeeded." As Abe Saperstein described it, "The Globetrotters carried around the world the American creed of sportsmanship and proved, once and for all, that sports [are] an effective common denominator." Despite the Globetrotters' high praise for their own efforts, it is still debatable whether the team helped change international opinions of American segregation, or if the team helped deepen the stereotypic images of people of African descent during their European, South American, and Middle Eastern jaunts.[17]

Around the World with the Harlem Globetrotters is filled with anecdotal asides that attempt to reveal how Zinkoff believed the Globetrotters positively depicted American race relations. In reference to the team's trip to Paraguay, Zinkoff argued, "The plainly evident respect, admiration, and comradeship between the members of the two teams, one coloured and one white, was somewhat of a surprise to many Paraguayans whose ideas of the role of the American negro had been influenced by stories of race riots, social discrimination, etc. The visit of the Globetrotters thus pointed out a brighter picture of the Negro place in American life." Nonetheless, Zinkoff's text also undermines the glowing description of the experiences of the Globetrotters.[18]

Zinkoff repeatedly tried to highlight the "brighter picture." However, by detailing the various high-risk playing conditions that the team endured in a comedic fashion, he also illustrated the extreme danger that African Americans had to navigate as Globetrotters. In the past, the team had played games in such improbable places as a hayloft, a church basement, and a drained swimming pool. During the 1952 world tour, the team played many games under hazardous conditions, including during a driving rainstorm in Reims, France, wearing vinyl rain hats and jackets, while holding umbrellas; a concrete floor in Liège, Belgium; a dirt playing floor in Holland; a bullring in Madrid, Spain; and a clay tennis court in San Remo, Italy. Zinkoff told a tale about a game at the Nostra Oltemare Arena in Naples that affirms the dangers the team faced. After noticing that the playing surface consisted of a thin sheet of plywood laid over an open orchestra pit, Saperstein still decided to play the game, according to *Around the World with the Harlem Globetrotters*. Early in the contest, one of the Globetrotters, William "Rookie" Brown, fell through the plywood and landed on the stone flooring below.[19] Rather than expressing horror at this unfortunate and dangerous incident, Zinkoff depicted it as merely the latest zany, unpredictable incident in the career of the Globetrotters.

Zinkoff attempted to defuse the situation by recounting a conversation aboard the team bus after Rookie Brown fell seven feet to the ground:

> Aboard the bus which carried us to Rome, where we were to enplane to Athens, Greece, a horrible thought suddenly struck Rookie Brown. "Suppose I hadn't been in possession of the ball when I fell through the floor," he said. "Nobody might have seen me fall. And maybe ten years from now somebody in Abe's office would ask, "Whatever happened to Brown?" And somebody else might say, "Brown? Let's see. Haven't seen him since Naples in 1952. Come to think of it, there was a hole in the floor at Naples. Maybe Brown fell into it. Next time we go there, let's take a look." "Brother," Rookie concluded, "am I glad I had the ball when I took that dive!"

This conversation seems laughable. Not because of the comedic tone in which it is presented, but rather because it seems like a highly implausible exchange. One would suspect that Brown would have been angered by the playing conditions that the team had to endure during this trip.[20]

The "Official" Narrative

Arguably, Zinkoff's most difficult yet important task was to erase the team's linkages to the long-standing minstrel tradition in the United States because it had the potential to undermine the new Cold Warrior narrative. Zinkoff and Saperstein developed historical tales to suit their agenda. Nonetheless, the origins of the Globetrotters and their comedic style of play continue to be shrouded in controversy. According to the "official" history of the Globetrotters, Abe Saperstein coached a team named the Savoy Big Five in their first game in November 1926 before a mere twenty people at the Savoy Ballroom in Chicago. During the ensuing weeks, the team never drew the large numbers of fans they were expected to attract. Eventually, the underpaid, disgruntled players feuded with the team's business manager. The disagreement caused three members of the African American squad—Walter "Toots" Wright, Byron "Fat" Long, and William "Kid" Oliver—to break away and form a new team. The players reportedly asked Abe Saperstein to be their coach. Saperstein eventually changed the team's name to the Harlem Globetrotters. *Harlem* identified the players as African Americans; *Globetrotters* gave the impression that the team had traveled extensively.[21]

There are several inaccuracies in the "official" narrative. As Ben Green points out in his groundbreaking book *Spinning the Globe: The Rise, Fall, and Return to Greatness of the Harlem Globetrotters,* the Savoy Ballroom did not exist in November 1926. Consequently, it was impossible for a team named after the ballroom to exist. It was not until December 1927 that the *Chicago Defender* introduced the team that would ultimately become known as the Savoy Big Five. The team played before an impressive crowd of twelve hundred fans and dance participants during its first game on January 3, 1928. Rather than folding quickly, the Big Five continued to be a major force on the basketball landscape for many years. Furthermore, no evidence exists to suggest that Abe Saperstein had served as the coach for the Savoy team. To the contrary, early records show that the team's first coach was Dick Hudson, who was replaced by Al Monroe after the team's initial season.

Former players, journalists, and scholars have challenged other aspects of the "official" version of the Globetrotter creation story. In *Elevating the Game: Black Men and Basketball,* Nelson George argues that Dick Hudson, the Big Five's African American business manager and coach, thought that a white man would more readily obtain bookings in Wisconsin and Minnesota than an African American promoter. Consequently, Saperstein was employed as a booking agent in 1926 in exchange for $100 and 10 percent of the booking fee. Originally hired to book ten games, Saperstein overbooked the Big Five and created the Harlem Globetrotters in order to fulfill the engagements that the Big Five could not keep, according to Nelson George.[22] Then by raiding the Savoy Big Five of its best players, Saperstein contributed to the weakening of the Savoy team while strengthening his own. However, aspects of George's account have also been challenged.

Ben Green agrees with George's claim that Saperstein was hired as a booking agent. However, he argues that it was not the Savoy Big Five that Saperstein overbooked; rather, Saperstein had been contracted to book games for a team called "Tommy Brookins's Globe Trotters."[23] Tommy Brookins, an African American and local basketball legend in Chicago, maintained that he started the team and was upset when Saperstein admitted that he booked as many games as he could and then formed another squad to fulfill the additional engagements. However, shortly after confronting Saperstein, Tommy Brookins decided to disband his team in order to pursue a singing career. He and Saperstein parted ways on amicable terms, as Saperstein continued to book games for the Globetrotters.

In *Spinning the Globe,* Green corrects one of the most important misconceptions regarding the Globetrotters when he reveals that Abe Saperstein was not the owner of the Harlem Globetrotters when the team first began competing in 1929. He maintains that Abe Saperstein and the five players were equal partners. They split the gate evenly, with Saperstein receiving a double share to help cover expenses. However, by 1934 most of the players from the original team had retired. Saperstein had spent years developing and cultivating essential relationships with promoters and newspaper reporters. As the original players began to retire to seek other opportunities, the new and remaining team members were not prepared to challenge Saperstein's ensuing power grab. Sensing that the new players were at his mercy, Saperstein announced changes to the team's financial structure and decision-making processes in 1934. Rather than receiving a percentage of the gate, Saperstein told his players, they were going to be paid $7.50 per game. This monumental shift had the effect of reducing the players to employees rather than equal partners, while Saperstein elevated himself to the principal decision maker and owner. As Green suggests, "From this point on, no player would be indispensable, and the most important member of the Harlem Globetrotters would be their owner, Abe Saperstein. . . . Players would be seen as cogs in the machine to be replaced with newer or better parts."[24] Saperstein's concentration of power also gave him the leverage to move the team into more racially sensitive terrain, including minstrel-based clowning. The incidents, myths, and fabrications surrounding the Globetrotters' introduction of "tricky" basketball are as nebulous as those surrounding Saperstein's consolidation of power within the organization.

According to Saperstein-Zinkoff lore, the Globetrotters were limited to conventional basketball from their inception until an unfortunate incident occurred during a 1939 game in Woodfibre, British Columbia, Canada, which led to the team's incorporation of "tricky" basketball antics. As the Globetrotters warmed up for the game, hecklers in the stands taunted the African American players. Runt Pullins, the starting point guard, is reported to have gathered the team together and said, "Let's pour it on these wise guys." With the Globetrotters leading 112–5, "the crowd of burly, irate, liquor-fueled loggers [were] on the brink of violence." Social critic Nelson George poignantly reminds us that "we have to remember that Saperstein's Trotters played . . . in a world where the lynching of black males for 'reckless eyeballing' of white women was still commonplace. . . . [T]he idea of five black men rolling into . . . town, kicking [butt] and getting paid could not have been the easiest sell."[25] Sensing the ugly mood of the crowd, the players reportedly began to perform tricks with the basketball. Runt Pullins dribbled the ball between his legs with a broad smile; Inman Jackson whipped a behind-the-back pass to Kid Oliver, who tossed the ball into the air and caught it on the back of his neck, then let it roll down his arm. Saperstein maintained that the wide grins of the Globetrotters helped reinforce the notion that they did not mean any harm to the white onlookers. As the legend goes, Saperstein encouraged his team to include the fancy dribbling and ball handling as a regular facet of their playing style.[26]

Although it is true that once the team began to incorporate "tricky" basketball the clever antics were utilized only toward the end of games, there are several questionable aspects of this legend. By suggesting that Woodfibre, British Columbia, Canada, was the instigating site for the racial tension that led to the allegedly spontaneous performance of elaborate, intricate, and difficult feats with the basketball, Saperstein was attempting to divert attention away from the history of racialized humor that placed the Globetrotters within the long-standing minstrel tradition in the United States. Canada, long reputed as a society more favorably disposed to racial egalitarianism, is a relatively surprising place from which a U.S.-based team would have to learn how to navigate a racially charged environment.

With the exception of the game in Woodfibre in 1939, the threats of violence, as well as actual instances of violence, have been erased from the Globetrotters' official narrative. However, basketball games pitting an all-black team against an all-white team occasionally became contests where racial prejudices and antagonisms were expressed. Although documentation is scarce, there are several important allusions to the team's involvement in hostile encounters and potentially volatile skirmishes within the United States prior to the alleged 1939 incident. Two of the documented incidents involved the Harlem Globetrotters and teams from Minnesota: the Minnesota Coaches and the Barnsdall Millers. In one instance, on December 16, 1935, in Rochester, Minnesota, the Globetrotters experienced a rare loss to the Minnesota Coaches, 40–25. The local newspaper, the *Post-Bulletin,* described the game as "one of the roughest exhibitions of basketball" the town had ever witnessed. The game had devolved into an exhibition of "blocking, hacking, gouging, tripping, and clipping," in which only "flagrant violations such as slugging, kicking an opponent while he was down and biting resulted in penalties."[27]

Similarly, on January 30, 1933, the Globetrotters won a tightly contested game against the Barnsdall Millers, 36–32. Ill feelings had been evident between the Globetrotters' leading scorer, Inman Jackson, and a Millers player identified only as "Roberts" in the press account. Immediately after the game, according to the *Northwest Monitor,* a local paper, Jackson "pushed Roberts and when the Barnsdall player turned, Jackson struck him in the nose, breaking it. One of the spectators stepped into the breech and as he did so, Jackson swung again and . . . started for the dressing room on the run. A riot threatened until police stepped in and separated the players from the milling crowd." The narrative presented by the *Northwest Monitor* based on eyewitness accounts from fans who had attended the game clearly suggested that Jackson, the Globetrotter, was the aggressor. Within the article, there is a reference to a skirmish in 1931 between the Globetrotters and another team from Minneapolis that may have precipitated this melee.[28]

The implicit suggestion of the legendary game in Canada was that the "new" tricky style of play alleviated racial tension or, at least, calmed tense environments. However, there is evidence to suggest that the opponents and fans were not seduced by the tricks but embarrassed and enraged by them, which could further heighten already perilous situations. For example, during a March 1944 game between the Globetrotters and the Oshkosh All-Stars attended by more than eleven thousand spectators, according to the *Chicago Defender,* the Oshkosh players "resorted to all sorts of rough tactics . . . [and] used their fists, elbows, and took swings at the Globetrotters as if the game was a battle royal." During the game, two white spectators were arrested for going onto the floor to participate in one of the game's many melees. With the Globetrotters leading 41–31 with six minutes remaining in the game, the Oshkosh All-Stars refused to continue. The *Chicago Defender* does not provide an explanation for Oshkosh's decision to forfeit the game. However, based on Globetrotter traditions at the time, it is quite clear that with a comfortable lead, this would have been an ideal situation for the Globetrotters to initiate their tricky act. Perhaps embarrassed by the Globetrotters antics, or perceiving the Globetrotters' display as a lack of sportsmanship, or simply frustrated by their impending defeat to the all-black team, the Oshkosh All-Stars walked off the court.[29]

Others have suggested that when the Globetrotters could not get a comfortable lead so they could begin clowning, it was a source of frustration for the Globetrotters. Indeed, as the team became noted for its brand of tricky basketball, it had to develop a comfortable lead in order to ensure victory, but also provide an entertaining show for the fans. However, when the team could not get a lead, it could have heightened the anxiety level of the team. Warren Perkins, who played for Fee's Rollerdome when the Portland-based team defeated the Globetrotters 39–30, believed that is what happened when one of his teammates was unnecessarily slammed into a brick wall near the court by a Globetrotter player who had been badly beaten on defense during a contest in January 1946. A fight ensued, and police officers had to restore order on the playing court.[30]

In addition to its entertainment value and soothing qualities, tricky basketball served a practical purpose: it gave the team an opportunity to rest its players during games. As the team became more popular, they increased their travel network to include all regions, but continued to maintain an insufficient seven-man roster. It was not uncommon for the Globetrotters to travel 300 miles by bus to play a game, then travel 150 miles to play a game the following day.[31] During the 1938–39 season, the Globetrotters played an astounding 161 games; the next season, they played 167 games. Since the team did not have more than two reserve players during the 1930s and 1940s, alternative means were needed to ease the burden of the players who were overworked. While one player dribbled around inferior opponents, the others relaxed and even went to the bench for a drink of water. Other times, while two Trotter players entertained the fans with a "series of machine gun–like passes," the other three laid beneath their basket, reading a newspaper or playing cards but, most important, resting. While the players appeared to be moving fast and expending large amounts of energy during the passing and dribbling exhibitions, their feet remained stationary.[32] As the team moved into a more elaborate form of entertainment, as Saperstein suggested, the Globetrotters could not sacrifice their identity as an excellent basketball team.

Further undermining the official narrative, there is tremendous evidence that suggests that the Globetrotters had been including trick shots and comedy in their games well before 1939. For example, in 1935 the local newspaper in Kelowna, British Columbia, listed some of the team's stunts: spinning the ball on one forefinger, rolling the ball up and down each arm, passing with one hand, performing underarm and overhead shots, and bouncing the ball from the floor into the basket. In Spokane, Washington, a 1935 newspaper described one of the gags that would become a Globetrotter staple: one of the shorter players would climb upon the shoulder of another player, and after receiving a pass, the elevated player would perform a slam dunk, an extremely rare occurrence at that time.[33] Rather than the product of a spontaneous incident, the Globetrotters' antics were rooted in contemporary popular culture and practices culled from a long line of other "tricky" teams within sports. Susan Rayl, whose work focuses on the Harlem Rens, an African American barnstorming basketball team that rivaled the success of the Globetrotters during the early twentieth century, suggests that showmanship was an important aspect of securing future dates for all traveling teams during the 1920s and 1930s.[34] The degree to which the threat of racial violence impacted the Globetrotters' move to incorporate comedy is debatable, but it is quite clear that the Globetrotters were borrowing from other cultural spaces.

The Baseball Roots of Clowning

Many of the Globetrotters' comedic sensibilities had been derived and adapted from black baseball, which had a long history of clowning. According to Sol White, an expert on African Americans in baseball during the nineteenth century, "Every man on a team would do a funny stunt during the game in the [eighteen] eighties and nineties." In addition to playing in league games, teams in the Negro Leagues began to compete against white small-town teams in the 1920s and 1930s to supplement their income. It was common practice to hold down the score to ensure return dates for the following year and to clown to keep the crowd amused. Ballplayers would bat one-handed, run the bases on their knees, and circle the bases in the wrong direction. Additionally, as a booking agent for barnstorming baseball teams during the 1930s and 1940s, Abe Saperstein was aware of the success of the Indianapolis Clowns, a team that at the height of their popularity in the mid-1930s attracted crowds of forty thousand to their games.[35]

The Indianapolis Clowns featured comedic antics that were clearly racialized. At the center of the Clowns' comedy routines was their first baseman. He would nonchalantly tag the base a split second before the runner reached safely. The lead clown would talk to the crowd, his pitcher, and the opposing team. After he joined the team in 1942, Reece "Goose" Tatum, who would be recruited by Abe Saperstein to star with the Globetrotters, was featured in the Clowns' capers.[36]

Wendell Smith, the dean of African American sportswriters during the 1940s, labeled the Clowns a "minstrel show" and asked African Americans to boycott the team's games. Despite Smith's call for a boycott, African American fans found the Clowns' routines entertaining. Between the fifth and seventh innings, the team engaged in skits designed to keep the crowd laughing. Baseball historian Donn Rogosin provides an apt description of a Clowns routine known as the "Fishing Act":

> Bebop [a mascot], Tut [another team mascot], and sometimes Goose Tatum pretended that they were fishing and rowing on a river that ran through the pitcher's mound. One of them looked up, and immediately a[n imaginary] bird "[defecated] in his eye." Then Tut caught a big [fish]. But after a struggle,

with victory almost in his grasp, he managed to fall out of the boat. . . . Tut tried to swim to safety, flailing the dirt around the mound. Little Bebop dragged the unconscious Tut ashore, but nothing revived him until Bebop removed his shoe and passed it daintily before Tut's nose.[37]

Another feature of the Clowns' act was their pepperball and shadowball exhibition. The infield players threw the ball to each other in an increasingly faster pace. Then they would discard the baseball and continue to go through the motions at a very fast pace. The link between the Clowns and the Globetrotters was explicitly demonstrated by the Globetrotters' adaptation of the pepperball routine. Replacing the baseball with a basketball and adding fancy passes, coupled with their musical anthem, "Sweet Georgia Brown," the team renamed its now world-renowned routine "the Magic Circle." Although it is clear that the Globetrotters were adopting ideas from black baseball, both sports were drawing from longer-standing minstrel traditions in the United States.

Perpetuating the Myths of Minstrelsy

Minstrelsy began in the early nineteenth century; by the early twentieth century, it was the most popular form of theatrical entertainment in the United States. During minstrel shows, white male performers blackened their faces with burnt cork and applied white makeup around their mouths and eyes as a means of replicated the degrading wide-eyed and smiling stereotypic images associated with African Americans. Minstrel shows featured jokes, eccentric dances, slapstick humor, and a stump speech. The stump speech caricatured black intelligence by using malapropisms and broken English to ridicule the idea that blacks were intellectually capable of grasping the complexity of the problems facing the nation. Mel Watkins has argued that minstrel audiences thought African American–inspired caricatures were funny, "only insofar as they engaged in a quaint, foolish, and childlike behavior, or stumbled over a language that they were only halfheartedly taught to speak and forbidden to read."[38]

The "happy darky fantasy" minstrel images of African American males served as a powerful alternative to the realities of the underlying brutality of the systems of slavery and Jim Crow in the United States. By embracing the ignorant, contented figure as a symbol of U.S. race relations, minstrelsy sought to express the alleged satisfaction of black folk with their social, political, and economic devaluation. Hence, minstrel images helped alleviate widespread fears regarding African American retribution for the injustices faced during slavery and Jim Crow segregation.[39]

The two most popular caricatures of African Americans to emerge out of the minstrel tradition were Jim Crow and Zip Coon. Jim Crow was usually depicted in a rural plantation setting and was characterized by his ignorant, slow-moving, slow-thinking, slow-talking, slow-to-anger, fun-loving demeanor. As Melvin Ely has argued, "Jim Crow was supposed to epitomize the plantation slave. . . . [H]e was physically grotesque, sporting a distorted version of African features, disheveled clothing, and a perpetual grin." He was depicted as an "ignorant emotionally childlike, fun loving creature endowed with an innate musical and rhythmic sense." Conversely, Zip Coon was parodied because of his self-conception as an urbanite dressed in "ostentatious finery and affected a graceful carriage; he boasted of his wide-ranging knowledge and of his magnetism among the fair sex." However, despite Zip Coon's pretensions, he was still widely associated with many of the attributes attributed to Jim Crow: "ignorance, musicality, a love of the sensual, and an outlandish appearance, including grossly caricatured Negroid features."[40] Most white Americans found these two stereotyped images appealing because they both presented black men as harmless and contented.

Similarly, radio's first serial and the most popular show nationally four months after its debut in 1929, *Amos 'n' Andy,* caricatured African Americans as cunning, dull witted, and incompetent. As historian Barbara Savage has suggested, one of the central common denominators with mass appeal during the 1930s was the stereotypic depictions of African Americans as infantile, shifty, and ignorant. Roi Ottley's words about the portrayal of African Americans in radio had relevance for all forms of popular culture at the time: "Until now, Negroes in radio have been mainly caricatures. They are usually hysterical servants frightened at ghosts—lazy buffoons—charmingly naïve children or menials rapturously enchanted by their white masters."[41] In addition to radio, stage presentations, and films, other sports teams had engaged in presenting African Americans in the minstrel tradition.

During the 1930s, the most popular African American movie star was Lincoln Theodore Monroe Andrew Perry. Better known as "Stepin Fetchit," Perry's minstrel-inspired brand of comedy depicted African Americans as coons, fools, and sambos. Fetchit was a tall, thin, dark-skinned man with a shaved head. Wearing clothes that were too large, he usually looked as if he was wearing clothes handed down to him, presumably from an affluent white benefactor. Physically, Fetchit often had a wide grin, which highlighted his extremely white teeth. Otherwise, he was noted for his head-scratching entrances accompanied by a dead-pan expression and his use of fractured language with an incoherent, whiny delivery. Furthermore, his shuffling gait seemed to reflect a lack of coordination, which placed heightened emphasis upon his huge shoes, slow pace, and flailing arms. Fetchit's act, like other minstrel acts, was designed to stress the inferiority of African Americans.[42] Fetchit's commercial success became one of the most important inspirations behind Saperstein's creation of a new position on the Globetrotter team: lead clown.

The Arrival of Goose Tatum

Before the arrival of Goose Tatum, the Globetrotters had incorporated fancy dribbling and a few comedy routines, but Goose Tatum became the team's first full-time court comedian. As Ben Green has argued, Tatum represented a new generation of Globetrotter players. The original Globetrotters had been reared in the North after their families had left the Deep South to seek opportunity in Chicago during the first great migration. After Saperstein had several incidents with city players in the early years, he focused on recruiting country boys, whom he believed to be more trusting, less sophisticated, and unlikely to challenge his authority.[43]

The genealogy of Goose Tatum's path to athletic and comedic stardom is murky, but it is clear that he developed his basketball skills relatively late in his athletic career. The skinny, lanky athlete had been a star baseball player for the Black Colonels and the Zulu Cannibal Giants: the Zulu squad played games wearing grass skirts and sometimes performed in whiteface. When Abe Saperstein spotted him in 1942, Tatum was the first baseman and lead clown for the African American Indianapolis Clowns. Saperstein decided to recruit Tatum and develop his basketball skills so that he could be a competent basketball player, while entertaining the crowds as the lead clown. However, before Tatum could get too involved in honing his basketball skills, he was drafted into the military.[44]

Goose Tatum was discharged from the military and returned to the Globetrotters in 1946. When Tatum returned, he began to develop most of the team's classic trick shots and comedy routines. For example, Tatum, who preferred the spectacular to the conventional, would flip the basketball backward over his shoulders into the basket. He would periodically stop the game and engage the crowd by initiating a devilish game of "hide-and-seek," or by posing for pictures in egotistically outlandish poses. One of his most hilarious routines involved him tiptoeing into the opposing team's huddle, listening to their strategy, and returning to the Globetrotters' huddle grinning broadly and divulging the other team's game plan. At other points in the game, he would stroll into the stands and sit on the lap of a spectator, borrow a hat, and sashay back to the court, score a quick basket, then head to the stands to return the hat and shake hands with the fans within arm's reach. These antics led social critic Nelson George to rightly maintain that "Tatum, more often than any other player, epitomized the childlike qualities that made even intolerant whites comfortable with the Trotters."[45]

Because of his desire to replicate minstrel imagery, Abe Saperstein preferred players with dark skin and ugly faces. Hence, the physical appearance of some of the team members was not merely happenstance, but reflected a concerted effort. As the team's humor became more racialized, Saperstein wanted his players to naturally resemble the cosmetically enhanced lips and eyes that were characteristic of minstrel artists. Tex Harrison, a Globetrotter player during the 1950s, remembered that on a trip to a southern town, Saperstein spotted an African American man with "glistening black skin, wide eyes, and huge lips walking down the street." "Stop the bus," the coach yelled to the bus driver. Saperstein got off the bus and asked the man whether he could play basketball. "No," the man replied. Undaunted, Saperstein told him, "Just get on the bus, we'll get you a uniform and teach you how to play." The man traveled with the team for a few weeks before Saperstein admitted that he was too uncoordinated to play for the team.[46]

As the team's chief clown and most recognizable player, Goose Tatum's physical appearance and mannerisms were the subject of constant ridicule and degradation. Tatum often employed big flashing teeth and widened eyes coupled with his large feet, slow-paced movements, and broken dialect. David Zinkoff, the team's manager, referred to Tatum as possessing "a charmingly bizarre appearance." Marshall Smith, a writer for *Life,* wrote a feature article about Goose Tatum for the March 9, 1953, edition: "Basketball's Court Jester." "A grotesque appearance, for which most clowns need elaborately incongruous clothes and makeup, is Tatum's natural birthright," Smith opined. "He comes equipped with tenuous, apelike arms. . . . [His hands] dangle loosely in the neighborhood of his knees. . . . [P]eople laugh at him on sight." Characteristic of the era, Smith believed that Goose Tatum's physical appearance and widespread racist assumptions that the slow-witted, lanky, simple-minded, ignorant, confused images that Tatum's antics reflected were beneficial because

Tatum would be able to entertain audiences predisposed to thinking about African Americans as overgrown children.[47]

Tatum had the gifts associated with great physical comedians: an elastic body and face, impeccable timing, charisma, a need to be an exhibitionist, and an appreciation and understanding of "the absurd." Goose Tatum's propensity to clown and romp around the court while making absurd faces and strange noises fed the belief that African Americans were the stereotypic "happy-go-lucky Negro clown oblivious to insult and humiliation." Or more pointedly, as Jack Olsen asserted, Tatum and the other Globetrotters "running about the court emitting savage jungle yells, shouting in thick Southern accents 'Yassuh, yassuh,' pulling sly tricks like walking with the ball when the white referee's back is turned . . . come across as frivolous, mildly dishonest children, the white man's encapsulated view of the whole Negro race set to the rhythm of Sweet Georgia Brown."[48]

Even the team's brand of competitive basketball invoked laughter and ridicule. Employing what John Christgau has referred to as a "merry-go-round" offense, the Globetrotters positioned Tatum, their primary ball handler, at the high post while three wing players circled around in a figure-eight formation while exchanging passes with Tatum. This simplified offensive strategy made a mockery of the complex strategies that other teams utilized in competitive games. The simplified offensive strategies implied that African Americans were not capable of grasping more complicated structures and patterns. In the early twentieth century, basketball was perceived as a thinking man's game, but by utilizing a cartoonish offense, the team was seen as supporting the suggestion that African Americans were mentally inferior.[49]

The Globetrotters' antics represented a subtle yet encompassing form of social control that limited the purview of African American achievement in American society. By making black masculinity the object of laughter, the goal was to strip the players of their masculinity, dignity, and self-possession. The stereotypic behavior became a means to attract white audiences without threatening the social order by suggesting that African Americans were the intellectual and social equals of whites. Consequently, the Globetrotters' humor was based on playing to the prejudices of white audiences.[50]

By making the white officials and the white opposing team the objects of their jokes, the Globetrotters appeared to control the balance of power. However, the team's humor gave credence to the notion that laughing, joking, and childlike behavior were proof of African Americans' supposed natural inherent inferiority.[51] The Globetrotters' comedic nature, which featured laughter, smiling, and a jovial atmosphere, suggested that African Americans were content with their status in America.

The Globetrotters and the Trickster Tradition

The discussion of the Harlem Globetrotters and their relationship to minstrelsy has dominated academic and popular discussions of the team's comedic and political significance. However, it is important to remember that the origins of minstrelsy emerged in white northern communities. While minstrelsy is a crucial lens through which we have to engage the cultural, social, and political meaning of the team, we also have to think about how the Globetrotters' humor and political salience are rooted within African American cultural practices. Cultural historian Robin D. G. Kelley utilizes James Scott's theory of the "hidden transcript" to examine forms of popular culture such as songs, jokes, folklore, and athletics that demonstrate how African Americans have used mainstream spaces to challenge dominant political structures in ways that are not always perceptible to mainstream audiences. In this case, the term *hidden transcript* refers to the ability of African Americans to see the suggested yet not explicitly subversive communication embedded in the comedic routines and antics of the Globetrotters.[52]

Trickster tales are among the most important and popular African American cultural products that contain hidden transcripts. Although other cultures produced trickster tales long before the transatlantic slave trade, African American trickster tales were undoubtedly influenced by the harshness of American slavery. Trickster tales suggested that the most effective means of challenging racial oppression was to seemingly accept the prevailing notions and fundamental assumptions of the dominant power structure, which defined African Americans as mentally inferior. Central to this process was the simultaneous use of furtive activities to undermine those assumptions. Hence, African Americans relied upon widespread perceptions of them as ignorant, lazy, and childlike to create spaces to confront white supremacy through guile, trickery, subterfuge, and deception. As John Roberts suggests in *From Trickster to Badman: The Black Folk Hero in Slavery and Freedom,* animal trickster tales were created to "serve as a model of behavior under artificially created conditions of destructive material shortages imposed on them by the power and control of the slave masters within a socio-political system that they did not accept as legitimate."[53]

Determined to enhance their ability to navigate the oppressive, racist conditions that confronted them, African Americans used trickster tales that emphasized the need to employ "amoral" actions such as stealing and lying as powerful weapons to defend themselves against the ravages of racial oppression. As Robert Falls, a former slave in Tennessee stated, "They learned us to steal." Thus, in the contexts of slavery and segregation, activities that oppressors thought supported derogatory ideas about African Americans were utilized as tools to attack the social order by undermining efficiency and productivity. Furthermore, these covert activities helped improve the material living conditions that confronted many African Americans.[54]

Black cultural commentators such as Frantz Fanon, W. E. B. DuBois, and Paul Laurence Dunbar have explored the meaning of the dual identities that African Americans maintained as tools of resistance. Arguably Dunbar's 1895 poem "We Wear the Mask" best captures the political utility of the subterfuge that trickster tales advocated:

> We wear the mask that grins and lies,
> It hides our cheeks and shades our eyes,—
> This debt we pay to human guile;
> With torn and bleeding hearts we smile,
> And mouth with myriad subtleties.
>
> Why should the world be over-wise,
> In counting all our tears and sighs?
> Nay, let them only see us, while
> We wear the mask.
>
> We smile, but, O great Christ, our cries
> To thee from tortured souls arise.
> We sing, but oh the clay is vile
> Beneath our feet, and long the mile;
> But let the world dream otherwise,
> We wear the mask!

Here Dunbar argues that rather than fighting to undermine dominant notions regarding their alleged inferiority, African Americans would benefit from stealthily deploying those ideas as techniques for survival and subversion. The ability to conceal one's true emotions was a necessary tool in the fight to maintain spaces of resistance. The slave aphorism "Got one mind for white folks to see another for what I know is me" captures the political utility of the concept. Therefore, central to the concept of masking was the reality that slave masters were unaware of the political nature of the masking. While African Americans engaged in covert trickery, whites often saw their actions as confirming the alleged subservience of African Americans.[55]

The Globetrotters' humor fell within the African American trickster tradition. Goose Tatum, the team's chief clown, frequently entertained by engaging in activities that clearly seemed to be at odds with the competitive ethos that was associated with sporting competitions. Tatum and other Globetrotters would dance, play leapfrog and modified baseball games, and incorporate elements of football into basketball games. Saperstein argued that the comedy routines helped deflect attention from the competitive nature of these contests, theoretically minimizing the level of hostility that the interracial contests could reveal.

In one of the team's most popular gags, Tatum would tiptoe to a patron in the first row. The sight of a tall, thin, dark-skinned African American male tiptoeing as if his slow, gangly movements made him undetectable caused the audience to laugh at the man whose actions made him hypervisible rather than invisible. Once Tatum reached his targeted customer, usually an older white woman dressed in a fur coat or an outfit that suggested her place firmly within the upper middle class, Tatum began to mimic the stereotypic walk of European aristocrats who were noted for their elitist walking style characterized by its pomposity. At the precise moment that Tatum engaged in this activity, his four other teammates attempted to stop the other team from scoring on the Globetrotters' defensive end of the court. Tatum's seeming disregard for the contest reinforced prevailing notions about the laziness and mental capacities of African Americans, which induced fits of laughter in the audience.

While Tatum's actions clearly buttressed many of the claims directed toward African Americans based on minstrel traditions, the conclusion of the gag suggests the trickster roots of the routine. The gag worked best when his four teammates were able to stop the other team from scoring. Once a Globetrotter forced a turnover or secured a rebound, he would toss the ball to the other end of the court, where Tatum, with a renewed focus on the game, stopped underneath the basket, awaiting the ball. Tatum, now standing under the basket alone with the basketball, would then turn his back toward the goal and nonchalantly flip the ball into the basket. Here, Tatum's actions offer several interpretations. By acting distracted, Tatum had lured the other team into believing that he was not an offensive threat to them, but by quickly reentering the playing surface, he was able to score an easy basket. However, by turning an easy shot into a difficult one, Tatum helped to minimize any animosity from the audience that would have resulted from his trickery.[56]

Tatum's nickname, "Goose," clearly falls within the trickster tradition. African American trickster tales often featured small nonthreatening animals such as hares, which would normally be considered prey for the more aggressive and predatory animals such as tigers, foxes, bears, and wolves. Thus, the trickster is represented as the harmless, weaker creature incapable of winning a physical confrontation with the larger animals. Similarly, given their vulnerable position in the dominant social order, it is understandable why people of African descent had to embrace strategies that reflected their defenseless status.[57] As nonthreatening herbivores whose diet consists of grains, marine vegetation, and grasses, geese are noted for their affability rather than ferocity. Because of their gentle nature, geese are preyed upon by seabirds and traditional trickster foes: coyotes and foxes. Geese have commonly been referred to as either stupid or humorous, gentle creatures; these descriptions were also closely aligned with the many U.S. minstrel depictions of African Americans.

In order to succeed in this racial climate, many blacks had to act within the trickster tradition to navigate U.S. racial politics. This is quite evident by examining the central role of the Harlem Globetrotters in the integration of the NBA. It is not a coincidence that several Globetrotters were among the first African Americans to be signed and drafted into the NBA. Taking advantage of one of the few spaces to display their basketball talent at the professional level, many of the Globetrotters made use of the opportunities to compete against the best white players to demonstrate that they could play the game at the highest levels. Indeed, the Globetrotters' two improbable wins against the Minneapolis Lakers were highly influential in the league's decision to integrate.

The Globetrotters won the World Championship of Basketball in 1940. This victory game gave the team a measure of credibility as a "legitimate" basketball team. However, it was the team's two successive victories against the Minneapolis Lakers in 1948 and 1949 that momentarily solidified the team's status as a premier basketball organization. During the first game, in 1948, the team came back from a halftime deficit and was able to keep the game's best player, George Mikan, in check. The Globetrotters won the sold-out game on a last-second shot by Ermer Robinson. To prove that their victory was not a fluke, they defeated the Lakers the following year by four points and even managed to incorporate some of their tricky plays. However, after these two improbable wins, the Lakers added Vern

Mikkelson to their roster, which already included two future hall of famers: George Mikan and Jim Pollard. Between 1950 and 1953, the Lakers won five straight meetings, embarrassing the Globetrotters in several contests, including an 84–60 debacle in Chicago Stadium before a capacity crowd of twenty thousand.[58]

The Globetrotters' two victories against the Lakers helped demonstrate that they remained a competitive basketball team despite their enhanced emphasis on comedic entertainment. By the beginning of the 1950s, the Harlem Globetrotters were grossing between two and three million dollars annually, making them the most successful basketball organization in the world. Simultaneously, the new National Basketball Association was having difficulty surviving financially. The Globetrotters agreed to play doubleheader games with the NBA in order to boost NBA attendance. The Globetrotters game would be played first, and then the second game would be played between two NBA teams. This arrangement helped keep the struggling league afloat. For example, on March 2, 1950, the Boston Celtics played a game against the New York Knicks before a capacity crowd of twenty-three thousand fans in the second half of a doubleheader that featured the Globetrotters in the first game. Three days prior, the Celtics had been able to attract only seventeen hundred spectators. Joe McKenney, a sportswriter for the *Boston Post,* was so unimpressed by the Celtics 81–72 victory over the Knicks that he labeled the game "dull." Whereas the Trotters had elicited cheers and laughs, the Celtics brought groans from their fans. Compared to the fancy dribbling, clowning, and trick shots performed by Saperstein's team, McKenney wrote, the Celtics were "dead on their feet . . . and the cheers of the crowd for the Globetrotters had long since stilled completely."[59]

However, three years into the joint effort between the Globetrotters and the NBA, and just six weeks after the doubleheader with the Celtics, the Globetrotters' relationship with the NBA changed forever. On April 25, 1950, at the NBA's draft, Walter Brown, the owner of the Boston Celtics, drafted Chuck Cooper in the second round. A hush fell over the crowd, and Brown was asked if he was aware that Copper was African American. At that point, Brown reiterated his selection. Ron Thomas argues in his book *They Cleared the Lane: The NBA's Black Pioneers* that Abe Saperstein had been the major stumbling block to integration in the NBA. Thomas suggests that the NBA's financial troubles and the league's reliance on the income from the Globetrotter doubleheaders made them sensitive toward the idea that signing African American players would be disruptive to their important relationship with Abe Saperstein. Nonetheless, two other

African Americans were picked in the later rounds of the same draft. The Washington Capitols selected both Earl Lloyd from West Virginia State in the ninth round and Harold Hunter from North Carolina Central in the following round. This was particularly troubling to Saperstein because all three of the drafted players had played with the Globetrotters earlier that year. In the cases of Cooper and Lloyd, both had played games with the Globetrotters earlier that month.[60] This new development signaled the end of Saperstein's virtual monopoly on the best African American basketball talent.

Despite the NBA's growing number of African American players, Abe Saperstein maintained an amiable relationship with the NBA until the late 1950s. Nate "Sweetwater" Clifton became the first African American to sign a contract with the league after the New York Knicks paid Abe Saperstein twenty-five thousand dollars for the rights to his services. Clifton started playing with the Globetrotters after two years' experience as a member of the New York Rens and the Dayton Mets. In 1948 the six-foot-seven, 220-pound Clifton was considered an imposing center by that day's standard. Saperstein maintained that he had decided to sell Clifton's contract to the Knickerbockers because Clifton was "too hard to handle." Alternatively, Clifton had been increasingly unhappy playing with the Harlem Globetrotters due to the constant travel and pay inequities. Although he had one more year on his contract with the Globetrotters, he informed Saperstein he intended to sign with the Knicks, who held his territorial rights. Sensing the bleakness of Clifton's dissatisfaction with the Globetrotters, Saperstein sold his contract. Despite these difficulties, it appears that the split between Clifton and Saperstein was amicable because Clifton frequently returned to the Globetrotters during the team's summer tours after completing the NBA season.[61]

In spite of losing Clifton to the NBA, Saperstein continued to fight for the services of the best black players during the 1950s. For example, a battle for the services of six-foot-eleven Walter Dukes of Seton Hall was waged after the court legend averaged twenty-six points per game, while leading Seton Hall to a then record twenty-seven-game winning streak. Dukes led the Pirates to the National Invitational Tournament (NIT) championship and was named the most valuable player. Because Dukes played at Seton Hall, he was considered the property of the New York Knicks under the territorial draft rights of the NBA. Nonetheless, the scarcity of quality big men made players with the imposing inside skills that Walter Dukes possessed prime commodities; upon entering the draft, Dukes had been rated among the three best collegiate centers. Ned

Irish of the New York Knicks had reached a salary agreement with Dukes when the Globetrotters offered twice as much money. Dukes signed with the Globetrotters. This was a major coup for Saperstein, who believed that Dukes would help maintain the reputation of the Globetrotters as a legitimate basketball team.[62]

Despite their comedic antics, the Globetrotters competed for the services of players like Walter Dukes because they wanted to be perceived as a first-class basketball team. To that end, the team initiated a tour with college players as a means of displaying their basketball talent. In April 1950, the Globetrotters inaugurated the "World Series of Basketball," a prestigious transcontinental tour pitting them against some of the best graduating college basketball players: Bob Cousy, Paul Arizin, Kevin O'Shea, and others. The College All-Stars were coached by the legendary Hank Iba, Ray Meyers, and Clair Bee. Basketball was not televised nationally, and the fledgling NBA did not travel west of the Mississippi; consequently, the "World Series" provided the only opportunity for parts of the nation to see the best ballplayers in the nation. The Trotters won the first series, eleven to seven, but realized in the first game that the clowning had to be held to a minimum if they hoped to win the series. Accustomed to amassing an early lead, then concentrating on their comedy routines, the Globetrotters found themselves confronted with a "zealous band of collegians" and had to struggle to ensure victory.[63] The stiff competition the Trotters faced on the tours, which lasted until 1962, provided them with an opportunity to demonstrate their status as a preeminent basketball team. However, the fans were often disappointed by the lack of shenanigans that plagued the series with the College All-Stars. Fans frequently sat in silence during the long stretches of conventional basketball, often leaving the arena disappointed at the lack of tricks and comedy routines.[64]

Arguably, the most competitive of the "World Series" was the 1952 tour. The Globetrotters won eleven of seventeen games in the Third Annual World Series of Basketball. A total of 201,755 fans saw the teams play sixteen games in fifteen days, including the largest basketball crowd since 1947: 20,047 spectators in Chicago. Additionally, they played before thirteen sell-out crowds, while breaking attendance records in seven major arenas, including Madison Square Garden, the San Francisco Civic Auditorium, the Denver Coliseum, and the Detroit Olympia. The games were extremely competitive: seven were decided by three points or less and ten by a maximum of six points, and two were sent to overtime. At the series' conclusion, the teams' scoring averages were 66.8 for the Globetrotters and 64.3 for the College All-Stars.[65]

In 1962 the World Series of Basketball ended. Interruptions in the tours in 1959 and 1960 due to the Pan-American and Olympic Games led to a decline in prestige. Additionally, the Globetrotters won fifteen of the sixteen games in 1962, and their dominance undermined the competitiveness of the series. The Trotters' combined record for the eleven tours was 144-66: a 69 percent winning percentage. During the duration of the World Series, more than 2 million fans attended the transcontinental games, and at the height of its popularity, the series overshadowed the NCAA Tournament, the NIT, and the NBA Finals. From its inception, the series had functioned as a barometer for Saperstein's ballplayers. Heretofore, the team had played novelty and comedic basketball for most of the year, but the World Series afforded them the opportunity to prove their legitimacy as basketball players. As a former Globetrotter noted, "When [the World Series] was terminated it was sad because we're not able to [prove that we were high-caliber basketball players]. . . . [T]his was the premise that we were built on—being great players, not clowns."[66] Although this is true, by the inception of the World Series of Basketball, clowning had begun to rival basketball as the dominant drawing card for the team. Understandably, by the end of the series, clowning had become entrenched as the Globetrotters' claim to preeminence.

Extending the Globetrotters' Audience

Because it was based on the Globetrotters and provided a compelling narrative of the team as Cold Warriors, the State Department supported Columbia Pictures' worldwide distribution of the film *The Harlem Globetrotters,* which was originally released in 1951 and starred Rookie Brown, the member of the Harlem Globetrotters who fell through the playing surface in Italy. The team's significance as symbols of racial progress caused the State Department to extend the range of the team's international influence. During the 1951–52 season, the Globetrotter organization played 333 games in the United States, Mexico, South America, Europe, Australia, and Asia. No matter how many games the team played annually, they would have been hard-pressed to match the number of people that they could reach through film.

U.S. Information Service (USIS) officials in Martinique, an island in the French West Indies, were excited by the Globetrotters' movie because they thought the film would enlighten members of the local populace who had been led astray by communist depictions of African Americans as downtrodden, persecuted, second-class citizens. Instead, the African

American athletes were portrayed as "well-dressed, well-paid, and well-fed Americans whose skill is admired by Negro and white fans alike."[67] Despite the rhetoric, the film was not an accurate reflection of life in the United States.

According to public affairs officer Stephen M. Carney, *The Harlem Globetrotters* stressed, albeit erroneously, that social mobility was readily accessible for African Americans.[68] In its attempt to provide a favorable impression of American race relations, the story presents contradictory images. For example, during one scene at a large university, a white professor attempts to convince Brown's character, Billy Townsend, the star African American basketball player and excellent chemistry student, that he should not abandon his promising academic future for the temporary high salaries of professional basketball. Commenting on this scene, Carney said that it "demonstrates the fact that Negroes are welcomed in American universities and that excellent career possibilities await them upon graduation." However, later in the film, Billy Townsend suffers a career-ending injury, and an official at a historically black university offers him a position at a black college. This scene reinforces the reality that segregated schools were ubiquitous in American society during the 1950s. In fact, most of the Harlem Globetrotter players had attended black colleges because access to other institutions was limited.[69]

Regardless of these inconsistencies, other scenes that feature the star player meeting his wife in an integrated hotel lobby, the comfortable living conditions of Billy Townsend's well-furnished apartment, and his one-thousand-dollar monthly salary are visual images that could be used to "refute communist-inspired distortions of the status of the America negro." Carney recommended that the film could be valuable to all posts where people were concerned with the treatment of minority groups in American society. Hence, both Carney and Zinkoff took liberties with the Globetrotters' cultural meaning.[70]

The Goose Is Loose

Was Saperstein merely capitalizing on the market's willingness to support a minstrel-inspired basketball team, or did he harbor racial animosity toward African Americans? Abe Saperstein fought hard to depict his team as a bastion of racial justice in sports. Notwithstanding the harsh environments that his team had to endure, Saperstein fashioned himself as "the Jewish Abe Lincoln." Consequently, he was shocked to hear anyone refer to him as racist. Many of the players he subsequently hired, including

Connie Hawkins and Meadowlark Lemon, found him to be paternalistic. "As long as you played the role of a grateful boy," Hawkins said, "Abe was good to you. . . . You had to let him know that you thought he was great."[71] Meadowlark Lemon developed a love-hate relationship with Saperstein: "[Saperstein] was the guy who made my dream come true. On the other [hand], I felt like I had to treat him as a father figure, a Santa Claus, to get anything out of him. I was in no position to demand or even ask. I had to be subservient and beg and plead to get a break."[72] Saperstein is reported to have made a number of statements that were demeaning toward his players.

Spinning the Globe chronicles a number of Saperstein's most offensive comments. Saperstein told a reporter at the *Seattle Times* in 1940 that a "negro is a natural entertainer." "Negroes are anything but bright" was his statement to Hal Straight of the *Vancouver Sun*. He also told Pete Sallaway, a Canadian reporter, that his team "can't think for themselves. I wonder just how far they would get if they didn't have me around to figure out" situations.[73] Lemon most poignantly summed up his eleven-year dysfunctional relationship with Saperstein when he said, "None of us really liked him, but for some reason we loved him."[74]

Despite the poor working conditions that the players endured, the Globetrotters continued to depict themselves as representatives of the American Dream. However, even after the Globetrotters began to travel internationally as representatives of racial progress in the United States, the team continued to schedule games in the segregated South. Tex Harrison, who joined the Globetrotters in the mid-1950s, remembered the grind caused by racial segregation: "We used to have to play two games—one for the whites and one for the blacks—and that was killing us."[75]

Abe Saperstein was notorious for advertising the high salaries that he paid his players, yet the financial compensation that the players received suggests that most of the African American players were underpaid and exploited. In 1954 the average Globetrotter's wage was $750 per month. This was far more than the salary of most African Americans. However, the Globetrotters were making far less than their counterparts in the NBA. Given the NBA's eighty-two-game schedule, compared with the two-hundred-game schedule of the main Globetrotter team, the fact that the Globetrotter players had to work much harder for far less compensation is troubling.[76]

More disconcerting for the Globetrotter players was the fact that the white College All-Star players who toured with the team during the 1950s often made more money than they did. Marques Haynes said in an interview with Joshua Wetterhahn, "I had been told [that white players were getting paid more than the Harlem Globetrotters] by several of the [white] players." Saperstein once explained the discrepancy in pay to Haynes by offering the offensive remark, "A Negro doesn't need as much money as a white man." By 1953 Haynes's and Goose Tatum's images were heavily featured in Coca-Cola advertising, but Abe Saperstein received most of the income from those and other advertising deals. Furthermore, David Zinkoff reveals that Saperstein considered the reported $40,000 that he annually paid Tatum in the early 1950s "a bargain." Years later Tatum disclosed that the most money he had ever been paid by Saperstein was the dismally low sum of $9,000. Hence, Saperstein's public inflation of his player's income masked the troubling reality. In *Around the World with the Harlem Globetrotters,* Zinkoff refers to Tatum as a "loner . . . [a] moody, almost morose, person." However, Zinkoff never acknowledges that Tatum's moodiness may have been related to his awareness of his economic exploitation. In fact, both Haynes and Tatum left the Globetrotters in the mid-1950s to pursue more potentially lucrative opportunities as players and owners of a competing barnstorming basketball team.[77]

The story surrounding Goose Tatum's departure from the Harlem Globetrotters remains shrouded in mystery. We know that Saperstein was upset with Tatum for missing several games, but why was Tatum absent? Zinkoff suggests that Tatum was a wanderer by nature. Although this was true, there are important circumstances that influenced Tatum's abrupt departure from the Globetrotters. Tatum did not show up at the games immediately following the team's first nationally televised game in March 1955. Perhaps the implications of the team's commercial viability finally dawned upon Tatum. Given his merger salary, it would not be surprising if he saw himself as being exploited by Saperstein. Sensing the possibilities of the emerging television market, it is quite possible that Tatum sought greater financial compensation.[78] These reasons are speculative, but it is probable that a 1955 lawsuit involving Tatum played a key role in his departure.

Shortly before Tatum's 1955 departure, Tatum along with his wife and several other friends filed a lawsuit against the Pan-American Cocktail Lounge after being refused service. Believing that their race was the source of the discrimination they faced, the lawsuit sought $21,000 in restitution for "great anguish and embarrassment." Despite the seemingly innocent capitulation to the demands of the racially charged comedic antics that he initiated and perfected, Tatum's lawsuit demonstrates that he had a profound sense of racial consciousness. It is unclear how Saperstein responded to Tatum's lawsuit. However, the serious charges that Tatum alleged were in contradiction with how Saperstein sought to depict the United States as a racially tolerant society to international audiences. Despite the fact that it is easily documented that the Globetrotters continued to compete before segregated audiences in the South through the mid-1950s, Saperstein maintained that his team reflected the openness of the American social order. To have his most high-profile athlete file a lawsuit that contradicted his pronouncements could have been a source of tension that contributed to both men's decision to sever their business relationship.[79]

Conclusion

The Globetrotters traveled throughout the world as examples of the State Department's evolutionary theory of improving race relations, which suggested that opportunity in America was available to talented and motivated African Americans, even under segregation. However, the team's comedic, minstrel-inspired antics suggested that black Americans were inferior and, consequently, unprepared for full integration. This argument would have been familiar to European audiences, who continued to be colonial masters throughout sub-Saharan Africa. Even after World War II, European powers continued to claim that their African colonies were not ready to govern themselves. Consequently, the Globetrotters fitted into preestablished racist notions that suggested that people of African descent did not have the capacity for self-government and were not ready to fully participate in the polity as equal citizens.

However, by 1954 African decolonization efforts had gained momentum, and the 1954 *Brown v. Board of Education* decision placed the United States Constitution behind the notion that all races were equal. As the NBA began to attract the most talented African American players, the Globetrotters' appeal as a professional basketball team waned. As the team lost its privileged position, the State Department developed a goodwill-tour program of its own, based in part on the government's success in promoting the Globetrotters abroad in the early 1950s.

3. Playing Politics

The Formation of the U.S. Cold War–Era Athletic Foreign Policy

With two of its best players sidelined with injuries, the team representing the United States lost to the Soviet Union—62 to 37—on January 28 before twenty-four thousand fans at the 1959 World Basketball Tournament in Santiago, Chile. After five minutes of play, the score was tied, 4–4. Then the Soviets gained control after inserting Yan Krumins, their seven-foot-two center from Latvia. His five quick points helped his team to a 25–14 halftime advantage. The Soviets capitalized on precise outside shooting and American foul trouble during the second half to cruise to an easy victory. The Soviet Union dominated every facet of the game: rebounding, shooting, ball control, and defense. Their intense zone defense frustrated the U.S. squad. At the game's conclusion, the disappointed Chilean fans littered the court with debris, coins, and fruit while chanting, "Russia, Russia."[1]

When the game ended, the ecstatic Soviets hugged each other and tossed their coach into the air, while the crowd cheered for the Soviets' first victory against the United States in an international basketball competition. After the game, the Soviet players who had been under strict training signed autographs and sat around their hotel's roof-garden swimming pool smoking cigarettes. The Soviets relaxed because they had accomplished their primary goal: gaining international prestige by beating the United States in a notable basketball tournament.[2]

In the two tournament games before the embarrassing loss to the Soviets, the United States barely squeaked by two mediocre teams: they defeated Puerto Rico by a single point and Bulgaria by a mere five points. The game following the Soviet debacle, the U.S. team was trounced by the Brazilians, 81–67, behind twenty-six points from their star player, Vladimir Marquez. The lackluster performance of the American team drew widespread criticism from members of Congress, newspaper columnists, American citizens, and the international community.[3]

At first glance, the poor exhibition of the U.S. team seems puzzling because the U.S. Olympic team had beaten virtually the same Russian team, 89–55, during their last meeting at the 1956 Olympic Games. However, the 1959 United States World Basketball Tournament team did not consist of any of the 1956 Olympians, many of whom had become professional basketball players. Additionally, none of the 1959 collegiate All-American players or future members of the 1960 Olympic team competed on the team sent to Chile. Since the tournament was scheduled during the collegiate season and while the military service championships were in full swing, the United States was not able to field a top-notch college or amateur squad.

Initially, the United States had decided not to participate in the tournament because it could not secure an elite team to compete. However, when tournament officials said that the absence of a team representing the United States would destroy the tournament, the Americans decided to send a squad. Unbelievably, the U.S. team was chosen based on responses to an advertisement for volunteers placed in an air force newspaper. The team was composed of eleven lieutenants and one airman second class, none of whom was taller than six-foot-five. Recognizing the poor quality of his team, the U.S. coach, Buzz Bennett, later said, "The night we played Russia we would have been beaten by the winner of the Indiana State High School Tournament. The Russians are good but any of the top 10 college teams in the United States would run them off the court."[4]

Throughout the World Basketball Tournament, the U.S. team was a grave disappointment. The domestic and international outcry over the disaster was swift and harsh. One newspaper reporter asked, "What happened? Some lame-brain [government official], who apparently doesn't know a hoop from a hula, [was] permitted to risk America's fading sports prestige in, of all places, South America where our diplomatic position has faltered considerably of late. . . . Those responsible should be brought to task."[5] Senator Henry Styles Bridges of New Hampshire drew a parallel between the fiasco in Santiago and the space race in a speech before Congress. "The United States is in direct competition with Russia in all aspects and on all fronts," the senator said. "Can you imagine the fuss and furor that would result if the United States government sent a group of college science students down to Cape Canaveral to take over the important job of beating the Russians in the race for space?"[6]

Everett Dean, who was stationed in nearby Uruguay on a coaching mission, stressed the political damage of sending a third-class basketball team to represent the United States: "[South Americans] cannot understand why the United States was willing to take a chance in losing 'face,' especially to Russia, in a country in which we are trying to improve our 'good neighbor' policy."[7] Dean's observations are important because they highlight how the South American nations interpreted the actions of the United States. Similar to other regions of the world, in South America sports competitions were crucial to national prestige and honor. In fact, a nation's prestige would change drastically based on a single performance in an international competition.

The American Public Affairs Office in Rio de Janeiro was bombarded with questions focused on why the United States did not send its best basketball team to the tournament. The embassy was hard-pressed to explain why domestic sports commitments took precedence over competing in an international basketball tournament that was trumped in prestige only by the Olympic Games. The embassy pointed out that a second-rate performance did the Americans more harm than good. For many "average, non-intelligent [men]-on-the-street, the Soviet victory was another indication of Soviet superiority."[8] The American public affairs officer in Brazil, John McKnight, concurred with the Brazilians: "This is big-league competition now—here, and everywhere else in the world—and bush-leaguers have no place in the line-up."[9]

The United States' lackluster performance was not a surprise to some Latin Americans, who saw the team's poor quality as evidence to support the oft-heard criticism that "Uncle Sam" looks down his nose at everything Latin American—that in the United States' opinion, second best is good enough for its southern neighbors. More specifically, by the United States not sending its best representatives, the actions were seen as slighting Chilean pride and displaying a lack of interest in Latin American countries. Conversely, the Russian victory in a basketball tournament in America's own "backyard" held tremendous prestige and potential political importance for the Soviet Union in its attempt to demonstrate genuine interest in Latin America.[10]

Recognizing the significance of the defeats, the U.S. Information Service in Lima, Peru, sent a dispatch to Washington, D.C., that chided the State Department for giving insufficient attention to the selection of the team, thereby causing an unnecessary loss of prestige because "there are many teams in the United States that would have defeated the Soviet team."[11] William Macomber Jr., the assistant secretary of state, wrote a letter to

Senator Lyndon B. Johnson explaining the limited involvement of the State Department in the selection process of the team that represented the United States in Chile. Macomber stressed that the department was not officially involved in the selection process and therefore could not be responsible for the results of the tournament. He went on to assert that a private-sector organization had jurisdiction over American basketball teams competing abroad. Like Senator Johnson, he hoped that the private sector would be "increasingly aware of the necessity of selecting only highly qualified athletes to represent the United States in international competition."[12] However, he did not suggest that the selection committee and the State Department cooperate to make sure that another embarrassing loss did not occur.

Unsatisfied with the official response, the Chilean embassy in Santiago emphasized that it was important for "Washington to influence, either directly or indirectly, the selection of only the highest calibre teams," especially when the Soviet Union was involved.[13] The importance that the embassy placed on this defeat can be understood through an examination of the place of sports in foreign policy, public relations, and propaganda during the Cold War. As I will detail below, through a series of attempts to improve the United States' image, particularly focusing on projecting an image of the social and political progressiveness of capitalism over communism, the government eventually turned to sports as an ambassador of U.S. values.

"Playing Politics: The Formation of the U.S. Cold War–Era Athletic Foreign Policy" explores the increased political significance sport received in the Cold War battle between the United States and the Soviet Union. After the Soviet Union rejoined the Olympic movement in 1952, sport became a crucial Cold War battleground. This chapter explores the 1950s athletic rivalry between the two superpowers and the athletic foreign policy that evolved around it, as well as how the United States developed a program of international athletic goodwill tours as a means to counteract the Soviet Union's successful implementation of its own athletic foreign policy program.

Sports served as a proxy for combat in the atomic age. By 1949 the Soviet Union had developed its own atomic bomb, breaking the United States' monopoly. As the United States and the Soviet Union reached a military stalemate, neither was able to dominate the globe using military force. Only after military crystallization did the two superpowers make use of sports in their quest to find creative avenues to improve their international image. I argue that through competing in international sports competitions, bringing foreigners to the United States, and sending athletes on goodwill tours, the U.S. government crafted a multifaceted propaganda program. Sports became a crucial Cold War weapon that deployed the notions of strength and cultural, political, and economic superiority over the Soviet Union. Projecting an image of racial equality became critical in this endeavor. After other goodwill trips proved to be lackluster, sporting tours eventually became important vehicles for this purpose.

Racial Spokesmen

One of the State Department's initial Cold War–era attempts to alter opinions of American race relations was to bring foreigners to the United States to witness American democracy firsthand. However, when some foreign visitors returned home praising American society, they faced rebuke. For example, C. P. Ramaswamy, an Indian citizen, said after his trip to the United States, "The spirituality of Americans should not be overlooked by those who emphasize American materialism." The Indian newspaper *Cross Roads* took offense to Ramaswamy's claim and charged him with proclaiming the virtues of the American system as a means to repay the State Department for his trip. A few weeks later, the same newspaper mockingly claimed that the execution of two African Americans was "evidence of American spirituality."[14]

Realizing that it would be impossible to bring all foreigners to the United States, the State Department developed programs to send American citizens, including African Americans, abroad. African Americans who projected middle-class values were recruited by the State Department to take international tours to speak about U.S. race relations. For most foreign nationals, these tours were their first opportunity to meet and interact with African Americans. The exchange programs were designed to balance negative depictions of African American life with more positive images. Consequently, the programs sought to highlight the accomplishments of individual African Americans as examples of American democracy. This practice allowed the government to assert that opportunity was available to African Americans with talent and motivation.[15]

The ideological preparation for the tours was minimal. The participants were encouraged to be truthful and forthright about their experiences in the United States. In accord with the precedent that had been established with Jackie Robinson's HUAC testimony, the only request that State Department officials made was that the individuals express confidence in the U.S. system of democracy to adequately redress the social, legal, political, and economic disparities in American society. Gertrude Macy, the general manager of the American National Theater and Academy's Cultural Exchange Service, said that the State Department "encourages a frank answering of questions, and we tell our performing artists, 'Don't conceal your views.'" Macy maintained that touring Americans were "advised not to wrap [themselves] in the flag."[16]

Max Yergan, who had been one of the highest-ranking African American members of the American Communist Party, was enlisted as a goodwill ambassador to Africa by the State Department in July 1952. Yergan, along with Paul Robeson, had cofounded the Council on African Affairs, an organization dedicated to obtaining American support for anticolonial movements in Africa. Yergan's attempt to protect the Council on African Affairs from communist infiltration, after attorney general Tom Clark placed the group's name on the list of subversive organizations that threatened to overthrow the U.S. government, caused an irreparable breach in his friendship with Paul Robeson. Because of his denunciation of many of Robeson's communist-leaning thoughts and his work on behalf of African liberation, he appeared to be an ideal goodwill ambassador. The State Department attempted to gain maximum exposure for Yergan's speech abroad, "The Trend in American Race Relations." Consequently, after he presented his speech to a crowd of three hundred audience members, the United States Information Agency (USIA) issued a special press release: "Yergan Says Trend in U.S. Race Relations Is Toward Full Civil Rights for Negroes." The State Department wanted to publicize Yergan's statement that he enjoyed "ever-expanding rights and privileges, which his grandfather, a Negro slave, could only dream of."[17]

During his trip to Africa, Max Yergan argued that "my people in America have chosen to cast their lot with democracy, because they believe it offers them the opportunity to achieve full equality." However, the effectiveness of Yergan's tutorial about the evils of communism was tempered when a member of the audience responded with a question: "If the Communists had made promises to the American Negro and broken them, had not the American Constitution done the same thing?" Referring to Yergan's speech, one local paper commented that "nobody in this country is going to swallow the vocal pills of outsiders who come here to teach rather than to learn." Many African nations were sensitive to Western paternalism, and many thought that the lecture tours were patronizing.[18]

Of all the crucial Cold War battlegrounds, India was the nation most preoccupied with American domestic race relations. Clifford Manshardt, a roving cultural affairs officer, said that when he toured India in 1952, he was constantly asked questions similar to the following: "Which race does America hate most?" Acclaimed African American author Jay Saunders Redding also toured India in 1952. Redding characterized the Indians as believing "American policy is opposed to the 'liberation and rise' of the colored peoples of the world, and that the treatment of Negroes in America is a demonstration of this." The predominant perspective that Redding encountered was that African American oppression was analogous to the Indian colonial past. On one occasion when he presented a positive image of American race relations, a member of the audience held up a copy of the petition "We Charge Genocide" and said, "What you say does not convince us in the face of this."[19] "We Charge Genocide" was a UN genocide petition prepared by the U.S.-based Civil Rights Congress, which documented hundreds of racially motivated incidents of violence, including lynchings in the United States.

The noted African American journalist Carl Rowan, who would later be named the director of the United States Information Agency by President Lyndon B. Johnson, took a twenty-three-day tour of India in 1954. The American Consulate in Calcutta called Rowan's visit "one of the most successful and rewarding Exchange Program projects to date." Throughout his tour, Rowan was asked about American race relations and America's postwar attempts to remake the world in its image. Rowan's tour was effective because of his willingness to "mix it up" with presumed communist sympathizers who attempted to derail his presentations by asking difficult questions, while audience members snickered aloud as demonstrations were held outside the venue.[20]

The speaking tours were not always successful. For example, the head of the Department of Languages at Howard University, Raleigh Morgan, was sent to North Africa as an educational and civil rights specialist. Morgan delivered his presentation, "The Social Situation in the U.S. Today," in several African nations. His presentation traced the historical background of the racial problem in the United States and emphasized how the problem was being addressed peacefully through the courts and the legislative process. The themes repeatedly stressed throughout his speech and during the question-answer session were that African Americans were in the process of being fully integrated into American social and economic life and that the civil rights movement was evidence that long-standing barriers were coming down. Morgan's presentation was referred to as a "failure" in the annual report of the American Embassy in Algiers, because by "presenting himself as an integrated Negro he could not dissuade his audiences from the notion that he had betrayed his people."[21] The speaking tours suggested that other nations were less inclined to be convinced of the sincerity of America's effort to end racial segregation by rhetoric than they would be by visual propaganda efforts.

Supreme Court justice William O. Douglas, surprised by the significance and importance of color consciousness abroad, realized the need to move beyond rhetoric. The first question asked at his initial press conference in New Delhi, India, during his 1950 visit was, "Why does America tolerate the lynching of Negroes?" Douglas's subsequent book, *Strange Lands and Friendly People,* expressed his post-trip views regarding how social transformation would take place in postcolonial Asia. "Neither wealth nor might will determine the outcome of the struggles in Asia, they will turn on *emotional factors* too subtle to measure," Douglas argued. "Political alliances of an enduring nature will be built not on the power of guns or dollars, but on *affection.*" Similarly, Robert McGregor, the American consul general in Leopoldville, Democratic Republic of the Congo, made the derogatory observation that the Soviet Union was having success in Africa because they were "skillfully playing on the emotions of those who do not think." McGregor's statement was designed to suggest that the United States needed to find ways to tap into what he termed "the new emotional, irresponsible, exaggerated and zenophobic [*sic*]" nationalism that was emerging on the African continent.[22] The ensuing sports tours would provide such an outlet, but not before the Soviet Union made significant gains using sports to further its own image.

The Cultural Offensive

During the late 1940s, the Truman administration acknowledged that propaganda characterizing the Soviet Union as the foremost advocate of peace and the premier defender of defenseless peoples was the Soviets' most powerful weapon in the struggle for worldwide influence. Sports were crucial to their efforts. In 1950 the Soviet Union sent thirty-nine thousand athletes, scientists, writers, artists, musicians, and ballet dancers abroad. The Soviets' 1950 budget for cultural exchange programs in France was estimated at $150 million. That's more than the United States spent in cultural exchanges worldwide. By 1952 the United States annually spent $88 million on propaganda, whereas the Soviets invested about $1.5 billion. The number of Soviet athletic teams sent abroad on goodwill tours increased from 29 trips in 1950 to 68 international tours in 1953. During 1955 the United States sent 15 tours abroad, but the Soviets far outdistanced U.S. efforts by sending 148 cultural and sport delegations around the world. As late as 1957, for every exchange conducted by the United States, the Soviet Union conducted 15.[23] The emerging Soviet cultural diplomacy juggernaut capitalized on the Olympic Games as a prime propaganda medium.

Once the Soviets reentered the Olympic Games at the 1952 Helsinki competition, the Games became a crucial arena for Cold War contestation. Consequently, after the United States won the unofficial medal count in the 1952 Helsinki Games, Senator John Butler of Maryland attributed American success to "our free system of government and vast educational networks [that] pave the way to athletic excellence." Before the 1956 Olympic Games, Senator Butler argued that American athletes were "living testimonials of the excellence and superiority of the free American system." Conversely, after the Soviets won the unofficial medal counts in 1956 and 1960, Premier Nikita Khrushchev used the same line of argument, claiming that "the triumph of the Soviet athletes is a victory for the man of the new Socialist Society."[24]

Although the Cold War contest between the United States and the Soviet Union elevated the international significance of the Olympic Games, this rivalry was not the beginning of the political use of the Games. Certainly, the Nazi Olympic Games in 1936 were quite politically charged. However, since the beginning of the modern Olympic Games in 1896, Mark Dyreson argues, many Americans viewed "Olympic performance as indicating how the United States ranks as a global power." By equating Olympic gold with national superiority, the United States had argued that victory proved the preeminence of American values and reaffirmed that the nation was "a city upon an hill" and that Americans were a "chosen people."[25]

For example, the battle waged between the United States and England at the 1908 Olympic Games in London illustrates how deeply rooted politics are in the Olympic tradition. At a time when the United States was challenging the British Empire's preeminence in world politics and in the global economy, the Games served as a symbolic battleground. The American contingent of athletes was angered during the opening ceremony of the 1908 Games when they noticed that the British had not displayed the American flag in the stadium, while the flags of all of the other competing nations were visible. The British explanation that a suitable flag could not be found did not ease the tense atmosphere. Ralph Rose, the shot-putter and flag carrier at the opening ceremony, refused to dip the U.S. flag as he passed the British royal box, which was a customary courtesy. As he passed the royal box, Rose is reported to have said, "This flag dips for no earthly king." Despite the fact that the British won fifty-six gold medals and the United States won only twenty-three, U.S. commentators still refused to acknowledge that the United States had been defeated. Rather, they claimed that the Games reflected the superiority of the U.S. athletes because the United States handily won the track and field competition. Consequently, the idea that sports had wider implications has been a long-held belief in the international community. However, the U.S. versus USSR competitions took that notion to unprecedented heights.[26]

On March 6, 1953, Soviet newspapers reported the death of Joseph Stalin. Stalin's death ushered in a new era characterized by the Soviets' repeated calls for peaceful coexistence. To that end, in the ensuing months the Soviets relinquished their claims on Turkey, helped end the Korean War, and reestablished diplomatic relations with Israel. The reversal of Stalinist policies, which became known as "the thaw," helped revitalize the international image of the Soviet Union. The Soviets' new openness avoided the antidemocracy tirades, along with the vilification, name-calling, and threats that had marked the Stalin regime. As James Vaughn has argued, the Soviets' new peace offensive caused "something akin to panic" for U.S. foreign policy makers.[27]

After Stalin's death, the expanded Soviet athletic program began to host local, national, and regional sporting events worldwide in an attempt to strengthen relations with communist countries, while creating friendships with democratic and other noncommunist nations. The "Soviet Cultural Offensive" championed the fraternal participation of the world's youth in sports and culture. Abbott Washburn acknowledges that the new approach was "one of the most effective psychological weapons that the Kremlin . . . unsheathed." Noted sports columnist Arthur Daley concluded that the Soviets were using "the toy department as a propaganda tool." The vast economic resources that the Kremlin had available for sports exchanges allowed them to increase their sports exchanges from the 40 delegations they sent abroad in 1952 to 237 delegations in 1963.[28] The Soviets were intent upon using athletics to display before the world the rapidity of its advancement.

Hence, the Soviets made effective use of international sport competitions as a weapon in the cultural Cold War. Athletics was one of the most publicly visible arenas in which the Russians were able to compete with the more economically advanced nations in the West. The Soviets were quick to claim that the impact of socialist sport "on the world sports movement was one of the best and most comprehensible means of explaining to people throughout the world the advantages that socialism has over the capitalist system." Winning athletic competitions and providing athletic demonstrations took on symbolic meaning, because athletic mastery was increasingly interpreted as a barometer to measure the appeal and success of an ideological or political system. For those who did not understand the complicated ideological differences between communism and capitalism, Russian athletic success conveyed an image of strength, accomplishment, and leadership.[29]

In the post-Stalin era, the use of sport as a foreign policy tool reached unprecedented levels, especially in developing countries. The Soviets' program pursued several key aims: displaying the perceived benefits of the Soviets' economic and social system, while promoting good relations with neighboring nations; enhancing the international status of the Soviet Union through international competitions; and garnering the allegiance of emerging countries in Africa, Asia, and Latin America. The Soviet effort included two policies that were adopted by the United States: sending coaches and athletes abroad as well as hosting competitions in the United States and other countries. However, the Soviets far outdistanced the United States in one key area: helping these countries solidify their sporting infrastructure by building sports facilities.[30]

Furthermore, the Soviets demonstrated their interests in the issues that were important to nations of color throughout the developing world by leading efforts to eradicate racial discrimination in sport. It was the Soviet National Olympic Committee that took the most strident steps within the International Olympic Committee to exclude South Africa from competing because of its apartheid policies in the early 1960s. The Soviets followed up their Olympic effort with support for the removal of South Africa from all international sports competitions. Because of the U.S. government's reluctance to embarrass South Africa, a key anticommunist supporter, the U.S. government remained publicly silent on South Africa's racial policies. Indeed, the Soviets reaped the benefits of their antiapartheid position in the developing world.[31]

After the Soviet success at the Helsinki Games, the ideological battles expressed through sports politicized the Olympic Games to unprecedented heights. U.S. pundits began to issue dire predictions about the impending triumph of the Soviet athlete and its larger implications. The notion that American defeat would cause the world to view America as physically "soft" created anxiety about how sports' success or failure would make the United States vulnerable in other areas and received great attention, particularly since 47 percent of those rejected for military service during World War II were rejected because of physical conditioning. The emerging Soviet athletic juggernaut threatened to replace the United States as the world's standard-bearer in overall athletic competence. Of particular concern was the rapidity of Soviet advancements. University of Michigan track coach Don Canham found the Soviet success awe inspiring. "In 1946, the Russians had nothing," Canham claimed. "They were the doormat of European track and field competition."[32]

The fear of the Russian sport offensive was evident in the mainstream press. The Soviets were interested in a "prolonged display of power and propaganda" that would reach its culmination at the 1956 Olympic Games in Melbourne, Australia, argued a *U.S. News and World Report* article, "Reds Hope to Rule Sports Too: 12 Million Athletes in Training to Beat the West." The Soviets had amassed huge victories against other nations in their national sports: ice hockey against the Canadians, skiing against the Scandinavians, and rowing against England. The former reclusive Soviet athletic program entered an unprecedented 150 international competitions in 1954. At their debut at the World Hockey Championships in March 1954, the Soviets won the tournament by defeating Canada easily, 7–2. In July the Soviet men and women won the World Gymnastics Championships, winning 10 of 14 events. *U.S. News and World Report* attributed Soviet success to a "big, grim, production-line business" that was run by "the supercoach, the state." The article concluded by arguing that the Russian athlete was fast becoming an "international advertisement for 'peaceful coexistence.'"[33]

"Russia Will Win the 1956 Olympics" was the provocative title of an October 25, 1954, *Sports Illustrated* article that predicted the Soviet team would be greatly improved over the team they sent to Helsinki in 1952. Don Canham argued that the Soviet team was only half as good as the team that the Soviets would be able to field in Melbourne in 1956. Canham noted the businesslike approach of the Soviet team. Rather than enjoying the thrill of victory and the satisfaction of competition, the Soviet team was depicted as stoic and "deadly serious."[34] The implication of these per-spectives was that the Soviet Union was imbuing athletics with rigidity, sobriety, and sternness that undermined the leisurely, pleasurable, and enjoyable aspects of amateur athletic participation. In essence, the Soviets were accused of perverting the meaning of sports.

Avery Brundage, the U.S.-born president of the International Olympic Committee (IOC), spent three weeks in Russia in 1954 after he was invited to attend the Russians' elaborate Annual Sports Parade. Brundage went to Russia to confirm that the Soviets were adhering to international amateur rules, and as a sports enthusiast, he wanted to observe the Russian sport infrastructure because of the Soviets' impressive results in international competition since they rejoined the Olympic movement. Brundage was surprised when the Soviet Olympic Committee invited him to attend the Annual Sports Parade because members of the communist press had denounced him as a "shameless, blood-sucking capitalist and imperialistic reactionary." Brundage decided to pay his expenses for the trip because he wanted to be free to criticize the Soviets, if necessary. Additionally, he did not want to afford his critics the opportunity to say that any positive statements regarding the Russians could be attributed to being "bought off."[35]

Having attended sports festivals worldwide, Brundage said that the beauty and magnitude of the Soviet sports festival were unmatched. "The Sports Festival was one of the finest organized events I have seen. It lasted five hours and went off without a hitch," Brundage noted. With more than thirty-four thousand participants from the sixteen Russian republics, the parade was a monumental undertaking. Brundage believed that the Soviets had adopted the values of Baron de Coubertin, who had resurrected the Olympic movement in 1896, a movement that preached that physical education and competitive sports programs made better citizens. Brundage maintained that Russia had adopted the program on a "national scale never before attempted, except by the Germans in the Thirties." Moreover, he concluded that the Russians had "placed all the power of the state behind it."[36]

"Every able-bodied citizen an athlete" was the goal of the Soviets' athletic endeavors. Consequently, the Soviets' national sports machine placed the national infrastructure behind the Olympic notion that sport participation made better citizens. The heavily state-subsidized Russian athletic programs were designed to develop their population for the physically demanding work that was required for military service, factory labor, and general health and well-being. Compulsory physical education courses were a component of the elementary school curriculum. The best athletes were funneled into one of the four hundred youth sports schools for teenage student-athletes. In addition to state support, labor unions allocated approximately one-fifth of their annual budget for athletic recreational facilities and activities.[37]

In order to gain entrance into the Olympic movement, the Soviets had to cease rewarding good athletic performances with cash prizes or material incentives. Despite Soviet efforts to comply with international regulations regarding amateur athletics, the Russian system faced widespread criticism in the United States. American journalists often defined a professional athlete as one who made his or her living because of athletic competition. They argued that there was very little difference between a Soviet athlete who trained at an all-expenses-paid sports complex and received a weekly "living expense" and a professional athlete in the United States. These efforts were frequently unfruitful. Sporting officials worldwide often pointed to the amateur status that was afforded subsidized collegiate amateur athletes in the United States and the Amateur Athletic Union teams created by U.S. business companies for their advertising value.[38]

Avery Brundage was a harsh critic of efforts to deceptively exploit sports for political means. Hence, he also went to the Soviet Union to investigate allegations of "state amateurism"—a charge that the Soviet state was paying athletes living expenses so that they could devote themselves wholly to athletic training. Brundage said that he did not see anything during his three-week visit that indicated that Russia was not adhering to international amateur rules. While in Russia, Brundage presented Nikolai Romanov, the chairman of Russia's Committee on Physical Culture and Sport, a cabinet-level position, with several articles written by former Soviet-bloc athletes who asserted that communist amateurism was "a sham and fraud." Romanov replied, "These men are deserters, traitors. Would you attach any truth to their statements if they had been Americans and turned against your country?" Brundage left the Soviet Union impressed by the Soviet athletic program and believed that it was abiding by international rules and regulations.[39]

The intense battle for Olympic supremacy at the impending 1956 Games led to an intensification of the symbolic importance attributed to athletics. A 1954 government-produced document titled "International Athletics— Cold War Battleground" stressed that the United States needed to respond to the onslaught of Soviet success in the sporting arena. The goal of the Soviets was clear: to "wrest world athletic supremacy from the United States," the report maintained. The communist countries invested significant amounts of money to train and enter athletes into sports events worldwide. In competitions that the United States did not participate in, the Soviets inevitably took the top honors. The U.S. government was concerned that the Soviets' success was "impressing on the minds of youth everywhere that communist youth [are] the new symbol of athletic perfection and that the myth of American sports supremacy has been shattered."[40] Referring to the Soviet athletic program, Abbott Washburn, deputy director of the United States Information Agency during the Eisenhower administration, said, "They don't really give a damn for sportsmanship or honest amateur competition, or international good will, although everything is done with great charm and in the name of these virtues."[41] Obviously threatened by the success of the Soviets' athletic program, Senator Butler of Maryland referred to the Soviet athletes as "paid propaganda agents" and "human weapons in the Communist conspiracy's cold war arsenal."[42]

Equally troubling was the reality that Soviet victories at international sports competitions were often won through default because the United States was not represented at many of the competitions. Worldwide speculation was that the United States did not send teams to compete because it feared defeat. The Soviets argued that the United States was too busy preparing for war and too materialistic to be concerned with attending international competitions. The reality was that the United States, the richest nation in the world, did not send representative teams because it did not allocate adequate funds for this purpose because it thought sports activities were the responsibility of the private sector. The secretary of the Amateur Athletic Union of the United States, the private group with jurisdiction over the international booking of American teams in sports such as basketball and track and field, reported that he was annually forced to decline approximately fifteen invitations to international meets he considered important to the effort to bolster America's worldwide image because adequate funding was not available.[43]

However, the Soviets' efforts were so successful that the State Department's Cultural and Athletic Exchange Program and the United States Information Agency were created to produce a counteroffensive to the Soviet Union's effective use of culture and athletics. Theodore Streibert, the USIA director, acknowledged that the agency was working against a "mounting tempo of Soviet propaganda and an increasing Soviet cultural offensive."[44] While admitting that the success of the Soviet exchange program was a strong incentive, U.S. officials sought to camouflage the political implications of the increased involvement in sports by publicly denying that competition with the Soviets was the purpose of the U.S. program.

Despite official rhetoric, the American efforts were clearly anticommunistic. In early 1955, a Reuters news dispatch quoted the father of Tenley Albright, the recently crowned U.S. and world women's figure skating champion. Mr. Albright acknowledged that the U.S. government had asked his daughter to make a goodwill tour "to combat communist efforts to gain influence, especially in countries that recently gained independence." In response to the story, an outraged Avery Brundage wrote to the United States Olympic Committee president, Kenneth Wilson, stressing that the United States had been "charged with adopting the same methods of the Communists."[45] As president of the International Olympic Committee, Brundage's protests against the U.S. State Department's sports practices received attention in the world press. Pressured to back down because his frequent attacks were contributing to a loss of American prestige, Brundage refused, maintaining his position that the United States was making a mistake by using amateur athletes as political agents. Brundage concluded his remarks by asserting that the United States needed to be careful, because "foreigners are not necessarily stupid." Notwithstanding the criticisms of the program, sports became an important Cold War battleground. The international prestige associated with the Olympic Games became a measuring stick for judging the success and strength of ideological systems. The American State Department played an increasingly important role in the promotion and support of international sports.[46]

Institutionalizing Athletes as Cold Warriors

In a 1954 meeting with President Eisenhower, U.S. ambassador to the United Nations Henry Cabot Lodge expressed his concern over the success of the Soviets' cultural offensive. Eisenhower then reported to his cabinet that he was going to ask Congress for special emergency funds for international affairs to counteract the Soviet efforts. Eisenhower reasoned that Congress "can't turn me down on a few million dollars for that purpose." The goal of Eisenhower's proposed program was to highlight the best of America's athletic, musical, and artistic accomplishments before the world, who would then presumably "extend their appreciation to the benefits of the 'free enterprise system.'"[47] While he was running for the presidency, Dwight D. Eisenhower, a former West Point football coach, had suggested that sports could be a peaceful means of waging the Cold War: "Diplomacy, the spreading of ideas through every medium of communication . . . friendly contacts through travel and correspondence and sports—these represent some of the political means to support essential programs for mutual military assistance and collective security."[48]

In 1954 Congress passed a bill allotting five million dollars for cultural exchange. The "President's Special International Program" was initially authorized to allow athletes, musicians, and artists opportunities to take part in international festivals, fairs, and competitions. This program operated on an emergency basis until August 1956, when Congress passed the International Cultural and Trade Fairs Participation Act of 1956, which gave full legislative sanction to the program. The tours became an integral part of the diplomatic ritual because diplomatic representatives valued cultural resources for representational purposes.[49]

The Cultural Presentations Program, the most significant component of Eisenhower's new plan, arranged tours of amateur and professional athletes, teams, coaches, and managers to foreign regions with the exception of Western Europe. Between 1954 and 1963, sixty-two groups of athletes, most of which were integrated, were sent to more than one hundred countries to perform demonstrations and conduct clinics. In its Cold War battle with the Soviet Union, the United States wanted to present to other nations the value of American ideals. Consequently, African American athletes were employed as the embodiment and personification of freedom and democracy. The implication that the State Department hoped people would draw was that if social mobility was possible for black Americans, other people of color worldwide could improve their social, political, and economic well-being by aligning with the United States in its effort to promote capitalist democracy worldwide. Ultimately, the State Department wanted other peoples to conclude that the best "guarantee for a promising future lies in close cooperation with the United States and the Free World."[50]

The State Department was adamant that sports tours sent to nations of color had to be integrated because athletics helped bridge the language barrier and "put the racial problem in the United States in a proper perspective." As propaganda vehicles, the visual images of the African American athletes and white athletes working together and the material condition of the black athletes made it unnecessary and, in many cases, undesirable for the athletes to verbally address the social condition of blacks in the United States.[51] The indiscriminate and often genuinely fraternal bonding, camaraderie, sportsmanship, and friendliness among the black and white American athletes were effectively contrasted with Soviet-promoted images of segregation that focused on incidents involving racial violence.

Sports were overwhelmingly popular on the African continent. The State Department–sponsored "Study of the Impact of Sports on Achievement of U.S. Foreign Policy Objectives" determined that 60 percent of all Foreign Service posts in Africa reported that the local emphasis placed on sports ranged from considerable to great. Fourteen African nations had a minister of sports or the equivalent. In fifteen other nations, the administration of sports was performed as a separate division of a broader ministry or department, most often the Ministry of Education. Given the evidence of the official importance of sports, the sports exchanges were judged to be instrumental to American efforts to gain greater influence in several African nations. For example, in Cameroon, the United States believed that these exchanges had helped to create a favorable impression, strengthening the idea that the United States was "friendly, willing to help, and willing to share their secrets." Based on similar successes, the Bureau of Cultural Affairs report "A Study of the Impact of Sport in the Achievement of U.S. Foreign Policy Objectives" concluded that "Africa is fraught with possibility."[52]

The State Department wanted to complicate the discussion surrounding the United States' treatment of African Americans by providing evidence that progress was taking place in America. It was important that the host nations were able to see depictions of American society that suggested that sports were at the forefront of improving the social position of African Americans. Andre Seddor, a Togolese journalist and director of the newspaper *Togo Oberservateur,* wrote that "it will not be by dollars [in aid] that Africa will judge the sincerity of the United States of America, but by the rehabilitation of the 15 million Negroes living there. The friendship of Americans for Africans must not be an exotic paternalism. It has to be sincere and true, beginning first with our brothers in their country."[53] Consequently, the State Department used athletic exchanges to represent American race relations in a favorable light to nations on the African continent.

The venue of sports was also appropriate because it was one of the first U.S. institutions to integrate during the Cold War, allowing the United States to point directly to America's social advancement. When Jackie Robinson integrated Major League Baseball in 1947, he helped position sports at the forefront of American racial reform. His success, coupled with that of his contemporaries in other sports, including Bill Russell in the NBA, Jim Brown in the NFL, and other racial pioneers in the American sports leagues, suggested that sports had accepted African Americans on an equal basis in the opinions of many Americans. The primary aim of the touring propaganda campaign was to convince the relatively tiny educated groups in the emerging nations that U.S. "policies and aims are in harmony with their own and will serve to advance their legitimate national aspirations."[54]

In addition to introducing others to the "American way of life," sports were utilized to help tie disparate groups together. Indeed, sports were a valuable tool for nation building, which attracted the attention of many African leaders. The new African sport ministries implicitly acknowledged that sports were an instrument of their foreign domestic policy during the Cold War. Athletic competition helped solidify ties between different ethnic groups within their societies. The feeling of community generated from participating on the same team and cheering for the national team helped provide avenues in citizen's everyday lives to connect them with national belief systems and social structures. The ability to generate intense emotions, and athletics' ability to identify a clear enemy, helped heighten and create a sense of group solidarity and cohesion that had not existed previously.[55] Nicholas Rodis, who served as the head of the Office of International Athletics in the State Department during the Kennedy administration, offered this assessment of sports: "Sports will tie a group of people together faster than many other ennobling principles. We believe that what is good for a new or developing country is good for the peace and stability of the world." Rodis also concluded that there would be a direct benefit to the United States when "these nations identify their progress with our help."[56]

Touring teams and individuals for the Cultural Presentations Program were usually recruited by the private organizations that had jurisdiction over certain sports. For example, the Amateur Athletic Union had jurisdiction over basketball and track and field, the two most popular sports for amateur athletic tours. Tour activities often included public contests or exhibitions, but emphasis was placed on teaching demonstrations and workshops for native athletes, youth groups, and coaches. A typical tour lasted approximately forty-five days and covered three to five countries.[57]

The American Specialist Program provided tours ranging from two weeks to one year for outstanding athletes or coaches. The more famous athletes usually visited a number of countries for two or three months, whereas the coaches and athletes who were not world famous tended to go to one country and stay from six to twelve months, organizing athletic activities and helping teams prepare for regional or Olympic contests. These tours often included demonstrations and workshops, but the emphasis of the program was on coaching. Based on the needs of a particular nation, the specialist might either develop the nation's capabilities in an individual sport by coaching the national team or help the country develop structures for its national sports program. Frequently, the specialist did both.[58]

Two of the earliest sports coaches sent abroad were track coaches, William Bowerman and Jack Mashin, who were sent to Pakistan in 1955. Before their arrival, Pakistani sports leaders were skeptical of athletic visits. Based on the previous brief tours of the track star Bob Mathias, the Pakistani viewpoint was that it was fine to see outstanding American sportsmen perform, goodwill was created, the United States received favorable publicity, but there were few lasting benefits from the standpoint of improved athletic standards and performances among Pakistani athletes.

The long-term nature of Bowerman and Mashin's visit helped quell their dissatisfaction. In fact, the visit of the American coaches was credited with the revitalization of the prestigious Karachi Annual Athletic, which had not been staged for the three previous years. The coaches' three-month visit was dedicated to the preparation of the military athletes for the Karachi meet. The tour was so successful that repeated calls were made by the vice chancellor of the University of Karachi, A. B. A. Haleem, and others for an American coach to be assigned exclusively to the Karachi colleges and universities for at least one year.[59]

The sports tours were helpful because they were often still welcomed when political relations were strained. One of the earliest goodwill trips sponsored by the American State Department involved the International Badminton Championships held in Singapore in late May 1952. The United States reached the finals against the team from Malaya (later renamed Malaysia), a nation where badminton was considered the national sport. When it became clear that the Americans would meet the Malayans in the finals, the newspaper scrutiny of the matches intensified throughout Malaya. The Malayans overwhelmingly beat the United States in seven of the nine matches to win the championship. Although the United States lost the match, the American Embassy in Singapore reported that "because badminton is so close to the hearts of almost all Malayans, it is doubtful whether any deliberate effort which the United States could have made to improve relations with Malaya could have been more effective." The report concluded that "the unintentional diplomacy of the members of the American badminton team, whose pleasant and unaffected manner, playing skill and sportsmanship were truly remarkable advertisements for the American way of life."[60]

As the American athletic exchange program became institutionalized, two of the points made by the embassy in Singapore would be altered. Rather than being unintentional, the United States began to make deliberate attempts to use sports to advance diplomatic ends. Furthermore, the success of the events would not be viewed as momentary shifts. Instead, they would be seen as one step in an evolutionary process to alter perceptions of the United States. However, for that moment, when falling rubber prices in Malaya had hurt the popularity of the United States, the American Embassy reported that the badminton match between the United States and Malaya supplanted the status of rubber prices as the lead story and helped to alleviate the tension between the two nations.[61]

Between 1952 and 1961, more physical education specialists were sent abroad than any other specialist group. In total there were 189 physical education specialist tours. In comparison, there were 84 musical specialist tours and 107 educational specialist tours. The tours were spread all over the globe: 47 were sent to the Near East, 37 were sent to Europe, 28 tours were sent to Africa, 46 tours were sent to the Far East, and Latin America received 31 tours.[62]

In addition to sending Americans abroad, there was a programmatic effort to bring foreign nationals to the United States. The Foreign Specialists Program brought athletic coaches, outstanding athletes, and physical education instructors to the United States, either as individuals or in groups. In addition to familiarizing them with American culture, the program allowed the specialists to increase their knowledge of the latest sports techniques. The average foreign specialist grantee spent two or three months on assignment in his or athletic field of interest, and then he or she was usually afforded another month to travel throughout the United States.[63]

Although controversial, the athletic goodwill tours were symbolic of the shift in the nature of foreign affairs in the post–World War II world. Foreign relations became accountable to the will of the people, as advancements in communications made the dissemination of information much easier. Thereafter, foreign relations experts could not be exclusively concerned with the opinions and thoughts of official representatives of nations. They had to pay particular attention to the people's attitudes, their state of progress and education, their level of information, and their hopes and expectations. According to Theodore Streibert, the director of the USIA, sports were one of the most important Cold War weapons during the mid-1950s. At a Senate Foreign Relations Committee hearing on the U.S. cultural exchanges, he testified that sports exchanges were "the most effective thing we're doing in the Orient."[64]

The leadership, conduct, and development of amateur athletics in the United States were traditionally handled by private groups and individuals, while the government functioned as "a sympathetic encourager." However, as I have detailed above, the United States increasingly became interested in athletics during the early 1950s because they had the potential to form impressions and attitudes in other lands about the United States, its culture, people, and the "American way of life." Because of athletics' ability to impact the international prestige of the United States, "physical fitness and amateur athletics have . . . been of interest and concern for the federal government." In fact, Republican senators Henry Styles Bridges of New Hampshire and Homer Capehart of Indiana joined with Democratic senators Hubert Humphrey of Minnesota and J. William Fulbright of Arkansas to share a fundamental criticism of the inadequate conduct and funding of the State Department's sports programs in the late 1950s. Nonetheless, it was universally agreed that while the government should supplement the activities of the private sector, the initiative, vigor, diversity, and dynamism of the private efforts were America's strengths. The government's program was designed around the presumption that "sports in the United States [are] best handled and managed by the private sector—not the government."[65]

The U.S. sports program was designed to prove to the world that American private sponsorship of athletics was superior to the Soviet state–sponsored program. Furthermore, in reality the U.S. government could not provide huge sums of money to support the country's efforts in international athletic competitions and exhibitions. Throughout the history of the U.S. athletic programs, this reality presented considerable difficulties. When more funds were needed for the sports exchanges, rather than suggesting greater government subsidization, assistant secretary of state Abbott Washburn suggested that a private committee made up of professional sports figures and other distinguished leaders should take on the responsibility of seeing that the United States had the best possible representation at the most important overseas competitions. He stressed that the "committee would work closely though informally and entirely unofficially, with USIA, CIA, and the State Department." Then the committee, using private funds, would provide the teams with transportation, accommodations, and equipment for the competition. Washburn's advocacy for greater private involvement is crucial because it highlights one of the central dilemmas that the State Department would continue to face in its athletic exchange programs.[66]

Within the early years of the program, it became evident that sports tours were among the most universally liked by the U.S. Information Service posts, because they were accepted by audiences. Additionally, they were among the least troublesome to arrange. U.S. ambassador Taylor Belcher, who was stationed in Cyprus and Peru, said that in his experience with sports exchanges, "Sports sell themselves . . . they are a real people-to-people program reaching right down into a cross-section of the community—touching the interest of people in all economic strata and all age levels." Belcher continued, "A first-class athlete has a message that everyone understands." Belcher did not elaborate on the message that the athlete carried; nonetheless, it can be reasonably assumed that he thought the exchanges were reflective of the character and vitality of the "American way of life."[67]

Playing Propaganda

The notion that sports were apolitical was crucial to the government's efforts, because the assumed inherent lack of ideological content minimized the vulnerability of sports to the charges of neocolonialism and cultural imperialism that plagued other American propaganda efforts. A report from the U.S. Embassy in Djakarta, Indonesia, suggested that because it was generally perceived to be "innocent of any political coloring, the general field of sports has always been one in which American assistance has not only been acceptable but eagerly sought after." The absence of overt political meaning helped make the tours more appealing to nations that were hostile to the United States or at least skeptical of American influence. For example, members of Congress and pundits were initially critical of the decision to send African Americans abroad as cultural ambassadors because they feared that this ploy would be readily denounced as propaganda. However, many foreign nationals were genuinely impressed by the material prosperity, training, and opportunities that athletic success suggested were available to black Americans.[68]

Propaganda theorist Jeremy Hawthorn's work provides a theoretical framework to understand why athletic tours were effective. Hawthorn maintains that effective propaganda hints at conclusions rather than drawing obvious connections. In the introduction to the edited work *Propaganda, Persuasion, and Polemics,* he argues that propagandists use implications and hints so that the audience perceives that it is actively considering and processing information, rather than "passively absorbing what is provided by a skilled persuader." In order for the propaganda to be effective, the spectators have to believe that their response is legitimate, based on facts, and derived from their own interpretation. Hence, the propagandist frequently uses nonverbal cues, Hawthorn argues, to encourage interpretation of evidence that has been presented in a "particular light, and relationships between them suggested. [Then] the audience is encouraged to join up the facts" in a manner that suits the needs of the propagandist. The expressed purpose of government-funded propaganda suggested that "implicit in the idea of 'submitting evidence' is the further idea that you let the audience draw its own conclusions." By not emphasizing explicit statements about progress in U.S. race relations, the athletic tours were able to maintain the illusion that the tours were sent abroad not for political reasons, but simply to entertain and cooperate in areas of mutual interest, thus masking the political implications.[69]

The potential emotional impact of the tours was a major drawing card. Antonio Gramsci argued that it was naive to think that people's political beliefs can be altered simply through logical persuasion; like-wise, behavior is not just the product of consciously weighed options. Consequently, involvement in rituals such as athletic competitions and exhibitions provided an opportunity to change perceptions, beliefs, and thoughts by impacting people's emotional state. Propaganda experts have argued that a chain of logical argumentation is often incomprehensible to crowds. The ultimate goal should be to move people emotionally, not just merely provide information. Hawthorn argues, "Action is triggered off more quickly and completely by emotional pressure than by rational agreement. . . . The association between successful persuasion and the ability to arouse an emotional response in one's audience is an intimate one." The basic notion is that human beings generally react instinctively, intuitively, or emotionally, not logically. Consequently, those who hope to persuade must make their case with strong emotional appeal.[70]

The power of symbols relies as much on their ability to stir emotions as their ability to lead the audience down a clear intellectual and ideological path. When emotional pressure is applied, in the case of the athletic tours by people in nations of color witnessing the success of African Americans in American society, it is believed that the people were more susceptible to being influenced. Applying anthropologist David Kertzer's arguments about ritual participation suggests that by attending and participating in the athletic events as spectators, the emotions of the citizens of the host nations would be aroused. The ultimate aim was to get the citizens to make a positive emotional investment in the images of integrated teams and successful African Americans as representative of American race relations. The larger goal was to convince skeptical audiences to attribute the positive feelings that were engendered at the sporting event to "the American way of life."[71]

American claims about the universalism of the American creed were buoyed by the notion that sports were a common interest of people world-wide and could serve as a means to promote mutual understanding and goodwill. The "Basic Guidance Paper" for the USIA reminded government officials that sports, music, graphic arts, theater, and literature were the best "way of reminding everyone of [the] common bond" shared through-out mankind. It was implicit in the government campaigns that athlet-ics reflected Western social systems. For example, the U.S. Consulate in Kuala Lumpur argued that the "promotion of sports will be one of the best means of keeping the youth of the New (Malayan) villages healthily occupied and away from the constant temptations which are directed towards idle ears by communist propaganda." Through participation in Western-sponsored sports, it was believed that the youth would identify with the larger political forces that were being expressed symbolically through the sports exchanges. Thus, sports were identified as a means of socialization to Western values. The sporting contest and exhibitions were analogous to mass rallies because they helped the participants increase their identification with the West and presumably increased the hostility and opposition to the Soviet Union, which was depicted as a threat to the extension of democracy worldwide.[72]

Sports were one of America's best foreign affairs assets because they provided an international common ground upon which the United States tried to impose its ideology. The Olympic Games had created emotional ties and a set of symbols associated with sports and universalism among the nations of the world, and the State Department wanted to reinterpret and take advantage of the connections and bonds that had already been forged. Indeed, foreign nationals who attended the exhibitions and games were supposed to come away with an appreciation of American ideals and an image of the United States as healthy, victorious, and altruistic.[73] Athletic accomplishments also suggested that the U.S. system was based on justice and fair play, which helped fuel the propagandistic interpretation that sporting exhibitions displayed America's commitment to creating a society where equal opportunity was a fundamental basis of society.

The United States employed sports as a means to gain entry into nations that, if not openly hostile to the United States, were not particularly interested in learning about the "American way of life." Sports tours were judged to be highly effective and widely accepted even in remote areas of the world. For example, in Libya sports were one of the major avenues of communication with young men because the national sports clubs were the primary social centers and outlets for their physical and mental energy. The United States sought to influence their ideas and thoughts by sending athletes and coaches to help advance track and basketball in Libya. Sports became an attractive arena to "break through the bureaucratic barriers posed between the American Embassy and the people of [the country]."[74]

The U.S. Embassy in Lisbon acknowledged that the Cultural Presentations Program was of great importance, particularly for public relations. In Portugal the press was highly censored, and United States Information Service press material was often unutilized. It was through cultural and athletic exchanges that the United States made the case against the notion that it was a purely materialistic country that lacked culture. The notion that America was devoid of culture meant that the United States needed to improve its image in order to assert its claim to leadership. As Secretary of State Dean Rusk argued, "The basic objective is to weave a fabric of intellectual, scientific, and cultural collaboration that will engage Americans and foreign people in common endeavors. This activity is extremely important for the long-range effect on the lives of nations. . . . [I]t is through this program as perhaps in no other way that we can take certain leadership in the change that is taking place in the world."[75]

The sports activities in East Asia during the late 1960s were judged in a highly favorable manner. In many of the nations, educational and other forms of exchange were not permitted; therefore, sports were the only available means to display American culture. For example, following the discontinuation of diplomatic relations with Cambodia in 1965, the American athletic coaches working in Cambodia were the last Americans asked to leave the country because of the significance of their work. It was recommended that despite an increase in hostility between the United States and many East Asian nations, the sports exchanges were to continue under certain conditions: individual athletes and coaches were to be used under noncompetitive arrangements; workshops, coaching clinics, or exhibitions were to be the principal activities; and, most important, sports were to be used primarily as "door openers" where other programs were not permitted.[76]

The targets of American sport propaganda were the youth worldwide, for whom the United States wanted to present an image of the nation as free, fun, modern, wealthy, open, and youthful. The State Department's Policy Planning Staff maintained that it was of the utmost importance that youth were one of the "principal, if not [the] primary target" of propaganda campaigns. Highly visible, cost-effective, and attractive to a broad mass of people, athletics and the international language of sports reached children and other audiences that diplomats simply could not. William Payeff, the acting public affairs officer at the U.S. Consulate in Hong Kong, maintained that "sports exchanges are one of the best possible methods, especially among youth, for achieving a better understanding of our way of life."[77]

As a 1964 report, titled "An American Specialist Program Directed to Youth," suggested, sports were one of the central avenues to reach youth. Based on a survey in which eighty-two Foreign Service posts responded, it was concluded that sports were arguably the principal issue that captured the attention of youth worldwide. In response to the question "What are youth interested in?" fifty-eight of the eighty-two posts said that the youth were interested in sports. By comparison, music and dance had twenty-nine affirmative responses each, and guidelines for organizing youth scouts, with twenty-eight responses, were judged to be the other most widely available ways to reach the young people.[78] The goal was to create rapport with college students, the potential future leaders in the emerging countries, who had not already developed hostile attitudes toward the United States.

The goal of the program was to influence the current and future leaders and decision makers of foreign nations. It was widely acknowledged that the benefits of the U.S. athletic exchange program would be evident in the long range: "The filtering down of impression from a society's taste-makers to the point where they become generally accepted is a slow and painstaking process. Old myths, fictions, and stereotypes die very hard."[79] The long-range aims of the program suggested that youth would also be an ideal audience, in particular the youth that showed the greatest promise of future leadership. The age of many of the touring athletes made them the peers of the best students attending universities worldwide. Seeing the best of America's collegiate students presumably highlighted the "American way of life."

Conclusion

As we have seen, the State Department finally recognized that transmission of messages through emotionally charged ritual dramatizations involving symbolism could be more powerful than the verbal declarations of spokespeople like Carl Rowan, Max Yergan, and J. Saunders Redding. State Department–sponsored cultural exchanges including athletic, musical, and theatrical tours were often more effective than speaking tours because they were less dogmatic and more subtle and appealed to people's emotions. Robinson McIlvaine, deputy assistant secretary for public affairs in the State Department, argued before a subcommittee of Congress's Committee on Appropriations about the value of cultural exchange. Referring specifically to a musical group, McIlvaine cited as evidence an article from the *Manila Chronicle,* a newspaper that publicly acknowledged its hostility to the United States: "Once in a while, America contrives to muster enough of her native genius to present to the rest of the world the best that she can give," the article asserted. The climax of the article claimed that the Philippines would not "care if the State Department bombarded us with invasions . . . of other American artists. . . . Should the United States Government adopt this propaganda as seriously and on as large a scale as it has adopted the program of military aid, all the evils with which America has been identified might be forgotten."[80] This article hints at the massive cultural exchange program that the Soviet Union had used to try to soften its international image, and the article argues that the United States had lost significant ground because of the success of the Soviet cultural diplomacy initiatives.

The U.S. goodwill-tour programs were initiated because the Soviet Union was having uncontested success with its athletic and cultural exchange programs. America's athletic goodwill tours were designed to counterbalance the success of the Soviets' program. However, the United States also sought to use its sports tours to showcase African American advancement. The following chapter juxtaposes international coverage of American race relations with foreign perceptions of touring African American athletes.

4. "The Good Negroes"

Propaganda and the Racial Crisis

In 1956 the State Department sent the University of San Francisco Dons men's basketball team on a summertime tour of Latin America. At the time of the tour, the Dons had won fifty-five consecutive games and had amassed an incredible 57–1 record on the way to back-to-back NCAA championships. The team was led by their All-American center, Bill Russell, a six-foot-ten African American, whose shot-blocking and defensive skills were the cornerstone of the team's domination. At the time, conventional wisdom held that defense was a time to rest until your team had the ball again, so most players did not expend energy jumping. Even when the occasional shot was blocked, the ball typically went out of bounds, which allowed the offensive team to maintain possession. However, Russell became adept at tipping the blocked shot to a teammate and initiating a fast break.[1]

Even as Russell's dominance propelled the Dons toward their first national championship, his coach, Phil Woolpert, perhaps too fixated on tradition, kept telling Russell that by jumping to block shots, he was "fundamentally unsound." Eventually, Woolpert came to appreciate and encourage Russell's innovation.[2] Two championships later, Woolpert, Russell, and the rest of the Dons were rewarded with a State Department–funded trip throughout Latin America.

The Dons' first stop was Guatemala, where they spent a hectic three days, winning their two games by an average of thirty-four points. Although the games were lopsided, the contests were "two of the best games of basketball ever played in this country," according to the U.S. Embassy's report. The highlight of the tour was the team's invitation to visit Guatemalan president Castillo Armas, an avid sports fan and recreational basketball player. After their visit with President Armas, the Dons appeared on the government-sponsored television station where a USIS film, *Foreign Sports in the United States,* aired before the station broadcast interviews with Guatemalan players and the Dons. Acting public affairs officer in Guatemala Maurice J. Broderick described the players' maturity, level of commitment to their tasks, and basketball skills as "noticeably outstanding."[3]

Throughout their tour, the Dons' effort was lauded. Harry S. Casler, the public affairs officer in Panama, said that the Dons "exemplified true democratic principles applied to the field of sports." The team conducted a well-attended clinic the day before it beat a tough Panamanian all-star team, 57–49, after the score had been tied at intermission. Similarly, the team was labeled the most successful venture arranged by the State Department's exchange program in El Salvador. Gene Karst, the public affairs officer in San Salvador, said that he had never come across a group of athletes who conducted themselves "in such a fine manner as the Dons," who made "great quantities of friends for the United States."[4]

On other tours in Latin America, close contests had engendered hostility toward the United States, as quibbles over officiating and player conduct had led some fans to leave games with their negative perceptions of the United States reinforced. On one occasion, the Dons had to come from behind to eke out a 43–41 victory in Asunción, Paraguay, against Club Olympia, the ten-time defending Asunción champion. Ten thousand fans watched as the Dons beat the stiffest competition they faced on their tour. In Paraguay basketball was a major sport played throughout the year. Rather than becoming hostile as the close game came to an end, the Paraguayans were ecstatic over the competitiveness of the home team.[5]

In additional to their basketball skills, the Dons were ideal goodwill ambassadors because their coach was a racial pioneer due to his extensive recruitment of African American players. Coach Woolpert started three African Americans on his championship teams: Russell, K. C. Jones, and Hal Perry. The coach, whom Russell referred to as "a fine and decent man," received hate mail and was called "Saperstein," a derogatory comparison to the founder of the Harlem Globetrotters because of his extensive use of African American basketball players. The talented African American star from UCLA Willie Naulls accompanied the Dons on their tour, so Woolpert was able to put four African Americans on the floor at the same time. The State Department was well aware of the potential political implications of Woolpert's progressive views.

In Guayaquil, Ecuador, Henry B. Lee, the public affairs officer, reported that every effort was exploited to "picture the racial mixture of the Dons" because a majority of the city's citizenry had black blood. The public display of camaraderie between the black and white players made the Dons' tours "worth more than hundreds of thousands of printed words" on U.S. race relations.[6] Such pronouncements made athletic goodwill tours important strategic undertakings during the Eisenhower and Kennedy administrations.

"'The Good Negroes': Propaganda and the Racial Crisis" explores President Eisenhower's and President Kennedy's widespread use of symbolic gestures in the realm of civil rights—including the extensive use of African Americans as cultural ambassadors. I argue that both administrations waged an unsuccessful battle to alter international perceptions of U.S. race relations, because the symbolic acts could not compete with the more "newsworthy" items of racial abuse such as lynching, battles over school desegregation, and other forms of political protest. To illustrate this point, this chapter focuses on the goodwill tours of Mal Whitfield and Rafer Johnson, both of whom were abroad touring in close proximity to the unrest in Little Rock, Arkansas, that was sparked by efforts to desegregate Central High School in 1957. By juxtaposing international coverage of Little Rock with the reception of Whitfield's and Johnson's tours, I suggest that the propaganda campaigns were not able to drastically alter international perceptions of U.S. race relations. Furthermore, I show how the failure of the propaganda campaigns was a contributing factor to the enactment of civil rights legislation in 1964 and 1965.

Brown v. Board of Education
Ushers in a New Era

At the height of the Cold War, African American athletic success continued to serve as a powerful example of racial progress. For example, Mal Whitfield, a dominant middle-distance runner, was a favored State Department cultural ambassador. Whitfield became interested in track when he sneaked into the Los Angeles Coliseum and witnessed Eddie Tolan's victory over Ralph Metcalfe in the 100-meter final at the 1932 Olympic Games. Whitfield credits that moment with inspiring him to pursue Olympic gold. Whitfield's dreams came true at the 1948 Olympic Games, where he won gold medals in the 800-meter dash and the 1,600-meter relay, while taking home a bronze medal in the 400-meter race. His victories made him the first U.S. serviceman on active duty to win

Olympic gold. He followed that performance with an impressive showing at the 1952 Olympics in Helsinki: a gold medal in the 800-meter dash and a silver medal in the 1,600-meter relay. Throughout his career, Whitfield established eighteen world records and became the first African American to be awarded the Amateur Athletic Union's prestigious James E. Sullivan Award as America's outstanding amateur athlete in 1954.[7]

In addition to his athletic accomplishments, Mal Whitfield displayed his loyalty to the United States during the Korean War, during which as a second lieutenant he flew twenty-seven combat missions. Because of Whitfield's athletic accomplishments and his military service, it was not surprising when the State Department asked him to take an international tour under its American Specialist Program to "enhance U.S. prestige . . . and assist in creating an atmosphere favorable to the acceptance of American friendship, goodwill, advice and possible assistance." The itinerary for Whitfield's 1954 tour contained nine destinations that were crucial Cold War battlegrounds: Belgrade, Yugoslavia; Lagos, Nigeria; Accra, Gold Coast; Karachi, Dacca, and Lahore, Pakistan; Rangoon, Burma; Athens, Greece; and Nairobi, Kenya.[8]

While abroad, Whitfield maintained a hectic schedule, conducting clinics, participating in exhibitions, showing films, and giving lectures. For example, during his stay in Karachi, Pakistan, he spoke before twenty-four different audiences: nine colleges and universities; two groups of instructors and athletes from approximately fifty high schools; three groups of Royal Army, Navy, and Air Force troops; and ten other mixed groups, with an additional twelve receptions, luncheons, and dinners in his honor. The U.S. Embassy in Karachi estimated that he personally addressed 11,500 local Pakistani citizens. His stop in Rangoon was also frenzied: he conducted four clinics, ran in a track meet, and spoke at several dinners in his honor.[9]

Whitfield's enthusiasm and hard work stemmed from his belief in the importance of sports as a vehicle for fostering peace. "Atom bombs cannot establish peace in the world, but goodwill visits of this kind [are] the only medium by which free and freedom loving people can hope to bring peace to the world," Whitfield stated in Accra. Undoubtedly, he shared the State Department's view that athletics could help improve the United States' international influence and reputation. His tour took on heightened importance because it occurred just weeks after the *Brown v. Board of Education* decision was rendered. Hence, Whitfield's tour provided the United States with a positive, progressive opportunity upon which the State Department was determined to capitalize.

The 1954 *Brown v. Board of Education* court decision was the most significant and celebrated moment involving race relations during the Eisenhower administration: a decision opposed by the president. The *Brown* case emerged out of the NAACP's decision to attack the logic of the 1896 *Plessy v. Ferguson* decision, which upheld "separate but equal" facilities for blacks and whites. On May 17, 1954, Chief Justice Earl Warren spoke for the unanimous Court—including three southern justices—when he asserted that separate educational facilities were inherently unequal. The symbolic importance of the *Brown* decision was enormous. The landmark case made civil rights a "different ball game," in presidential press secretary James Hagerty's opinion, because it overtly placed the power of the Constitution behind the African American struggle. Hence, the ruling severely undermined the legal underpinnings of racial discrimination. At the time, *Newsweek* labeled the decision "the most momentous decision in the whole history of the Negro struggle."[10]

President Eisenhower thought that the *Brown* decision was a mistake and would impair progress toward greater equality for African Americans. Eisenhower told his speechwriter, Arthur Larson, "I personally think that the [*Brown*] decision was wrong." Eisenhower did not believe that "prejudices, even palpably unjustified prejudices, will succumb to compulsion." He thought that the *Brown* decision artificially granted forced integration when whites needed more time to change their racial attitudes. As Carol Anderson has argued, in the "most delicate realm" of civil rights, Eisenhower believed that "time," "education," and "local control" were the best ways to address civil rights concerns. Consequently, his administration did not emphasize federal legislation, but rather stressed persuasion, patience, and passivity. In a 1958 critique of President Eisenhower, *Ebony* maintained that the president was elected because he had "the reputation of a great leader," but in reality he was "not inclined to get ahead of the public. He urges patience, and in effect asks Negroes to place their ultimate faith in time."[11]

Despite Eisenhower's misgivings, the U.S. State Department made sure that it reaped the propaganda rewards of the *Brown* case. Officials sought to cloak the decision in ways that reified the Constitution through patriotic rhetoric and by positioning it within the American Protestant religious tradition. For the State Department, this positive development affirmed the contention that the U.S. social system could facilitate racial advancement and gave credence to the image that the State Department tried to propagate in its athletic tours program.[12]

Within an hour of Chief Warren's reading of the ruling, the *Voice of America* radio program broadcast the news worldwide as a triumph for democracy. School segregation was one of the issues that most negatively impacted U.S. prestige among African nations. The Justice Department brief, which had been filed in the waning days of the Truman administration, expressed its support for the plaintiffs in the *Brown* case because of the international implications of U.S. racial strife: "It is in the context of the present world struggle between freedom and tyranny that the problem of racial discrimination must be viewed." Although the Court's decision did not specifically refer to the Cold War, the brief's observation that "hostile reaction [to American racial practices] among normally friendly peoples . . . is growing in alarming proportions" was a veiled reference to the international implications of continued race-based oppression.[13]

The *Brown* decision received favorable coverage worldwide. For example, the weekly newspaper *Afrique Nouvelle,* from Dakar, Senegal, which was adamantly opposed to racial discrimination, published an article titled "At Last!" The article greeted the news with enthusiasm, but prophetically predicted "desperate struggles" over its implementation. However, the article concluded that "all the peoples of the world can salute with joy this measure of progress." The positive responses to the *Brown* decision empowered U.S. propaganda experts because they suggested that the United States could win the hearts and minds of skeptical audiences.[14] Hence, in the wake of the *Brown* decision, the State Department intensified its propaganda campaign.

When originally asked to tour by Harold Howland, an officer at the State Department, Mal Whitfield maintained that it "was an opportunity that I, as a man of color, had never anticipated." However, in the post-*Brown* environment, the State Department wanted Whitfield to take a tour precisely because of his stature as a "man of color."[15] Consequently, the State Department was very interested in how U.S. race relations were contextualized on the tour. At a lecture in mid-January 1955 before a crowd of four hundred in Athens, Greece, Whitfield avoided U.S. racial issues in his address but highlighted two topics: the essential ingredients (sacrifice, hard work, team spirit, and determination) for championship-level performances and the role of athletics in the effort to foster peace, health, and contentment in the world. The embassy report noted that "the lecture itself was not impressive. It had obviously been prepared for any and every occasion, and had not been adapted to the local situation in any way."[16]

However, Whitfield was quite engaging during question-answer segments, particularly on questions involving U.S. race relations. For example, he was asked why the Sullivan Award committee did not honor Jesse Owens after his four-gold-medal performance at the 1936 Olympics. The U.S. Embassy was pleased to report that Whitfield "deftly turned his reply into a review of the immense progress made in the United States . . . toward race tolerance." In accord with the State Department emphasis on progress, he referred to his own selection as the 1954 Sullivan Award winner as evidence that the United States was moving "toward a final solution of the problem of race relations." Only years later in his autobiography did Whitfield reveal that he was not proud of being the first black American to receive the Sullivan Award: "The honor should have gone first to Jesse Owens, then to Harrison Dillard, then to me."[17] Whitfield also did not reveal to his audience that he had to use the servants' elevator to get to the Sullivan Award ceremony at the New York Athletic Club (NYAC), which barred African American membership.

Despite his treatment at the NYAC, Mal Whitfield's personal success as an African American was crucial to achieving his mission: altering international perceptions of the United States. His subtlety in addressing the United States' racial dilemmas caught the attention of Joseph C. Kolarek, the public affairs officer at the American Embassy in Belgrade, Yugoslavia. At a cocktail party where Whitfield met Yugoslav athletic leaders and athletes, he answered questions in a manner that was "of considerable propaganda value," according to Kolarek. By pointing out that the United States was a large nation with regional interests and attitudes about different sports and various other aspects of American life, he "indirectly but effectively made the point that the Negro problem in the United States is regional rather than national," claimed Kolarek, the host of the party. Kolarek judged Whitfield's visit as an "unqualified success," because Whitfield was a racial moderate who had a "hard-working, assured, and level-headed" demeanor and his athletic success commanded the respect and admiration of the Yugoslavs.[18]

The seemingly apolitical nature of the tour also helped consolidate and expand contacts with segments of the various nations' populations "that were not so receptive to other USIS activities." The public affairs officer at Dacca, Pakistan, Fentress Gardner, expressed a similar sentiment in her report about the track star's visit: "Dacca could use more visitors of this type, particularly of the young enthusiasts who are successful in their own field and who appeal to certain groups of students who are difficult to reach in other ways."[19] Gardner's observation reiterated the propaganda value of the sports tours' ability to engage young, nonliterate, and nonelite audiences.

By authorizing tours like Whitfield's, President Eisenhower demonstrated that he intended to craft narratives about the progress of African Americans rather than use the moral authority of the presidency and his executive power to drastically improve the living conditions of African Americans. Because Eisenhower was fearful of alienating southern whites, his involvement in civil rights was largely in the symbolic realm: he appointed African Americans to low-level executive posts, begrudgingly supported efforts to end segregation in Washington, D.C., and expanded U.S. propaganda efforts.[20] Eisenhower's most important accomplishment was helping eradicate lingering legally sanctioned segregation in the armed forces. As Michael Krenn has suggested, President Eisenhower's action made "American military personnel . . . actors in a public display of symbolic allegiance to the ideal of racial equality."[21] Although all-black units were abolished, African American servicemen were concentrated in menial jobs with limited mobility because of unequal educational opportunities and military seniority rules.

President Eisenhower's appointment of African Americans to visible yet noncontroversial administrative positions, often with international responsibilities, was a relatively inexpensive means to project an image of inclusiveness. For example, Lois Lippman joined the secretarial staff at the White House; Frank Snowden, a Howard University professor, became a cultural attaché in Rome; Clifton Wharton was named minister to Romania and became the first black chief of mission to a white country in 1958; Robert Lee Brokenburr, Charles H. Mahoney, and Archibald J. Carey were appointed to the American delegation to the United Nations; John B. Eubanks became the head of the Rural Improvements Staff for the U.S. Operations Mission of the International Cooperation Administration; and E. Frederic Morrow became the first African American to hold the position of administrative assistant to the president. As historian Robert Burk has argued, the strategic placement of blacks in nonthreatening positions in the executive branch "reflected the belief of high-ranking officials that the value of black government employees laid in their presence as symbols of national racial democracy rather than in their usefulness as policy makers."[22] Despite Eisenhower's hesitancy, the momentous victory that the *Brown* decision represented reinvigorated African American acceptance of Cold War–era limitations regarding acceptable criticism of the United States. In other words, some African Americans were encouraged to publicly express their faith in the ability of the United States to solve its racial problems because, as a positive development, the *Brown* decision provided an important counterpoint to the coercive McCarthy-era fearmongering.

Bandung and the Emerging Afro-Asian Bloc

On the heels of the *Brown* decision, twenty-nine decolonized states met in Bandung, Indonesia, in 1955. Despite their religious, political, and cultural differences, the fate of peoples still under colonial rule and the struggles of those still suffering from racial discrimination were the common bonds that united these nations. The African and Asian states articulated links between liberation movements in Africa and Asia with African Americans' struggles for civil rights in the United States. The Bandung Conference alarmed U.S. policy makers because it held the potential to reinvigorate African American attempts to articulate the oppression of African Americans as an aspect of the global fight against colonialism. The continued suspension of W. E. B. DuBois's and Paul Robeson's passports revealed the depths of State Department fears.[23]

Outspoken congressman Adam Clayton Powell from Harlem had suggested that the House of Representatives send a multiracial delegation of observers to illustrate U.S. support for the causes espoused by the nations meeting in Bandung. The Eisenhower administration refused. Powell's reputation as "Mr. Civil Rights" did not always endear him to Eisenhower. His reputation stemmed from his incessant calls for racial reform as a "highly visible member of Congress" and his repeated introduction of the "Powell Amendment," a legislative provision that withheld federal funds from racially segregated facilities. Since becoming a member of the House of Representatives in 1944, Powell challenged the United States to reconcile the "American dilemma" by eliminating racial discrimination. In this instance, Powell thought that attending the Bandung Conference could generate goodwill and demonstrate that the United States valued Asian and African nations as much as European countries.[24]

The Eisenhower administration wrestled with how it would respond to the conference. Their uneasiness with the ramifications of the meeting was evident in the suggested comments offered by Nelson A. Rockefeller, a White House special assistant. Rockefeller suggested that it should be clearly expressed that the United States was dedicated "to the principle that political freedom and independence is a basic right of all peoples has been confirmed by the consistent record of our history in terms so clear that they should require no reaffirmation." However, a few paragraphs later, the suggestion that the United States supported self-determination "for all people who wish to exercise it and *are able to undertake its responsibilities*" was problematic because most policy makers at the time did not think that sub-Saharan African nations were ready for self-rule.[25]

In the face of impending decolonization in Africa, the United States had sought to find a middle position between direct support of rapid decolonization and outright defense of continued white control: a daunting challenge. The U.S. State Department was fearful that the strong connection between the "free world" and colonialism provided the Soviets with advantages in the struggle over the "third world." Since all of the colonial governments in Africa and Asia were aligned with the free world, the United States had to balance its allegiance to the European colonial powers with its desire to influence former colonized peoples.

William Gowen, a U.S. intelligence officer, expressed his concern over the Soviets' ability to lure Asian nations into their orbit. Gowen surmised that the Soviets' return to Moscow as its capital was a repudiation of "St. Petersburg, the symbol of Europeanization."[26] Indian prime minister Nehru said that the thrust of Asian interest in communism was "based on the degree to which [Asian] deep-rooted anti-colonial impulse is ignored by the Western world." Clifton Daniels's front-page *New York Times* article "Soviet Justifies New Foreign Line" suggested that the Soviets were going to champion the cause of nationalism and independence worldwide. William Gowen thought that this approach would cause anti-Europeanism to expand. "Colonialism is used to inflame the racial pride of the Asiatic and unless we find an anti-Communist outlet for the same thing," Gowen argued, "the white man and *all his values* will be swept away and replaced, step by step, with Marxism. . . . What the hell are we going to do?"[27]

The United States' viewpoint that communism rather than starvation, inequality, or other quality-of-life issues was the overriding threat to stability was diametrically opposed to the perspective of the nonwhite people in the third world. The Soviet Union took an alternative approach to the issues important to former colonized nonwhite people. The Soviets realized that in underdeveloped countries, past or present, white domination was a greater reality than either the Soviet menace or capitalist expansion because both failed to specifically address the problems of poverty, disease, illiteracy, and colonial bondage. Therefore, the Soviets made repeated calls for complete national independence and self-determination in all colonial areas.[28]

Congressman Powell viewed the Bandung Conference as a perfect forum to express the commonalities between the goals and values of the

United States and those of the Asian-African bloc. After Eisenhower rejected his proposal, Powell paid his own expenses to attend the Bandung Conference. At Bandung, before a crowd of five hundred reporters, Powell said that "racism in the United States is on the way out. Second class citizenship is on the way out. . . . [I]t is a mark of distinction to be a Negro." Communist reporters were flabbergasted and displeased with Powell's depiction of U.S. race relations as a narrative of progress. Although he was an outspoken voice in the fight to end racial discrimination in the United States, Powell through his actions at Bandung revealed that he was willing to adhere to the oft-heard notion that "politics stops at the American shore." During a postconference meeting with Eisenhower, Powell explained that he went to Bandung "to give living proof to the fact that there is no truth in the Communist charge that the Negro is oppressed in America." When Powell returned to the House of Representatives for the first time after the conference, he was greeted with a standing ovation from his peers, many of whom were ardent critics of the Powell Amendment. Powell's statements in Bandung reflected the aims of the State Department's propaganda campaign. As Nikhail Singh has argued, "Powell gambled that sugary words abroad would enhance his bargaining power at home."[29] In essence, his overseas performance, although controversial, demonstrated that many African Americans were willing to accept their role as Cold Warriors in exchange for substantive change in the racial landscape. This is important because it is too easy to see African Americans who publicly praised the United States abroad during segregation as political puppets, but the reality is that many of them demonstrated a keen understanding of the political nature of their pronouncements. Yet high-profile instances of racial injustice continued to trouble international audiences. Abroad, school segregation caused the most damage to U.S. prestige.

The Challenges of Little Rock

Two of the most highly regarded African American goodwill ambassadors—Mal Whitfield and Rafer Johnson—were abroad in close proximity to the eruption of violence in Little Rock in September 1957. The United States would have been hard-pressed to find athletes who better personified the ideals of amateur athletics, had better "bridge-builder" personalities, and were more devoted to being "team players" than Whitfield and Johnson. Just weeks before Little Rock garnered international attention, Mal Whitfield traveled to North and East Africa—Tunis, Tunisia; Tripoli,

Libya; Nairobi, British East Africa; Kampala, Uganda; Monrovia, Liberia; and Freetown, Sierra Leone—on a State Department–sponsored tour.[30] Whitfield faced a hectic schedule in order to maximize his brief visit. For example, while in Libya on July 18, 1957, he began his day with a lecture and demonstration for Libyan police cadets at 8:30 a.m. and concluded with a 9:30 p.m. film session and presentation at an athletic club.[31]

His second tour helped generate goodwill toward the United States on several fronts: the United States was praised for taking an interest in the success and development of emerging nations, and he demonstrated the improving place of African Americans in American society. Records were broken everywhere that Whitfield conducted clinics. Howard Russell, an officer at the U.S. Embassy in Nairobi, said that even more important than his athletic accomplishments were Whitfield's "friendliness and willingness to do anything requested of him which made friends for him and for the United States throughout the country. He cheerfully worked 12 to 14 hour days and seven-day weeks without a single complaint. His effectiveness could hardly be exaggerated." William C. Powell, the public affairs officer at the American Embassy in Monrovia, said that Whitfield helped improve Liberian appreciation of African American advancement, because he was "a representative American Negro whose contribution to the American way of life is recognized throughout the world."[32]

The community development sports officer in Nairobi, R. H. W. Bachelor, was so impressed with Whitfield's work in Nairobi that he wrote that Whitfield possessed "the gift of spreading the gospel of Democracy and Christianity through the medium of Athletics." An injury hindered Whitfield from competing at a meet, but the disappointed crowd was treated to his instruction. Whitfield was at his best when working directly with the athletes. He demonstrated his personal, practical workout. He playfully demonstrated several common faults that track athletes made; his energy and enthusiasm "had the crowd in fits of laughter." Thereafter, he demonstrated how these faults could be remedied. His presentation earned a rousing ovation. His excitement was infectious as he tried to help athletes develop perfect technique, and his influence was evident as participating athletes set ten new records at the Coast Championships held in Mombasa. The local communities openly gave Whitfield the credit for their improved performances.[33] Whitfield was so highly regarded by State Department officials that he was offered an administrative position, which he gladly accepted and thereafter served in various countries on the African continent.

Rafer Johnson, arguably the greatest athlete in the world in 1957, was on a goodwill tour of Southeast Asia in the midst of the Little Rock incident. During the 1950s, before television came to dominate spectator sports, track and field was much more popular in the United States and worldwide than it is today. Hence, Johnson was one of the United States' most high-profile athletes. At the time of his tour, Rafer Johnson was the world recorder holder in the decathlon, a grueling two-day track and field competition that entails demonstrating expertise in ten athletic events—the 100-meter dash, the long jump, the high jump, the 400-meter dash, the shot put, the 100-meter high hurdles, the discus throw, the pole vault, the javelin throw, and the 1,500-meter run. The wide-ranging skills that a champion decathlete had to display caused many worldwide to label the world's best decathlete as "the world's greatest athlete."

Equally important to Rafer Johnson's success as a goodwill ambassador were his nonathletic qualities. Although much of Johnson's acclaim, success, and adulation would come after his 1957 goodwill tour, the personality traits that led one admirer to label him an "uncommonly decent, ethical, and likable man" were already well evident. Johnson, an honor student, attended UCLA on an academic scholarship, and he was chosen as UCLA's student body president during his senior year. Furthermore, Johnson would be awarded the James E. Sullivan Amateur Athletic Union memorial trophy in 1960 after being voted the runner-up in 1956 and 1958. The Sullivan trophy was awarded to the "amateur athlete who by performance, example, and good influence did most to advance the cause of good sportsmanship during the year."[34]

Perhaps the highest testament to Johnson's preeminence as a sportsman was his selection as the flag carrier for the United States at the opening ceremony of the 1960 Olympic Games in Rome. Traditionally, the person chosen for that honor was the oldest Olympian or the competitor who had had the most success at previous Olympic contests. When Johnson was chosen to carry the flag, he had not yet won a gold medal, and there were nine Olympians competing in their fourth Olympic Games. When Louis J. Wilke, a member of the United States Olympic Committee (USOC), was asked why the committee had broken with tradition, he said, "We thought Rafer represented the best in Americanism. We not only felt he was probably the greatest all-around athlete in the country, but also an example of your finest traditions." Furthermore, Johnson was the first African American given this honor.[35]

Even as superb athletes and individuals like Whitfield and Johnson generated enormous goodwill toward the United States worldwide, the violent and contentious battles over implementation of the *Brown* decision undermined the story of progress that the State Department crafted. The most notable example focused on Little Rock, Arkansas. On September 2, 1957, Arkansas governor Orval Faubus announced that integration would not proceed the following day at Central High School in Little Rock. Faubus authorized a National Guard contingent to bar the entrance of nine black students who had been selected to integrate the school. Faubus's actions were puzzling because Little Rock had a moderate mayor, Governor Faubus's son attended an integrated college, and in 1948 Arkansas had been the first state in the South to integrate a public state university without being prompted by a court order.[36] Furthermore, after the *Brown* decision, the Little Rock School Board had developed a plan for gradual desegregation of its public schools: high schools would be integrated in 1957, junior high schools in 1960, and elementary schools in 1963. Additionally, Governor Faubus did not have a history of race-baiting.

After the African American students were prohibited from entering Central High School on September 3, the federal district court ordered desegregation to take place in a ruling the following day. An assembled angry mob caused the troops to again deny entrance to the black students seeking enrollment. Each day a larger white mob gathered to make sure that troops turned away any African American students seeking to integrate the school. As Faubus's use of state armed forces to oppose the authority of a federal court brought the most severe test of the Constitution since the Civil War, newspaper and television reporters arrived to cover the latest maneuvers, making the crisis the "first on-site news extravaganza of the modern television era."[37]

After weeks of political wrangling, the federal district court repeated its order to Governor Faubus to stop obstructing school desegregation at Central High School. With a hostile white crowd assembled, eight African American students entered the school through a side door on September 23. Upon hearing the news, the assembled crowded estimated at between five hundred and two thousand strong grew more agitated. Groups of white students exited the school. Then Little Rock mayor Woodrow Wilson Mann ordered the black students removed at midday because he feared violence. The next morning Mayor Mann called White House aide Max Rabb, the president's adviser on civil rights, to plead for the deployment of federal troops to stifle mob violence at the high school. Aware of the international implications of the situation, the mayor argued that his call for help was in the interest of "democracy worldwide."[38]

By authorizing the use of one thousand troops from the 101st Airborne Division to keep order in Little Rock, President Eisenhower became the first president since Reconstruction to use armed troops to support the constitutional rights of African Americans. In a televised speech to the nation, President Eisenhower partly defended his use of troops because communist media outlets were using the Little Rock incident to portray the United States as a "violator of those standards of conduct which the peoples of the world united to proclaim in the Charter of the United Nations." President Eisenhower estimated that it would be difficult to "exaggerate the harm that is being done to the prestige and influence" of the nation abroad. Indeed, photographs and newspaper articles about Little Rock made front-page news internationally. As Mary Dudziak has suggested, in 1950 the State Department publication *The Negro in American Life* suggested that slavery should be the benchmark by which the nation's progress in race relations should be judged. However, after 1957, Little Rock became the new measuring rod for progress.[39]

The Little Rock incident, which occurred as the United Nations General Assembly was discussing Soviet aggression in Hungary, hurt the moral position of the Western world. The Soviet press seized upon the incident as a means to discredit American condemnation of Soviet actions in Hungary. One Moscow paper ridiculed U.S. ambassador to the United Nations Henry Cabot Lodge's speech on the crisis in Hungary, because as he discussed the ideals of civilization, humanity, and the rights of man, U.S. newspapers "report unbelievable crimes and violations of the most elementary human rights which are taking place" in Little Rock. Another article leveled a charge of hypocrisy: "White-faced but black-souled gentlemen commit their dark deeds in Arkansas, Alabama, and other Southern states, and these thugs put on white gloves and mount the rostrum in the United Nations General Assembly, and hold forth about freedom and democracy." In a telephone call to the attorney general, Herbert Brownell, Secretary of State John Foster Dulles was concerned that the situation would severely hamper U.S. foreign policy objectives and be more detrimental in Africa and Asia than the Hungary issue was for the Soviet Union. Aware of the political fallout, U.S. officials strove to distinguish Little Rock from Hungary by asserting that national authority in the United States had been used to "expand the freedom and equality of the individual," whereas the Soviet Union used its national authority to suppress rights and freedoms.[40]

By contrasting the international coverage and reception of Johnson's tour with that of Little Rock, it is clear that the State Department tours were not able to reverse the ill will that high-profile racial incidents caused. For example, the week of Eisenhower's meeting with Governor Faubus in Rhode Island, Johnson was in Colombo, Ceylon, where his visit

was overshadowed by Little Rock. At an afternoon weekend meet, Johnson won all seven events he entered and broke four Ceylonese records:
100 meters, javelin, discus, and shot put. The *Ceylon Daily* contained a
glowing description of Johnson's performance, claiming that "he came,
he saw and he conquered." Johnson was lauded for his athletic preeminence but also his exemplary behavior, willingness to sign autographs,
and fraternization with the local citizens.[41] Nonetheless, Little Rock was
a front-page news story in the local press.

Rafer Johnson saw himself as a moderate on the question of racism
in the United States. "Confrontation was simply not my style," Johnson
maintained. Instead, he believed that he "could do the most good by maintaining a positive image." Johnson's basic philosophy was that for "change
to be lasting and meaningful it had to take root in individual hearts and
minds." Hence, his "quiet, modest disposition," coupled with his impeccable sense of sportsmanship, made him a potentially valuable asset to have
abroad as the Little Rock crisis intensified. In his autobiography, Johnson
described how he handled questions regarding U.S. race relations abroad:
"I never minimize our problem, but I tell people abroad that there is a
lot being done to alleviate the problem." His approach was the preferred
approach among State Department personnel because he expressed his
faith in the American capitalist-democratic system to solve the nation's
racial problems.[42]

The violence at Little Rock brought scorn upon the United States from
all over the world. Reports from the United States Information Agency
suggested that in many parts of the world, Little Rock lowered international impressions of American race relations. However, in other instances
where impressions were already low, Little Rock confirmed and solidified
previously held unfavorable attitudes. For example, an editorial from the
newspaper *Suluh Indonesia,* published in Djakarta, Indonesia, said that
Little Rock made it difficult to believe "U.S. Western Democracy is an
invaluable thing which should be introduced all over the world." A U.S.
diplomat asserted that before Little Rock, Israel had been "the enemy"
in the Middle East, but the violence in Arkansas over school integration
made the United States "the enemy." Little Rock became so synonymous
with U.S. race relations that Vice President Richard Nixon was greeted
with chants of "Little Rock" as a hostile crowd attacked his motorcade in
Caracas, Venezuela, in May 1958.[43]

Foreign allies of the United States who had been tolerant and understanding of U.S. efforts to address racial discrimination found their ability
to bridle their criticism of the United States strained. Robert P. Chalker,

the American consul general at the embassy in Amsterdam, reported that Dutch sentiment was concerned because the incident and the corresponding "weakening of America's moral leadership in the world indirectly hurts America's allies," since racism was contradictory to the values of liberty, equality, and equal opportunity. An article published in a Canadian magazine asked, "Is Little Rock any of our business?" The article argued that Governor Faubus's actions caused as much harm to Canada, Britain, and Western Europe as they did to the United States, because for nations in Africa and Asia, "the most important thing about a white man is the way he treats a colored man, and of course they tend to judge a white man by his neighbors and friends."[44]

It was popular during the 1950s to assert that racial discrimination in the South continued because of the constitutional division of power among federal, state, and local governments, an arrangement that the Eisenhower administration claimed precluded federal interference in matters under state control, such as criminal justice and education. Given the global reach of U.S. power, many foreigners were unconvinced of the sincerity of this position. One French citizen told the noted African American historian John Hope Franklin at a seminar in Salzburg, Austria, "It appears to the outsider that federalism stands in the way of nothing that the national government actually wants to do; but it is always used as an excuse for the national government's not protecting the rights of Negroes." Others publicly wondered how the United States planned to convince the world of the advantages of democracy when it could not get Governor Faubus to obey the laws of the land.[45]

In an attempt to ameliorate the damage caused by the violence in Little Rock, Christian Herter, the acting secretary of state, distributed a memo to American embassies worldwide, titled "Overcoming Adverse Reaction to the Little Rock Incident." Herter's advice to place the events at Little Rock into perspective by stressing specific progress that had been made in race relations and reminding the world that discrimination was not unique to the United States was a preferred method of dealing with racial crises in the Eisenhower administration. Believing that Little Rock had been misinterpreted and misunderstood, Herter suggested that it be emphasized that the crisis arose because of the "force and strength of the American people's insistence upon complete equality." Herter advised that it be noted that in thirty-one of the nation's forty-eight states, "public school integration was a reality."[46] Although this was factually true, there were still great disparities in the educational opportunities available to the average African American.

Interestingly, Secretary of State Herter expressed his belief that African American athletes were a "great value" to the government's effort to alter international perceptions of American race relations. The American consul general in Dakar, French West Africa, proposed that an effective response to Little Rock "would be the sending to Black Africa of American Negro athletes and athletic teams. . . . The Africans at this stage are insatiably interested in sports." Although Little Rock was damaging, a USIA report gauging post–Little Rock opinions about American race relations revealed that even after the violent incident, most nations, with the exception of France, believed that the status of African Americans had advanced over the previous decade. Athletics was listed as one of the reasons for the perceived rise in status among African Americans.[47]

A close examination of the press coverage reveals that the meaning associated with Rafer Johnson's tour at the height of the Little Rock controversy was co-opted by the Ceylonese as a means to critique American race relations. Such was the case when the *Times of Ceylon* suggested that Ceylonese sports fans should attend the meets in which Johnson was competing, because it would be a show of sympathy "for all Negroes handicapped by the color of their skin." Thus, the Ceylonese citizens expressed their kinship with Johnson based on their mutually shared oppression at the hands of white imperialists, rather than as advocates and supporters of the American democratic-capitalistic system.[48] The tours, which had been heralded as effective means to manipulate international perceptions of U.S. race relations, especially before the 1955 Montgomery bus boycott ushered in the modern-day civil rights movement, faced significant challenges, as the violent battles that accompanied the civil rights movement received unmatched press coverage and other interested parties attempted to co-opt the meaning of the tours.

The challenges that increasing racial violence posed were evident in a 1957 State Department report, "Treatment of Minorities in the United States—Impact on Our Foreign Relations," which was completed after the violence in Little Rock became international news. The civil rights bill passed in 1957—the first of its nature in eighty-two years—authorized the creation of a Civil Rights Commission to serve as a liaison between Congress and the State Department. Understanding the foreign policy implication of domestic civil rights, the commission asked the State Department for a report regarding the extent to which treatment of minorities impaired the country's relationship with other governments and how communist-bloc countries took advantage of racial unrest in their propaganda campaigns. The thirty-five-page report made several important observations:

1. American race relations helped shape foreign attitudes toward the United States. Therefore, shortcomings had an indirect impact based on how the issue swayed public opinion.
2. The central focus of foreign nations on American racial issues centered around the plight of African Americans. Awareness of progress based on successful desegregation was increasing, but *high-profile incidents of racial strife and struggle . . . overshadowed reports of progress.* The emotional impact, coupled with sensationalistic press accounts, continued to dominate international discussion of U.S. race relations.
3. Interest was highest in Africa and Asia, where racial discrimination in the United States was linked with white colonialism. Interest in Europe was largely based on the reality that the gap between American principles and practice gave a powerful weapon to the communists, who used discrimination to discredit Western democracy.
4. The issue weakened the United States' moral position as the "champion of freedom and democracy" and reinforced doubts about the nation's interest in the welfare of others, particularly peoples of color.
5. Because the issue received wide attention in noncommunist press, the Soviets no longer produced much original material on the subject. Instead, Moscow quoted and reprinted articles from the *New York Times* and other publications to increase the credibility of its attempt to expose the "American way of life" as morally bankrupt.[49]

This report is significant because it suggested the limitations and ineffectiveness of the approach advocated by Secretary of State Herter in his memo "Overcoming Averse Reaction to the Little Rock Incident." Whereas Herter and other leading State Department officials thought that the international public would find the State Department story of progress believable and satisfactory, this report suggested that examples of progress were not able to sufficiently counteract the damage done by instances of racial violence and oppression.[50] This report expressed the limitations of the goodwill tours as propaganda weapons. It suggested that the United States had to take more aggressive measures to combat the international problems that racial oppression caused the United States. Despite the evidence that the tours were not effectively countering foreign impressions of the United States, President Eisenhower continued to suggest that slow progress was the best means to enact civil rights reform. Therefore, as the Eisenhower administration came to a close, it tried to counterbalance incidents of racial violence such as the repression of the sit-in movement with more positive examples of racial progress.

The Kennedy Administration Faces the "Race" Question

African American athletes were still prominently featured in State Department propaganda campaigns at the end of the Eisenhower and the beginning of the Kennedy administrations because sports were still perceived to be at the forefront of improving U.S. race relations. Relatedly, the majority of African American athletes were still willing to express faith in the evolutionary approach to U.S. race relations, which stressed the notion of progress. For example, although Muhammad Ali, formerly Cassius Clay, would become a role model for the athletes who sought to use their athletic preeminence for black uplift, his words and deeds at the 1960 Rome Olympic Games suggested that he was supportive of the Cold War rhetoric about the social significance of African American athletic success. Cassius Clay won the gold medal in the light heavyweight boxing division at the 1960 Olympic Games. Shortly after the award ceremony, a Russian reporter asked him how it felt to win glory for a nation that did not allow him to eat at Woolworth's in his hometown of Louisville, Kentucky. "Tell your readers we've got qualified people working on that problem," Clay answered, "and I'm not worried about the outcome. To me, the U.S.A. is still the best country in the world, counting yours." Clay concluded his comments with a derogatory reference to Africa that he would later come to regret: "It may be hard to get something to eat sometimes, but any how I ain't fighting alligators and living in a mud hut."[51]

Clay's response to the Russian reporter suggested that he was an heir to the political legacy established and strictly heeded by former African American heavyweight boxing champion Joe Louis, who defined "acceptable" behavior for a generation of African American athletes. Louis strove to be approachable, deferential, integrated, sensitive to white sensibilities, and uninvolved in controversial racial politics. One of the costs of inclusion was that the majority of African American athletes during the 1950s maintained a low profile and avoided controversy.[52] Clay's comments at the 1960 Rome Olympic Games characterize the general attitude that prevailed among African American athletes from the late 1930s through the early 1960s. African American athletes were willing to express faith in the ability of the United States to successfully solve the racial problems. Clay and others like him believed the notion that the nation was advancing and saw themselves as instruments of progress. Their continued, collective willingness to adhere to the sanctioned notions regarding "progress" reflected black America's faith that increased social, political, and economic opportunities were forthcoming, and the election of President Kennedy was seen as a catalyst to make their aspirations reality.

On the issue of civil rights, before assuming the presidency, Kennedy's record was uneven. Kennedy supported antilynching legislation, southern school desegregation, and a strong Fair Employment Practices Commission, and he was the first New England member of either house of Congress to appoint an African American to his staff. Kennedy's call to Coretta Scott King, when her husband had been sentenced to hard labor for a minor traffic violation, helped tip a close election in his favor. As Charles Hamilton has suggested, John F. Kennedy's symbolic act helped give "legitimacy to Martin Luther King and the civil rights struggle at the highest levels of government."[53] African Americans perceived this act as a potential sign of Kennedy's commitment to civil rights reform. However, in order to win the presidency, Kennedy needed the support of African Americans, but he also needed the southern white vote. Despite pressure to champion civil rights reform, Kennedy moved cautiously.

Despite his campaign promises to end discrimination in federal housing with the "stroke of a pen," Kennedy failed to sponsor a civil rights bill or issue a sweeping executive order or support the civil rights movement's assault on segregation during the first two years of his presidency. Frustrated African Americans mounted an "Ink for Jack" campaign to remind Kennedy of his promise. After assuming the presidency in 1961, John F. Kennedy continued and expanded the presidential pattern of giving token appointments to African Americans. Kennedy's failure to pursue aggressive civil rights reform during his first two years in office made African Americans skeptical of the president's intentions. Furthermore, the president had given only grudging support for the March on Washington. In fact, during his first two presidential years, President Kennedy sought to curry favor with southern whites. Consequently, the president who during his 1957 southern tour was touted as "Dixie's Favorite Yankee" appointed William Harold Cox, a Mississippi segregationist who openly referred to African Americans as "niggers," to the federal bench. Even Martin Luther King grew impatient with Kennedy and accused him of "aggressively driving only toward the limited goal of token integration."[54]

The Cold War context is crucial to understanding Kennedy's concern with domestic race relations. After seventeen nations gained their independence in 1960, the need for reform became imperative. His primary concern with the civil rights struggle was limiting the political fallout abroad caused by the contentious nature of efforts to defeat southern segregation by calling for moderation on both sides and, most importantly, limiting the "social instability" that civil rights–related violence engendered. For example, the president urged a halt to the Freedom Rides because they were damaging the nation's image on the eve of his meeting with Soviet premier Nikita Khrushchev. Thus, as Thomas Borstelmann has argued, "Kennedy fit the description of Martin Luther King's notion of the 'white moderate' who agreed with the goals but not the direct action methods of the movement, who felt as if they could set the timetable for another's freedom, and were more devoted to order than justice."[55]

President Kennedy's hesitancy on civil rights reform led Donald Wilson, the deputy director of the USIA, to issue a dire prediction as he addressed a meeting of the Woman's National Democratic Club in Washington, D.C.: "We are no longer coping with isolated incident. Where the span between a Little Rock and an Oxford could be marked by months and years, now we are witnessing a massive effort throughout the nation, and there will be no long pauses which allow us to slip into apathy." Wilson's insight suggests the sense of urgency that he and other officials believed was necessary to overcome the international damage caused by racial violence.[56] The incident at Birmingham was the key catalyst for change in Kennedy's approach to civil rights.

Birmingham, Alabama, also known as "Bombingham," was the most segregated big city in the United States. The city had endured eighteen racial bombings and more than fifty cross-burning incidents in a six-year span ending in 1963. Years later Martin Luther King explained the reasoning behind choosing Birmingham as a battleground in the national civil rights struggle. "If successful [the battle would] break the back of segregation all over the nation," King said regarding the Birmingham campaign. Or as the Reverend Wyatt T. Walker later explained, "We decided on Birmingham with the attitude that we may not win it, we may lose everything. But we knew that as Birmingham went, so went the South." In the wake of a failed effort to desegregate Albany, Georgia, the civil rights movement needed an "audacious" victory, because questions were being raised about the viability of nonviolence as a tactical method.[57]

Bull Connor, Birmingham's commissioner of public safety, had been relatively restrained the first few weeks of protesting, which denied the civil rights agitators the type of confrontation that usually resulted in extensive press coverage, aroused the interest of northern liberals, and provoked the disdain of international communities. However, after city high school kids were recruited as marchers, Connor permitted police dogs, fire hoses, and police batons to disrupt the march on May 3, 1963. Vivid images of teenaged African American youth being washed down the street by high-pressure water hoses and images of police dogs tearing clothes from the bodies of march participants were broadcast on television news programs worldwide that evening and filled newspapers the following morning. Police dogs and water hoses became symbols of the systemic oppression of African Americans, especially throughout Africa.[58]

As the violence in Birmingham escalated, the representatives of thirty African nations were meeting in Addis Ababa, Ethiopia, at the founding conference of the Organization of African Unity. The group passed a resolution expressing the "deep concern aroused in all African peoples and governments by measures of racial discrimination taken against communities of African origin living outside (Africa), and particularly in the United States." Images of police dogs attacking African Americans had a deep impact in many regions of Africa, largely because they were reminiscent of colonialism and apartheid. One Nigerian writer was so outraged that he suggested that the United States was becoming "the most barbarian state in the world." Incidents like Birmingham led one poll to suggest that 78 percent of Americans thought that U.S. domestic race relations were hindering U.S. foreign policy objectives.[59]

Three weeks after violence erupted in Birmingham, Secretary of State Dean Rusk addressed the international significance of racial abuses before a meeting of the National Foreign Policy Conference for Nongovernmental Organizations on May 27, 1963. The Georgia native addressed an audience of three hundred representatives of private organizations concerned with foreign affairs. Rusk argued that the international implications of U.S. racial discrimination were analogous to running a race "with one of our legs in a cast." The purpose of Rusk's presentation was to solicit the help of nongovernmental organizations in avoiding the racial confrontations that he said were "not representative of America, should not be necessary in our kind of society, and [do] us deep injury abroad." The secretary of state made the powerful statement that helping quell racial outbreaks would be the best way that domestic organizations interested in international relations could help U.S. foreign affairs.[60]

United States Information Agency deputy director Donald Wilson was also called upon to make a public statement about the international implications of U.S. domestic racial tensions. On June 10, 1963, Wilson delivered a presentation titled "Racial Strife: The Overseas Impact." Wilson began his speech by recounting examples of media criticism that the

Birmingham violence engendered in nations in Africa, the Far East, the Middle East, Latin America, and Europe. "Since the dark days of the Nazi Gestapo—no such barbaric and merciless repression has been seen as in Birmingham," one unidentified source was quoted. Internationally, U.S. democratic rhetoric was negatively juxtaposed against images of dogs snarling at defenseless African Americans and of police officers using batons to pin African American women to the ground. Wilson reiterated a familiar point: "[Racism] puts our professions of freedom and democracy in doubt; it more than any other, makes suspect our motives and aspirations."[61]

The quest to present the disturbances in "perspective" by emphasizing success stories was hampered, because as news items they were, according to Wilson, "competitively slow." Wilson and the USIA had reached the same conclusion that the State Department had reached six years earlier after the violence in Little Rock. The recommendations from the report "Treatment of Minorities in the United States—Impact on Our Foreign Relations" had not yet been acted upon by Eisenhower or Kennedy. Because images and descriptions of vicious dogs, water hoses, and dilapidated ghetto housing facilities were more striking, they were much more likely to be considered news than the quiet, peaceful, and successful efforts to integrate. Consequently, Wilson advocated swift action: federally protected access to public facilities, the right to vote, decent housing, and equal employment opportunity. The USIA deputy director supported his claim by arguing that "words will not enlist the world's confidence in this country as a bastion of democracy. Only action can do this."[62]

The following day, President Kennedy delivered a nationally televised address detailing his plan to eradicate segregation. Proclaiming that it was the nation's time to live up to the promises of the Constitution, Kennedy expressed the need for congressional action by advocating three general legislative proposals: a public accommodations law, authorization for more effective intervention in school desegregation lawsuits, and tougher voting-rights provisions. The president's uncharacteristically fervent speech placed his support behind civil rights, in part because the battle against communism required an end to racial tension in the United States.[63]

A State Department–produced "Memorandum for the President" distributed shortly after the president's speech began by praising the president because "national and international acclaim of your forthright statement on civil rights has been remarkable." However, the memo predicted that the racial situation was "fraught with danger" because "the determination of Negroes to achieve their constitutional rights is equal to the determination of those who would deprive them of these rights." The report stressed the need for the government to pursue "sustained and vigilant action." Warning the president that there would probably not be a "cooling off" period, the report suggested that the president's aggressive commitment to solving integration problems would be in the best interest of the nation.[64] Despite President Kennedy's best efforts to utilize "citizen diplomacy," goodwill tours and other international programs could not sway international public opinion given the violent responses that civil rights activists encountered.

The United States had engaged in extensive cultural foreign relations for more than twenty years before the Kennedy administration, but never on the scale that was reached under President Kennedy. Expanding educational and cultural exchange had been one of the major recommendations of the 1960 Eisenhower-sponsored Sprague Committee report that reviewed government-sponsored informational programs. In programs oriented to tap into the nationalistic fervor abroad, Kennedy increasingly sought to use sports as a means to enhance the prestige of the United States. With the Kennedy administration's active support in 1961, Congress enacted the Mutual Educational and Cultural Exchange Act, otherwise known as the Fulbright-Hays Act. This bill superseded most of the previous legislation in the area of cultural affairs and created the Bureau of Educational and Cultural Affairs to broaden these programs. Politically, the cultural programs were seen as a means to counterbalance the administration's seemingly hostile pledge to "fight any foe" in the struggle against communist expansion with a softer, friendlier side.[65]

President Kennedy further emphasized sport as a propaganda vehicle by signing an executive order that authorized the creation of the Interagency Committee on International Athletics in 1963.[66] Executive Order 11117 acknowledged that sport "might have a potential effect upon the foreign relations of this Nation." The principal function of the committee was to make recommendations to the president and the secretary of state. The chairman of the committee was Nicholas Rodis, the special assistant for athletic programs in the State Department. The committee included representatives from among the most significant and innovative agencies in the Kennedy administration: the Justice Department, the President's Council on Physical Fitness, the Department of Defense, the United States Information Agency, and the Peace Corps.[67] The Peace Corps was Kennedy's most high-profile contribution to the nation's exchange programs.

Just six weeks after he assumed the presidency, Kennedy signed an executive order and committed $1.5 million from his discretionary fund to establish the Peace Corps. Kennedy's swift action helped galvanize U.S. citizens who were moved by his inaugural speech, in which the young, charismatic leader issued a call to service to which many citizens responded. In words that echoed the best intentions of the Peace Corps and the cultural exchange programs, the president's inaugural speech asked U.S. citizens to prioritize the collective needs of the nation and the world above their individual desires. The overwhelming response to the president's plea helped secure a $40 million appropriation and the passage of the Peace Corps Act in September 1961. The large financial investment acknowledged how important foreign exchange programs were as a means to pursue U.S. foreign policy objectives.[68]

The Peace Corps worked to promote development around the world by sending American citizens to host nations to provide technical expertise, middle-management skill, and manpower to solve problems in several core areas: education, agriculture, engineering, and health professions. Volunteers were asked to live abroad for two years while completing their work projects and to build "bridges of friendship" between the United States and Africa, Asia, the Middle East, and Latin America. Applicants were subjected to standardized tests, personal interviews, and two months of training that focused on global development as well as the host country's language and culture. Similarly to those sent abroad through the cultural exchange programs, Peace Corps volunteers were expected to use their time abroad to help develop "mutual understanding" between the United States and host nations.[69] By this U.S. policy makers meant that the volunteers were to help convince their hosts of the benefits of the U.S. capitalist, democratic system.

Sport was also utilized as a key component of Peace Corps initiatives. It was the organization's policy to send volunteers only to countries that requested them and only for the purposes outlined by the host country. By the end of 1964, more than 250 volunteers were running sports programs, teaching health and physical education, or coaching teams. All Peace Corps volunteers were trained on the best coaching techniques for the most popular sports in the countries to which they were assigned because sport was acknowledged as a means of building lasting relationships. The Peace Corps had a contractual agreement with the American Association for Health, Physical Education, and Recreation (AAHPER) to provide and train physical educators. A mid-1960s recruiting poster specifically sought physical educators: "Those interested in helping to develop, expand, and strengthen physical education and athletic programs in other lands have an opportunity to use their special skills in the AAHPER Peace Corps

Projects." The poster listed the potential assignments that were available to the volunteers: teaching positions in secondary and university physical education programs as well as coaching assignments at the club, regional, and national athletic-team levels. Perhaps most significant, Peace Corps officials found that sport-related volunteers were less likely to be accused of acting as spies. Therefore, sports were employed as a means to enter countries that had rejected other Peace Corps overtures.[70]

The program served as an ideal space for the president to pursue his anticommunist campaign by tapping into the youthful idealism of many of his supporters. During the 1960 presidential campaign, Kennedy invoked the Cold War and the Soviets' exchange programs as important rationales for the Peace Corps. Kennedy sought to use the program to demonstrate that U.S. ideals could help defeat the Soviet "missionaries," who, theretofore, far outnumbered U.S. citizens sent abroad during the early days of the Cold War. However, after he assumed the presidency, Kennedy's official pronouncements sought to deny that the volunteers were "instruments or agents of the Cold War or American foreign policy." Despite the concerted effort to conceal the political importance of the program, the Peace Corps was seen as a propaganda venue through which the United States could attempt to address international concerns regarding racial injustice as the civil rights movement continued to garner international headlines.

Because U.S. racial struggles continued to influence international perceptions of the United States, the Peace Corps was compelled to acknowledge the centrality of the issue. By the mid-1960s, Peace Corps volunteers were given instruction on the civil rights movement in the United States because it was the issue that most placed volunteers on the defensive. A 1961 Peace Corps report acknowledged that volunteers' being "asked about civil rights matters is a foregone conclusion." In its attempt to make sure that volunteers were adequately prepared and knowledgeable about the struggle, the program had volunteers watch televised coverage of the strife. Additionally, the training program included several lessons devoted to the subject: "Know Your Little Rocks Facts," "Integration: Token or Reality?" and "Significant Achievements of the American Negro." Despite these efforts, the program had one glaring problem: the lack of African American volunteers. Only 2 of the first 100 volunteers were African American. Only 4 of the initial 120 volunteers sent to Africa were of African descent.[71]

As one of the measures to improve the number of African American participants, the Peace Corps turned to one of the nation's most high-profile African Americans to travel abroad during the early Cold War, Rafer

Johnson. Attorney General Robert Kennedy asked Johnson to consider the possibility of working with the Peace Corps after Kennedy was the keynote speaker at an awards ceremony that honored Johnson. During his acceptance remarks, Johnson expressed his desire to continue working in international relations and foreign exchange programs. At the time of the ceremony in 1961, Johnson was at the height of his international acclaim after winning the decathlon at the 1960 Olympic Games in Rome. As a Peace Corps spokesman, Johnson's principal task was to recruit volunteers, especially African Americans who shared his moderate racial views. As one who sought to "shed light" on the "common humanity" of blacks and whites, by "maintaining a positive attitude," Johnson was positively viewed as someone to whom many African American citizens with similar worldviews would respond. However, despite Johnson's and the Peace Corps' best efforts, the number of African American volunteers never exceeded 7 percent of the 13,000 volunteers send abroad during the early years of the program.[72] Notwithstanding Kennedy's best efforts to extend and improve the exchange programs, decisive legislation was essential to alleviate international condemnation of U.S. racial abuses.

Conclusion

Five months after he began actively advocating for the passage of a strong civil rights bill, President Kennedy was assassinated. A week later, President Lyndon Baines Johnson stood before a joint session of Congress and admonished them to pass the bill as a memorial to the slain president. After months of congressional haggling, Johnson signed the 1964 Civil Rights Act on July 2, 1964. The act banned discrimination in employment, federally assisted programs, public facilities, and public accommodations. The federal government was given the power to initiate lawsuits to desegregate school districts and to withhold federal funds from reluctant school districts. The Equal Employment Opportunities Commission and Community Relations Service were created to mediate discrimination problems. After the passage of the law, it was no longer legally permissible to discriminate based on the grounds of race, color, religion, or national origin.[73]

Civil rights activists considered the passage of the 1964 Civil Rights Act a huge victory for the civil rights movement because it went beyond mere symbolic declaration, and the walls of segregation in public accommodations fell with very little resistance in the South. International support and praise for this advancement came from across the globe and created an environment in which many government officials felt as if they had gotten the upper hand on the racial issue in the United States. Some went so far as to assert that the 1964 act completely eradicated racism from American society. However, the emergence of the Black Power movement would shatter that illusion.

5. Black Power

International Politics and the Revolt of the Black Athlete

There were several unsuccessful proposed efforts to organize African American athletes to boycott the Olympic Games because of the persistence of racial discrimination. The outspoken African American activist Dick Gregory in 1963 unsuccessfully proposed a boycott of the 1964 Tokyo Olympics. A year later, the idea was resurrected. However, the new proposal came from an unlikely source: Mal Whitfield, the conservative Republican and former Olympic track champion. Whitfield had repeatedly toured internationally as a goodwill ambassador who embodied the State Department's emphasis on racial progress. At the time of his suggestion, Whitfield was employed as a health and athletic adviser to the Nigerian government. "Let's Boycott the Olympics" was the shocking title of an article Whitfield wrote for *Ebony*'s March 1964 edition. Whitfield asserted that his State Department–sponsored travels abroad were a prime motivation for his call to action. As he tried to "tell the story of democracy," the three-time gold medalist asserted that he reportedly faced several questions: "Why are you here trying to sell us on democracy when there is no democracy for your kind in America?" "Why are you in front of us talking about what sports can do for integration when some of the best athletes in the world are American black athletes, yet they are accepted only to a point?" State Department reports had expressed relief at the skillful ways Whitfield addressed these legitimate concerns when he toured throughout Africa, Asia, and other parts of the world. Undoubtedly, State Department policy makers could not have predicted Mal Whitfield's discontentment and activism.[1]

The impetus for Whitfield's new aggressive posture was the delayed passage and filibustering of the civil rights bill that was languishing before Congress in early 1964. He believed that it was "time for American Negro athletes to join in the civil rights fight—a fight that is far from won, despite certain progress made during the past year." Describing the "conspicuous" absence of wide-scale involvement by athletes in the battle for racial equality, he argued that drastic actions needed to be taken to ensure that greater rights were granted to African Americans. Arguing that "it is time for America to live up to its promises of Liberty, Equality, and Justice for all, or be shown up to the world as a nation where the color of one's skin takes precedence over the quality of one's mind and character," Whitfield issued a conditional challenge to potential African American Olympians. The former Olympic champion said that if civil rights legislation was not passed by the time the Olympic Games began in October, African Americans should stay home.[2]

Whitfield's suggestion elicited few responses from both the African American and the white communities. Consequently, the Olympic-boycott idea did not receive widespread support. Most of the African American athletes were sympathetic with his frustration, but unwilling to seriously consider forfeiting their Olympic dreams. Ultimately, significant civil rights legislation was passed in 1964 and 1965. Nonetheless, many of the problems plaguing the African American community continued to persist. Consequently, some elite African American athletes, including Lew Alcindor and Tommie Smith, were willing to seriously contemplate boycotting the 1968 Mexico City Olympics.

"Black Power: International Politics and the Revolt of the Black Athlete" explores the altered domestic and international landscapes that caused African American athletes to challenge the State Department's propaganda regarding the meaning of African American athletic success. After the passage of civil rights legislation in 1964 and 1965, many Americans believed that the nation's racial problems had been solved. However, after the civil rights movement gave way to the more rhetorically aggressive Black Power movement, the nature of protest in the African American community was altered. I argue that the protest gestures of Tommie Smith and John Carlos in Mexico City were a direct response to the State Department's use of African American athletes as propaganda tools. Furthermore, I show that these athletes saw themselves as picking up Malcolm X's mantle and mission. These athletes were heavily influenced by Malcolm and believed that their actions were the equivalent of taking the United States before the United Nations on charges of violation of international law. Perhaps most significant, this chapter analyzes the minimalist response from the U.S. government to the protest gestures of Smith and Carlos to demonstrate how and why international pressure ceased to be a dominant impetus for racial reform in the United States by 1968.

The Roots of the Olympic Committee for Human Rights

Tommie Smith, a world-class sprinter and student at San Jose State University, was in Tokyo for the World University Games in the fall of 1967. A Japanese sports reporter asked Smith about the likelihood of a black boycott of the upcoming Summer Olympic Games. "Yes, this is true," Smith responded. "Some black athletes have been discussing the possibility of boycotting the games to protest racial injustice in America." The American press reported the brief exchange widely.[3] Many young African Americans applauded Smith's sentiments. However, many Americans were confused by his statement, dismissing him as childish, ungrateful, and unpatriotic. Unsettled by the personal attacks, Smith made an appointment to meet with Harry Edwards, his professor in a Racial Minorities course at San Jose State University. The meeting led them to decide to further survey the "attitudes of other world-class athletes toward a revolt of black athletes over the problems facing black athletes and the black community in general."[4]

Harry Edwards had been a collegiate discus thrower and basketball player at San Jose State College, where he earned a bachelor's degree in sociology. Instead of pursuing an athletic career, Edwards began working on a doctorate degree in sociology at Cornell University. As he was completing his graduate education, Edwards was invited back to his alma mater, San Jose State, to teach in the Sociology Department. As a former student-athlete, Edwards was sensitive to the housing discrimination, low expectations, and hostility that African American student-athletes experienced at the college. Edwards worked with the student-athletes on campus to draw attention to their plight. In the aftermath of his efforts to force San Jose State to address the concerns of the African American student-athletes, Edwards helped organize the Olympic Committee for Human Rights (OCHR) in October 1967. The aims of the OCHR were to extend the political power of African American athletes to address racial injustice in the United States.[5]

By the mid-1960s, it was widely accepted that sports were at the vanguard of African American social advancement and the embodiment of how a just society was ordered and maintained. Consequently, sports participation was viewed as a cornerstone of what Brenda Gayle Plummer has labeled "the Age of Negro Firsts," by which she refers to the era in which African Americans gained unprecedented access to positions of influence, honor, and high prestige. Theretofore, the successful integration of the National Football League, Major League Baseball, and the National Basketball Association was said to be advancement for the race: proof that the United States was becoming more egalitarian. Manning Marable termed this widely held belief "liberal integrationism." The notion suggested that "if individual African Americans are advanced to positions of political, cultural, or corporate prominence, the entire black community will benefit."[6] Thus, sports became a stage to dramatize the American liberal democratic system's emphasis on *individual merit*. The two pinnacle virtues of the merit-based system were fair play within the rules of the system and that individual achievement was the fundamental building block of the American social system. The predominant belief was that any talented and motivated individual could succeed in American society.

Furthermore, African American athletic success was used to suggest that racial injustice was not an impediment to the advancement of individual African Americans. This interpretation gave legitimacy to existing racial inequalities in American society during the Cold War and civil rights era. Athletic achievement suggested that if African American masses were competitive, disciplined, hardworking, and patriotic, loved America, and believed in God, the American Dream would be available to them. This line of reasoning reinforced the perception that African Americans were to blame for their own disproportionately high poverty levels, unemployment, and limited opportunities. Hence, the ability of a few black athletes to achieve athletic success seemed to validate the American way of life for many Americans. For example, Martin Kane, then a senior editor at *Sports Illustrated*, wrote, "Every black child, however, he might be discouraged from a career with a Wall Street brokerage firm or other occupational choices, knows he has a sporting chance in baseball, basketball, football, boxing, or track. [He] has something real to aspire to when he picks up a bat or dribbles a ball." Kane's assessment had been widely accepted among all segments of the population because it offered hope in the face of outright and persistent racism.[7] This line of reasoning had been used to provide some limited means by which African Americans could still identify with the American Dream.

Throughout the 1950s and 1960s, the sports arena had perpetuated a vision of itself as being above racial antagonism. It deceived itself. Using more intricate, subtle social and political mechanisms, the sports world sought to keep African Americans complacent and complicit by advocating blind faith in the mere presence of blacks in athletics as a means to alter the American racial structure. The OCHR increasingly argued that despite the prevalent claims about sports as an antecedent for racial integration, sports had not done a lot to alter racist perceptions and the structure of the American social order. A widely read 1968 series of articles in *Sports Illustrated* focusing on "the black athlete," written by Jack Olsen, discussed the plight of the African American athlete on college campuses and professional athletes. Olsen's articles indicated that African American athletes felt the same despair that characterized the discontented masses in the urban ghettoes. Olsen wrote, "Almost to a man African American athletes were disgruntled, dissatisfied, and disillusioned."[8]

The reality that a critical mass had been reached in each of the three major professional sports leagues yet the promised advancements had not trickled down to the masses caused the OCHR to seriously consider the possibility of organizing a boycott. By 1968 approximately one-half of all professional basketball players were African American. Additionally, roughly one-third of all professional football players and one-fourth of all professional baseball players were African American. Between 1954 and 1964, African American athletes had won seven of eleven National League batting championships and led the league in home runs eight of those years. As African Americans became more visible in athletics, their mere presence ceased to be a positive, progressive racial force. Their success did not have the same symbolic meaning. The black athlete increasingly became "part of the status quo, the expected, the taken for granted."[9] Consequently, the "silent symbol model" of athletic behavior exhibited by Jesse Owens and Joe Louis was now interpreted by a new generation of black athletes headed by Tommie Smith, Harry Edwards, and Lew Alcindor as hindering racial advancement and as a form of legitimization of existing racial inequalities.

The Boycott Idea and the Backlash

Increasingly, the OCHR began to assert that the best way to use sports to achieve the political and social goals of the black community was to protest against American society rather than to celebrate it. Hence, by the late 1960s, sports not only reflected Black Power's critique of U.S. racism, but also helped shape the politics of the struggle. Jack Scott, a political activist, believed that America was not prepared for the change in behavior of the black athletes. Scott argued that society had "mistakenly assumed that the docility and acquiescence common in [African American] athletes of the past was an inherent quality rather than a posture" adopted as a means of survival in the racist sports world.[10]

Harry Edwards and Tommie Smith met with more than two hundred participants in a Sunday-school room at Second Baptist Church in Los Angeles on Thanksgiving Day, November 23, 1967, at the Western Regional Youth Conference. The theme of the conference was "Liberation Is Coming from a Black Thing." Four of the five world-class athletes who were present at the meeting—Tommie Smith, Lee Evans, Otis Burrell, and Lew Alcindor (later known as Kareem Abdul Jabbar)—spoke in support of the boycott. Alcindor, who was the leading scorer for the two-time defending NCAA men's basketball champion UCLA Bruins, addressed the two hundred assembled athletes to discuss the possibility of a black boycott of the 1968 Olympic Games. "Everyone knows me," Alcindor began. "I'm the big basketball star, weekend hero, everybody's all-American. Well, last summer I was almost killed by a racist cop shooting at a Black [man] in Harlem. He was shooting on the street—where masses of Black people were standing around or just taking a walk." The crowd was mesmerized as he continued, "But [the police officer] didn't care. . . . I found out last summer that we don't catch hell because we aren't basketball stars or because we don't have money. We catch hell because we are Black. Somewhere each of us has to make a stand against this kind of thing. This is how I take my stand—using what I have. And I take my stand here." Harry Edwards maintained that Alcindor's statements were "the most moving and dynamic . . . [and] memorable" words spoken in behalf of the boycott idea. The attendees gave Alcindor a five-minute standing ovation. Ultimately, the two hundred assembled attendants, including fifty athletes, decided to support an African American boycott of the Mexico City Games.[11]

The day of the meeting, the *San Jose Mercury News* reported that Tommie Smith said that he was "quite willing not only to give up participation in the Games but my life if necessary if it meant that it will open a door or channel by which the oppression and injustice suffered by my people in America can be alleviated." Smith received a lot of hate mail, telephone calls, confrontations in public, and death threats for his position. The famed *Los Angeles Times* sportswriter Jim Murray compared Smith to a "child who holds his breath to make his parents feel bad." Smith was warned his aggressive posturing would alienate the white people who were empathetic to the plight of black folk and antagonize white racists nationwide.[12]

The arguments against the boycott accepted the notion that civil rights gains through sports participation inevitably reflected a gradualist yet effective approach. Consequently, the OCHR was accused of trying to artificially speed up the natural evolutionary process. No longer content to be the apolitical "good Negro," the potential boycotters wanted to counteract the notion that sports participation mitigated the harshness of American racism, to alter the political outlook of black athletes, and to control how the United States would have to confront the racial issue before the world. The OCHR's rejection of moral suasion was consistent with the ideas that were at the core of the Black Power era.

In their 1965 treatise, *Black Power: The Politics of Liberation in America*, Stokely Carmichael and Charles Hamilton argued that racism was a subject that "America would much rather not face honestly and squarely." For most liberal white Americans, racism was embarrassing; to others, it was inconvenient; and for some, it was confusing. Carmichael and Hamilton argued that approaching the racial divide in any of these manners was "a luxury." Consequently, *Black Power* claimed that for blacks to "adopt [white Americans'] methods of relieving our oppression is ludicrous." Instead, African Americans needed to first reject the simplistic expressions that reflected white America's nonchalant and apathetic attitude toward racism: "Granted, things were and are bad, but we are making progress"; "Granted, your demands are legitimate, but we cannot move hastily. Stable societies are best built slowly"; "Be careful that you do not anger or alienate your white allies; remember, after all, you are only ten percent of the population."[13] By accepting the language and tone of white liberals, African American civil rights leaders implicitly supported white notions that the slow movement toward full equality was satisfactory progress.

The increasing rejection of moral-suasion tactics suggested that Malcolm X was replacing Martin Luther King as the role model for black activists in the late 1960s. In Malcolm X, the youngsters found justification for confronting the "pervasiveness and perversity of white racism." Malcolm X was the "archetype, reference point, and spiritual advisor" for the OCHR. Unlike Dr. King, Malcolm X refused to rely upon the notion that the collective white soul of America could be redeemed. Malcolm rejected appealing to the national conscience by arguing that "America's consciousness is bankrupt." Arguably, what made Malcolm X most popular, particularly after his death, was his rejection of the conciliatory tactics of the civil rights movement. Malcolm's presence provided a counterpoint to the mainstream's unswerving certainty about the inevitability of the nation's path to racial progress.[14]

One of the principal factors that distinguished Black Power–era activist-athletes from their counterparts in the civil rights era was their rejection of the Myrdallian analysis. Noted author Charles Silberman argued, "The real tragedy is that there is no American Dilemma. White Americans are not torn and tortured by the conflict between their devotion to the American creed" and racial abuse, as Gunnar Myrdal suggested in his 1944 classic, *The American Dilemma.* Myrdal characterized the American creed as a belief in the "ideals of the essential dignity of the individual human being, of the fundamental equality of all men, and of certain inalienable rights to freedom, justice, and a fair opportunity."[15] Rather than being troubled by the moral problems posed by racial injustice and racial discrimination's blatant contradiction with the American creed, the OCHR and similarly minded athletes suggested that white Americans were more concerned about how racial protest threatened peace and destabilized law and order.

African American civil rights leaders had accepted Myrdal's notion and used it as a basis for reform, but as Carmichael argued, an appeal to the morality of American society cast African Americans "in the beggar's role, hoping to strike a responsive chord." The willingness to rely upon white America's conscience revealed to Carmichael that the civil rights movement was operating from a powerless base. For Carmichael and Hamilton, appeals to the conscience of white America were based on the misguided notion that "a black minority could bow its head and get whipped into a meaningful position of power." Carmichael and Hamilton termed that perspective "absurd." Carmichael said that "this country does not function by morality, love and nonviolence, but by power."[16]

Media reaction to the proposed boycott was overwhelmingly negative. The response of Charles Maher, a *Los Angeles Times* columnist, reflected the white backlash that frequently accompanied Black Power–era protests. Maher asked, "What can [a boycott] accomplish for the American negro? Suppose that all negro athletes refuse to compete for the United States in the Olympics and that the U.S. squad is so weakened it finishes behind Ecuador. Will the white majority in the United States then be disposed to treat the Negro more generously? Or will it be angered and resist the Negro's demands even more resolutely? We suspect that the latter response is far more probable and that the Negroes who voted Thursday to become athletic dropouts will bring their people less good than grief."[17] Anticommunist sentiments ran high, and most Americans viewed an Olympic victory over the Soviet Union as a matter of national honor that was more pressing than the concerns that the OCHR stressed. Conservative governor Ronald Reagan of California spoke against the boycott, saying that it would be "harmful and injurious to race relations."[18]

Those who lashed out at the OCHR pointed to the passage of the Civil Rights Act of 1964 and the Voting Rights Act of 1965. Yet the persistence of slums, ghettoes, poverty, and racial discrimination exposed the limitations of legislative reform. The fundamental assumption that limited the purview of the civil rights movement's emphasis on appealing to white moderates was the notion that equal protection of constitutional rights would afford African Americans equal opportunity to acquire wealth, stature, and prosperity. However, civil rights laws alone could not sufficiently mitigate the effects of past discrimination: economic disparity and lingering prejudice.

The removal of the legal impediments led Americans to assert that the market and civil society would fully integrate African Americans in a relatively quick period. The equalization of laws, rules, and norms meant that individual African Americans would be able to rise or fall according to their ability and initiative. However, the OCHR, and other Black Power activists, began to affirm that although legal restrictions had been removed, racism remained institutionalized and visibly demonstrated by urban poverty, limited educational opportunities, and restrictive hiring practices, thus hindering the upward mobility of most African Americans. Living outside of the South, and directly unaffected by the recent legislation, urban African Americans sought to force American society to shift the battle from recognition and protection of formal equality to a broader critique of the American economic and political system.[19] As Kenneth B. Clark, an African American psychologist, noted, the persistence of the ghetto made it brutally clear how little society valued black people.[20] The resulting protests emerged because of the inferior conditions of urban African American life: the denial of dignity, inferior housing, unemployment, and limited government services.

Those who were willing to acknowledge the fundamental problems underlying black discontentment suggested that African Americans take their grievances to the courts and ballot box. This perspective left the fundamental problems—joblessness, inadequate housing, poor wages, and institutionalized racism—unacknowledged, unaddressed, and unaltered. Furthermore, it did not appreciate the fact that the protests were a challenge to the notion that American establishments—the courts, traditional political parties, the police, and educational institutions—were, as constituted, capable and willing to redress the problems facing racialized urban areas.[21]

A 1967 University of Michigan survey showed that white interpretations of Black Power differed markedly from African American perspectives.

The study found that almost 60 percent of whites interviewed associated Black Power with violence and destruction, racism, and black domination. "The Negro wants to enslave the white man like he was enslaved 100 years ago. They want to take everything away from us—We'll all be poor," said one white respondent who foresaw an African American attempt to wrestle control of America away from white America. Another weary respondent complained, "Blacks won't be satisfied until they get complete control of our country by force if necessary." Not surprisingly, only 9 percent of African Americans held similar beliefs.[22] As William Van Deburg has argued, the "passion for self-definition better represented the views of the average Black American than did the frustrated cry 'get whitey.'"[23]

Most whites were unwilling or unable to see that Black Power's militant posturing was a tactical means to draw attention. As the *Los Angeles Times* recognized, African American leaders "find that they draw more attention when they hint or threaten a 'long, hot summer.'"[24] For example, as part of his effort to gain media exposure, Harry Edwards had been advised by his friend and mentor, the African American journalist Louis Lomax, whom Edwards described as having a "flair for the dramatic and [abiding] appreciation for the character and power of the electronic media," to replace his traditional suit and tie with clothes that would capture the attention of the nation's African American youth. Lomax revealed to Edwards that his suit and tie, coupled with his Ivy League graduate degree, made the media, students, and the public think that he "was just another middle-class Negro with something to say about civil rights." Shortly thereafter, Edwards began to wear "pseudo-revolutionary" clothing: a black cap, work boots, black jeans, African beads, dark sunglasses, and a black jacket "with an occasional book of matches pinned to the front." The new image drew enormous media attention. He acknowledged that he sometimes had a difficult time keeping "a straight face, standing before crowded auditoriums, under blazing television lights, delivering a lecture developed for my race relations class from a rostrum festooned with reporter's microphones, or bombarding White Americans with rhetoric calculated to outrage." He continued, "When I couldn't bedazzle them with brilliance, I bamboozled them with bull." Thereafter, Edwards would frequently incorporate inflammatory language—"Uncle Tom," "white man's nigger," "honky," "cracker administrator"—throughout his presentations. Edwards's transformation represents an important shift. Rather than appealing to the conscience of white America, Black Power advocates targeted white fear.[25]

After the boycott announcement, *Track and Field News* conducted an analysis of the media responses of African American track competitors, which revealed that the athletes had mixed feelings about the boycott. In the ensuing days, there were twenty-seven world-class athletes quoted in the press: none pledged unequivocal support for the boycott, four said they would boycott if asked by certain leaders, three said they would go with the majority, eighteen said they planned to compete. Triple jumper Art Walker was firm in his opposition to the boycott idea. "I believe every person has to do what his conscience tells him to do," Walker stated. "Mine tells me to go to the Olympics."[26] Ralph Boston, a 1964 Olympic champion, said he planned to participate: "What boycott? I've put too much time and effort into track and field to give it up." Articulating the uncertainty that many athletes had, Boston asked, "Do Negroes owe this sacrifice to the cause? Will a boycott advance the cause? If it doesn't is it fair to ask the athletes to make the sacrifice needlessly?" With divided support among the athletes, Edwards sought the help of civil rights leaders.[27]

Harry Edwards met with Louis Lomax to discuss the future moves of the Olympic Project for Human Rights, the official name of the organization serving as the organizational unit of the boycott effort. They decided to bring the Reverend Dr. Martin Luther King Jr., the president of the Southern Christian Leadership Conference, and Floyd McKissick, the director of the Congress of Racial Equality, aboard as advisers. Edwards, who had momentarily been a member of the Black Panther Party, decided to turn to these two pillars of the integrationist philosophy for guidance. Although the eventual protest has been remembered as a watershed moment in the Black Power movement, it is important to note the important continuity that the boycott effort shared with other civil rights tactics. King was supportive of the OPHR because it employed nonviolent direct-action methods. King, and other civil rights activists, had demonstrated the viability of protests, boycotts, and other nonviolent confrontations as a means to foster social change. Furthermore, it is important to note King's attempt to shift the battle for racial equality after the passage of the Civil Rights Act in 1964 and the Voting Rights Act in 1965. Having achieved equal protection under the law, Dr. Martin Luther King and other advocates attempted to shift the civil rights movement in the direction of the eradication of poverty and urban blight.

On December 15, 1967, in the conference room of New York City's Americana Hotel, Edwards, with Dr. King and McKissick at his side, presented the OPHR's six demands. The OPHR called for the restoration of Muhammad Ali's title, removal of Avery Brundage as the chairman of the International Olympic Committee, curtailment of participation of all-white teams and individuals from South Africa and Southern Rhodesia in the

United States and all Olympic activities, the addition of two black coaches to the men's track and field coaching staff, the appointment of at least two black people to policy-making positions on the United States Olympic Committee, and complete desegregation of the New York Athletic Club.[28]

For the OPHR, the plight of Cassius Clay–Muhammad Ali epitomized the shifting attitudes of African American athletes and the need to reject the premise that athletic success could insulate African Americans from racism. Notwithstanding his positive assessment of American race relations at the 1960 Olympic Games in Rome, Clay ultimately helped establish a new precedent among African American athletes. Rather than adopt an accommodationist perspective, the generation influenced by Ali would be willing, even expected, to offer a harsh critique of American racism. In fact, one's position on civil rights, Black Power, and even Vietnam was evident based on whether the dethroned champion was referred to as "Ali" or "Clay" after he changed his name and political philosophy.[29]

On February 26, 1964, the day after Cassius Clay became the heavyweight champion of the world by defeating the heavily favored Sonny Liston, he held a press conference. In the Veterans Room of Miami's Convention Hall, the jovial exchanges between Clay and the media ended when one reporter asked if he was a "card-carrying member of the Black Muslims." "Card-carryin'," Clay responded, obviously uneasy with the term *card-carrying,* which reminded him of McCarthy-era communist-baiting, and *Black Muslim,* which was offensive to members of the Nation of Islam: "What does that mean? I believe in Allah and in peace. I don't try to move into white neighborhoods. I don't want to marry a white woman. . . . I know where I'm going and I know the truth, and I don't have to be what you want me to be. I'm free to be what I want." Clay's statements were designed to explain to the media that he did not intend to cater to their vision of whom he should be, whom he should represent, and whom he should follow. His stand suggested that he would break from precedent and the role American society envisioned for him.[30] Clay determined that he was going to help chart a new course for African American athletes, a course chosen and navigated by the athletes themselves and primarily responsive to the needs and desires of the shifting political temperament of the African American community.

In March 1964, the World Boxing Association (WBA) temporarily stripped the newly named Muhammad Ali of his championship for "conduct detrimental to the spirit of boxing." It was obvious that his religious and racial beliefs were reasons for the proceedings against the champion. The Nation of Islam differed from other civil rights organizations because it refused to appeal to the conscience of white America; instead, it sought to establish community control in African American neighborhoods. Its approach threatened most white Americans and was deemed too radical by many African Americans.[31] However, the WBA's steps were effectively nullified when three major athletic commissions (New York, Pennsylvania, and California) refused to support the WBA.

Several years later, Ali would find himself embroiled in an international issue when he refused to enlist in the military. After he was informed that his draft status would be reclassified, making him eligible for the draft, Ali's response, "Man, I ain't got no quarrel with them Vietcong," became his most celebrated and most detested statement. His declaration came at a time when most Americans supported the Vietnam effort. Jimmy Cannon, Red Smith, and Arthur Daley, three of the nation's most respected sportswriters, condemned Ali's statement. Red Smith, who like other reporters refused to address the champion by his new name, wrote, "Cassius makes himself as sorry a spectacle as those unwashed punks who picket and demonstrate against the war." Other rebuking statements labeling Ali a traitor and pariah were voiced by several members of Congress. Furthermore, the Kentucky State Senate issued a statement that blamed him for bringing "discredit to all loyal Kentuckians and to the names of the thousands who gave their lives for this country during his lifetime." Ultimately, Ali was stripped of his title. Louis Lomax referred to the decision to vacate Ali's title as a "total castration of the black people in this country."[32] Missing Lomax's point, noted white journalist Red Smith wondered if Lomax would feel the same way if another African American won the title. Lomax's hyperbolic statement was designed to illustrate that "sport status was a fragile platform the white man could always take away." Lomax was suggesting that if U.S. officials could take away Muhammad Ali's title simply because they disagreed with his political views, then sports had not significantly altered the social landscape because African Americans were operating from a powerless position.[33]

Most likely, Ali would not have been asked to bear arms; instead, the military would have allowed him to reprise the role Joe Louis performed during World War II while he was the heavyweight champion. As an enlisted soldier, Louis conducting boxing exhibitions for the troops stationed abroad. Consequently, Ali's refusal to comply suggested that his resistance was motivated by more than a fear of facing armed combat. Ali was emphatically taking a political stand. Ali joined Dr. King in Louisville to campaign for fair housing and spoke about his refusal to enlist: "No I am not going 10,000 miles from home to help murder and burn another poor nation simply to continue the domination of white slave masters of the darker people the world over. . . . If I thought going to war would bring freedom and equality to twenty-two million of my people, they wouldn't have to draft me," Ali said. "I'd join tomorrow."[34]

A group of prominent African American athletes, including Bill Russell, Lew Alcindor, and Jim Brown—three of the most famed and politically involved African American athletes—met with Ali to discuss his opposition to the war. Emerging from the meeting, satisfied with Ali's religious and moral convictions, the assembled athletes decided to publicly support Ali's stance. Ali's battles with the American government helped usher in a new consciousness among black athletes that did not accommodate white America and defied the dominant rhetoric regarding racial progress rather than reinforcing it.[35] Muhammad Ali's position would be instrumental in the shifting politics that called into question the presumptions and values of the civil rights movement.

The OPHR demands were sent via telegram to Arthur Lentz, executive director of the U.S. Olympic Committee. Lentz correctly replied that the USOC could not meet the demands because several of them were out of their jurisdiction. The World Boxing Association, which stripped Muhammad Ali of his title, was not connected with the USOC; Brundage was elected to his post by more than one hundred nations. Lentz also informed the OPHR that the USOC members were elected by a vast variety of organizations, such as the National Collegiate Athletic Association, Amateur Athletic Union, and National Association of Intercollegiate Athletics. Avery Brundage simply replied to the demands by claiming that the boycotters would be making a mistake and that there were enough talented white athletes to win gold medals for the United States anyway. On another occasion, Brundage labeled the idea of a boycott "foolish," because the Olympics was the "one enterprise against all forms of discrimination." However, he also offered the inflammatory remark that Jesse Owens was "a fine boy" and should be considered for a spot on the USOC Board of Directors.[36]

Bud Winter, Tommie Smith's coach at San Jose State, expressed concern about the drastic nature of the protest idea: "I am appalled Negro athletes have been driven so far as to consider boycotting a movement that epitomizes the very thing for which they are fighting." Winter's comments reflected a widely held position that the Olympics were the wrong target for protest. The Olympics were seen as historically being a force at the forefront of racial progress. Sportswriter Red Smith labeled the Games "the Negro's best friend" and argued that Olympic participation, not abandonment, would be most beneficial to the cause of black athletes.

Olympism stood for and "fostered peace, international understanding, and harmony among the races," Brundage believed.[37] There were several perspectives challenging the boycott idea: black participation in sport was good for African Americans and race relations; a boycott was un-American; the Olympics were a humanitarian gathering of individuals, not a place for members of groups or factions; and politics did not have a place in the world of sports. As sociologist Doug Hartmann has argued, the main arguments against the boycott were individualism, patriotism, and antipolitical sport idealism.[38]

Jackie Robinson, whose efforts to integrate Major League Baseball paved the way for the widespread integration of professional athletics, initially did not favor the boycott because he did not think that it was practical. Robinson stated, "I admire these youngsters for their determination, but I don't think there are enough athletes to make it worthwhile. I wouldn't do it myself." However, Robinson began to think more favorably about the subject provided that "the leadership is right and their motives are correct." As the issue continued to draw large media interest, Robinson supported the boycott idea because the boycotters were applying the moral-suasion tactics advocated by Martin Luther King. Thus, Robinson was able to articulate a relationship to the larger civil rights struggle.[39]

Conventional wisdom suggested that African American athletes could have the greatest impact on race relations by letting their athletic accomplishments speak for themselves. African American heroes such as Jesse Owens were welcomed and embraced by white Americans because they displayed quiet and patient personalities, articulated conservative viewpoints, advocated moderation, and were unwaveringly patriotic. Owens was from a generation that believed that black people were proving themselves "qualified for full citizenship by uncritical accommodation to white definitions of the situation, to white characterizations of what was right, what was fair, [and] what was best." The mind-set was that African Americans should be willing to suffer humbly until black people were able to win over the hearts of white Americans. As journalist Kenny Moore has argued, "Owens seemed to glory in overcoming obstacles. He preached that if a man worked hard, if he endured racial taunts the way Jackie Robinson and Joe Louis had, he would succeed, he would win the white man's respect and things would change." Furthermore, Owens's assertion that he had made it in spite of racism reinforced the notion that racial obstacles were not a severe impediment to the advancement of individual African Americans in American society and validated hegemonic ideals about equality in American society.[40]

Similar to Owens, other former African American gold medalists, including Rafer Johnson, Ralph Metcalfe, and Mal Whitfield, expressed sympathy for the OPHR's concerns but did not think that the boycott was the best forum for demonstrations. Whitfield, altering his perspective from 1964, maintained that the Olympics should not be a protest forum in the battle for increased civil rights: "It would be wrong to boycott the Olympics which have given Negro athletes so much international recognition. . . . Members of the so-called boycott movement have not been able to give any solid reason for such a move." When Jesse Owens first heard about the potential boycott in October 1967, he issued a sensitive yet deliberate statement. "We have been conscious of racial problems for many years," Owens commented to a group of reporters. "But it is no good dropping out of the Olympics. We have to be there, we have to be everywhere it counts." However, Owens soon began to offer more frequent and fervent objections to the boycott. On television appearances, public lectures, and radio programs and in the printed press, he argued that African Americans could "bridge the gap of misunderstanding more in athletics than anywhere else." He adamantly rejected the utilization of the Olympics as a battleground for increased civil rights.[41]

Jesse Owens along with other prominent older African American athletes such as Rafer Johnson, Roy Campanella, and Don Newcombe made regular media appearances condemning the boycott idea. These athletes expressed faith in the American sports myth. Sports were deemed a "panacea promising salvation, not just for star Black athletes but for the Black masses as well." These athletes argued that athletic participation helped diminish racism, made black people more acceptable to white Americans, and were a "citadel of interracial harmony, a shining example illuminating the route toward a more humane society."[42] These views received strong condemnation from Harry Edwards and other boycott sympathizers.

John Carlos argued that Jesse Owens's experiences after he returned stateside after his historic four-gold-medal performance at the 1936 Berlin Games suggested that sports had not sufficiently altered white American attitudes about African Americans. The way in which Jesse Owens had been treated exposed the limitations of "good behavior" and "preparation." For example, Avery Brundage barred Jesse Owens from competing as an amateur after he refused a request to tour Europe immediately after the 1936 Olympics. One of Owens's most embarrassing moments occurred at halftime of a soccer game in Havana, Cuba. On December 26, 1936, Owens defeated Julio McCaw, a thoroughbred horse, in a 100-yard race around a wet track in a race promoted by Owens's white American entertainment agent, Marty Forkin. Years later Owens remarked that the event made him feel like "a spectacle, a freak." Owens told an interviewer in 1971, "What was I supposed to do? I had four gold medals. There was no television, no big advertising, no endorsements then. Not for a black man, anyway." Given Owens's experiences with American racism, young athletes had a difficult time understanding why he attacked their position. Nonetheless, Owens continued to assert that he did not think that "the pride which our black athletes have in themselves and their country will allow them to do anything to embarrass the United States in so conspicuous a world arena."[43]

Black Power advocates derisively labeled those who attacked them as "Negroes" and argued that they supported the status quo. Harry Edwards, who had a banner that said "Traitor (Negro) of the Week" with a photo of Jesse Owens beneath it, said that black athletes had been expected to "play the role of the responsible Negro, the good Negro, no matter what else was going on in the black world. The Black athlete was the institutionalized Tom, the white man's nigger." On another occasion, Edwards maintained that Jesse Owens "belongs to another generation, a controlled generation."[44] Eldridge Cleaver also challenged dominant interpretations of the role of black athletes. Cleaver claimed that "whenever a crisis with racial overtones arises, an entertainer or athlete is trotted out and allowed to expound a predictable, conciliatory interpretation of what's happening." He termed this phenomenon an effective "technique of Negro control."[45]

Edwards saw the Mexico City Games as an opportunity to signal a historic shift. Owens, whose four-gold-medal performance at the 1936 Olympic Games made a mockery of Hitler's Aryan-supremacy theories, symbolized the era in which black athletes' passivity was seen as "a credit to the race." Edwards announced that the boycott would end the use of the success of black athletes "in a fun-and-games [festivity] propagandized as the epitome of equal rights so long as we are refused those rights in white society."[46]

Reshaping the International Narrative

As the boycott gained momentum, the OPHR clarified its objectives. The organization's goals were "to protest the persistent and systematic violation of black people's human rights in the United States; to establish a standard of political responsibility among black athletes vis-à-vis the needs and interests of the black community; and to make the black community aware of the substantial hidden dynamics and consequences of their sports involvement." Harry Edwards sought to put more pressure on athletes to see that by simply being represented in the sports arena was not enough to effect racial change. He asked athletes to make their prestige, influence, and stage a force for the improvement of all African Americans. Arguably, the most important OPHR goal was to expose America's historical exploitation of black athletes as political propaganda tools in both the national and the international arenas.[47]

Malcolm X, whom Harry Edwards labeled "St. Malcolm," was clearly one of the people who had helped shape Edwards's thinking. Edwards gleaned five essential directives from Malcolm X. Malcolm preached that African Americans had to control their community, resources, and institutions; use any means necessary to achieve these goals; develop an ethic that would unify them and prevent outsiders from assuming control of black movements and communities; "recognize that their primary enemy was, is, and has always been the legally established institutions and government of the United States of America and anyone—Negro or white—who supports those institutions or that government in its efforts to maintain the status quo"; and resist the standards defined by white America. Instead, black folk needed to define themselves and control their definition of white America as well.[48]

Malcolm X's rhetorical style and content were evident in Edwards's speeches. When Edwards discussed the global significance of race, he was parroting the words and tone of Malcolm X. For example, Malcolm's influence is obvious in the following passage in which Edwards critiqued U.S. imperialism: "The crackers are losing all over. In Vietnam, Thailand, Laos, Bolivia, all over. The blue-eyed devil is in trouble. The third-world power—black, red, yellow, brown—is taking the white man apart in chunks. We must get the cracker off our backs, by Olympic boycott, by out-and-out revolution, by whatever means."[49] Perhaps Malcolm X's greatest influence upon Edwards was Malcolm's attempt to dramatize U.S. racial issues before an international audience.

Malcolm X had traveled throughout Africa in 1964 and had begun to fully understand the magnitude of State Department and United States Information Agency propaganda regarding African American advancement. Malcolm X believed that the U.S. propaganda agencies had waged a successful campaign to manipulate African perceptions of U.S. race relations. He maintained that the mission of the USIA was to make "the Africans think that you and I are living in paradise, that our problems have been solved, that the Supreme Court desegregation decision put all of us in school, that the passage of the Civil Rights bill last year solved all of our problems, and that now that Martin Luther King Jr. has gotten the peace prize, we are on our way to the promised land of integration." He asserted that African American leaders had made a grave tactical error by not developing a communications network that would allow African American leaders to provide African leaders with the latest developments in American race relations, in an attempt to counter State Department releases, which were overly positive and implied that injustices faced by African Americans were rapidly being eliminated.[50]

Malcolm X's main mission during his travels throughout Africa was to get the independent African nations to pressure the United Nations to censure the United States because of racial oppression. On July 17, 1964, Malcolm X addressed the First Ordinary Assembly of Heads of State and Governments at the Organization of African Unity in Cairo, Egypt. Malcolm X called the independent African heads of state "the shepherds of all African peoples everywhere." By doing so, he wanted to get the assembled delegates to see the "African American problem" as an "African problem." He declared his intent to internationalize the plight of African Americans as a human rights violation, so that it would not merely be confined to the domestic jurisdiction of the U.S. government. As a precedent for his intended action, Malcolm X maintained that if South African racial abuses could be subject to UN action, then the oppression of African Americans could also be brought before the international agency. He then issued a plea to the assembled delegates: "We beseech the independent African states to help us bring our problem before the United Nations, on the grounds that the United States Government is morally incapable of protecting the lives and the property of twenty-two million African-Americans."[51]

At his first press conference with the American press upon his return to the States, Malcolm X continued to maintain that African Americans had a "strong, airtight case to take the United States before the United Nations on a formal accusation of 'denial of human rights'—and that if Angola and South Africa were precedent cases, then there would be no easy way that the U.S. could escape being censured." Malcolm continued to contend that the African American civil rights struggle needed to be elevated to an international human rights struggle. "El-Hajj Malik El-Shabazz," one of the most influential chapters from his acclaimed autobiography, is dedicated to making a compelling case for the need to internationalize the African American struggle. Although convinced of the need for this dramatic action, Malcolm X concluded that the "American white man has so thoroughly brainwashed the black man to see himself as only a domestic 'civil rights' problem that it will probably take longer than I live before the Negro sees that the struggle of the American black man is international."[52]

If one looks closely at Edwards's reasoning behind the proposed boycott, one can see that Edwards saw himself and the OPHR as trying to pick up Malcolm X's mantle. At the November 1967 meeting, Edward made his intentions clear: "This is our way of pointing out that the United States has no right to set itself up as a leader of the free world. . . . We're going to put this question before the United Nations. We want to take it out of the sphere of civil rights and bring it into the sphere of human rights." On another occasion, Edwards stated, "We want to get this problem into the world court." Presumably, he was talking about the "court" of international opinion. In his autobiography, Edwards would later write that Smith and Carlos's protest "was the only route both accessible to Blacks and promising an *international* protest platform, an escalation long advocated by many of the more militant spokesmen in the Black struggle who saw the oppression of black Americans, not as a domestic civil rights issue, but as a violation of *international human rights law and principles.*" Edwards was right to point out that many 1960s black spokespeople were interested in the internationalization of the American race issue.[53] Most would attribute the late-1960s push to draw global attention to the problems in the United States to Malcolm X's initiatives.

The OPHR was determined to reconstruct dominant interpretations of race relations in American culture. The U.S. athletic goodwill exchange programs helped Harry Edwards deepen his understanding of the political nature of black athletic participation in the international arena. "The United States government has taught us well," he observed. "In the ideological wars with other world powers, the U.S. State Department has time and time again used athletes—both professional and amateur—as political adjuncts."[54] The political potential that he saw exemplified by the U.S. State Department–funded tours illustrated the need for African American athletes to provide a counternarrative to the State Department propagandization of athletics as representative of a just American social system.

The pattern of using black athletes and coaches as evidence of American democracy was still a matter of official State Department policy in the mid-1960s. For example, the State Department sent Joe Yancey on his sixth department-sponsored trip—an eleven-month goodwill tour of Latin America—during 1965–66. One department report said that "Yancey is perhaps the greatest non-salaried globetrotting athletic coach in the world today." Another telegram praising Yancey's work enthusiastically declared that "Yancey was a superb coach and great ambassador of good will. No task too arduous; no trip too long, he gave of himself unstingily, willingly and with devotion to his craft." Joe Yancey had coached Olympic teams from four nations, including Jamaica and the Bahamas. Even the head coach of the American national track team labeled Yancey's job with the 1952 Jamaican team the greatest coaching job he has ever seen. Nonetheless, the United States Olympic Committee never saw fit to award him with the opportunity to serve as the coach for the United States Olympic Track Team.[55] Slights such as those experienced by Yancey increasingly drew the disdain of African American athletes.

The desire to counteract the U.S. government's propaganda campaign as well as a sense of community obligation and the realization that the futures of African American athletes and the African American masses were intertwined and interconnected had a tremendous impact on many athletes. Edwards spoke of the seriousness of the issue:

> We must no longer allow this country to use Black individuals of whatever level to rationalize its treatment of the black masses . . . to use a few "Negroes" to point out of the world how much progress she has made in solving her racial problems when the oppression of Afro-Americans in this country is greater than it ever was. . . . We must no longer allow the Sports World to pat itself on the back as a citadel of racial justice when the racial injustices of the sports industry are infamously legendary. . . . [A]ny black person who allows himself to be used in the above manner is not only a chump—because he allows himself to be used against his own interest—but he is a traitor to his race. He is secondly, and most importantly, a traitor to his country because he allows racist whites the luxury of resting assured that those black people in the ghettoes are there because that is where they belong or want to be.[56]

Edwards was arguing that those who were still beholden to the notion that individual success was an advance for the race were deluding themselves and contributing to the oppression of African Americans. Bill Russell, one of the 1960s' most outspoken critics of the American athletic sporting scene, agreed with Edwards: "To say that I am an example of the greatness of the country—that's not true. Because I feel to be honest with myself and with the people I deal with, that I'm an exception."[57] Increasingly, African Americans during the Black Power era came to respect athletes and sports figures such as Russell and Edwards who were involved in the community.

The New York Athletic Club's track and field Olympic warm-up meet provided a crucial opportunity to test the OPHR's organizational potential because the meet was one of the most prestigious in the United

States. The NYAC had forced Mal Whitfield to use the service elevator
when he was honored at the club as the first African American recipi-
ent of the Sullivan trophy, which was annually given to the nation's best
amateur athlete. It was the club's custom to give memberships to medalists
in the Olympic track and field events, but Whitfield and other African
Americans were repeatedly denied memberships. Hence, Edwards called
a boycott of the February 1968 meet as a means to "regain some of the
dignity that black athletes had compromised" by competing at a club
where they were not permitted to shower. Edwards marked the NYAC
boycott as "the end of an age when Afro-American athletes would compromise black dignity for a watch, a television set, a trophy, or merely
the love of competition."[58]

The NYAC decided to hold the meet despite the threat of a boycott.
Attendance fell by 50 percent, as track powerhouses Georgetown and Vil-
lanova, all of the Ivy League schools, all of the New York high school teams,
and O. J. Simpson boycotted. Additionally, the Russian team withdrew.
Their withdrawal was magnified because they were to be the first Russian
team to compete in the United States since a protest against American
policy in Vietnam in 1966 hindered a meet involving the two nations. With
the absence of the Russian team, the meet lost its international credentials and lure of an East-West showdown. Performances were mediocre,
and only nine African American athletes competed: five of them were
from the University of Texas–El Paso. UTEP's Bob Beamon warmed up
in the locker room and made only one attempt in the long-jump competition. Sufficiently satisfied that his initial jump would not be matched or
bested, Beamon packed his bag and left. In the aftermath of the boycott,
the NYAC decided to cancel the meet rather than integrate. "The NYAC
meet emerged as a formal coming out party for the politics of race within
sport," Amy Bass has argued, "indicating further that a large scale boycott
enterprise by African American athletes was feasible."[59]

The importance of the NYAC boycott took on heightened meaning
because the day before it began, the International Olympic Committee
announced that it planned to allow South Africa to send a team to Mexico
City. South Africa had been barred from competing in the Olympics in
1963 because it did not allow interracial competition. Interior Minister
Jan de Klerk made the government's position clear when he announced
that South Africa would not allow nonwhites to represent the nation in
international sporting competitions, despite international condemnation
of South African policies as antithetical to Olympic values. After several
meetings and visits to South Africa, the IOC announced that it was satis-

fied with the progress that South Africa had made by allowing African Americans to represent the country at the Olympic Games, but the country still refused to have integrated Olympic Trials. The condemnation of the IOC decision was swift.[60]

Within hours of the IOC announcement reinstating South Africa, six African nations announced that they intended to boycott the Games. The international boycott movement continued to gain steam as other African nations announced they would not participate. The Supreme Council for Sports in Africa, which helped develop continent-wide sports policies for thirty-two African nations, voiced its support for the boycott. By the time that the IOC acknowledged that "it would be most unwise for a South African team to participate," on April 21, 1968, in a meeting in Lausanne, Switzerland, almost forty African nations, the Soviet Union, and several Middle Eastern nations had announced that they were considering boycotting the Olympics. Emboldened by the success of the NYAC boycott and the temporary reinstatement of South Africa, Edwards was able to make impassioned pleas to those who questioned whether the Olympics were an appropriate venue to challenge racial injustice. However, once South Africa was barred, the boycott movement lost some of its momentum.[61]

At the Olympic Trials in Los Angeles, talk of a boycott continued, but a definitive course of action could not be reached. Only half of the twenty-six African American male athletes who made the team said that they would boycott. The boycott idea received a tremendous blow when Jim Hines and Charlie Greene said that they planned to compete in the high-profile men's 100-meter dash at the Mexico City Games. At the trials, there had been speculation that Greene and Hines might be willing to support the boycott idea because they wore OPHR buttons. However, Greene made his thoughts regarding the boycott well known: "They're just buttons. They show sympathy for an idea. They definitely don't mean a boycott." Greene did admit that he had the opportunity to speak with Harry Edwards and had developed an admiration and a level of respect for him. Nonetheless, Greene's decision to compete was based on his identification as an American citizen. "I am American, and I'm going to run," he adamantly maintained.[62]

Athletes began to argue that the boycott should be canceled if unanimity could not be reached, because the lack of unity would be harmful. At a meeting of black athletes held at the Olympic Trials, it was decided that the boycott would be called off. Athletes realized that they would be replaced by other black athletes who did not stand for the principle of using sports as a vehicle to highlight the oppression of African Americans. Although the boycott was off, a number of black athletes remained committed to the idea of using the Games to stage some form of protest.[63]

The athletes began to explore various ways to draw attention to the treatment of African Americans. Some suggested that all of the athletes should refuse to stand on the victory platform during the playing of the national anthem to illustrate the systemic exclusion of African Americans from aspects of American society. Others recommended that the participants refuse to participate in any event after the opening ceremonies. Furthermore, it was proposed that the athletes should deliberately finish last in every event to embody the "last place" position of blacks in American society. It was even suggested that the athletes crawl out of the starting blocks. Although all of these options were rejected, the athletes left with the agreement that each athlete would "do their own thing."[64]

As part of his effort to garner media attention, Edwards was not forthcoming with the media during press conferences after the track athletes had overwhelmingly rejected the boycott idea at the Olympic Trials. Edwards announced, "We are going to tell white people nothing about their Olympic team at this time. . . . At this particular point, our strategy is chaos." Although the boycott effort had been aborted, it made the plight of African Americans and the role of black athletes headline news and stirred debate, and Harry Edwards's efforts helped lay the foundation for the subsequent protest gestures that occurred at the 1968 Mexico City Olympic Games.[65]

Protests in Mexico City

On October 12, 1968, the Olympic flame was lit in Aztec Stadium. More than seventy-eight hundred athletes from 119 countries attended the opening ceremonies of the first Olympics to be held in a Latin American nation. On the second day of competition, African American athletes were involved in protests. The Jamaican sprinter Lennox Miller won the silver medal in the 100-meter dash; he along with the bronze medal winner, American Charlie Greene, and the gold medalist, American Jim Hines, whose 9.95 time was the first sub-10.00 time and a new world record, refused to have their medals presented by Avery Brundage. The three medalists had asked who was going to present the medals. When they were informed that it would be Brundage, their indifferent attitude suggested that an alternative presenter be used. Instead, the medals were presented by Lord David Burghley of England. Because they had refused to take their medals from Brundage, attention focused on Americans Jim Hines and Charlie Greene at the victory ceremony. As the American national anthem began, both stood sedately, facing the American flag. Despite their conformity on the victory stand, their gesture aimed at Brundage inspired other black American athletes to assert that if they won, they did not want the IOC president to present their medals either.[66] It was Olympic custom to have members of the IOC board present the medals to winners from their home nation. Tommie Smith asked his wife, Denise, to purchase a pair of black gloves, in case he was forced to shake hands with Avery Brundage on the victory stand. At this point, it was uncertain whether a more substantive protest was going to take place.

The competition for the men's 200-meter dash began on October 15. Tommie Smith ran a 20.3 in the first qualifying heat, tying the Olympic record set by Henry Carr four years prior in Tokyo. The record was eclipsed a few heats later when the relatively unknown Australian Peter Norman ran a career-best 20.2. Then Tommie Smith tied Norman's mark in the next heat. There was serious doubt whether Smith would be able to compete in the 200-meter final the next day because he had pulled an abductor muscle in his groin during the semifinal, in which he ran an impressive 20.1.

Known for his slow starts, Tommie Smith did not show any discomfort after emerging from the starting blocks at the finals of the 200-meter dash. Trailing John Carlos after 60 meters, a burst of speed propelled Smith to victory in world record time: 19.83. The next two to cross the finish line, Carlos and Norman, were both clocked at 20.0; however, Norman was awarded the silver medal and Carlos the bronze.[67]

Dressed in black stockings but no shoes, a black glove on one hand each, and Tommie Smith wearing a black scarf around his neck, Smith and Carlos, the gold and bronze medalists, took their positions on the award-ceremony dais. With their medals displayed around their necks, the two athletes, along with Peter Norman, who wore an OPHR badge on his jacket, turned to face the American and Australian flags. As "The Star-Spangled Banner" began playing, Smith and Carlos raised their black-gloved fists and bowed their heads in "silent defiance of American prestige and Olympic protocol."[68] As the crowd, including twenty thousand Americans, recognized their gesture, booing and jeering followed. The booing continued as the two athletes left the stadium, causing Smith and Carlos to defiantly raise their fists again.

As Amy Bass has reported, Smith granted sports announcer Howard Cosell an in-studio interview the following day in which he explained the significance of the protest gesture. The two black gloves and the arc that they formed when the two fists were stretched into the sky symbolized

"the power within black America" and "black unity." Smith's scarf signi-
fied "blackness," while the black socks, worn without shoes, stressed the
poverty plaguing black America. Later, John Carlos would add that the
bowed heads represented praying for black Americans. When asked if he
represented all black athletes, Smith responded, "I can say I represented
black America." Cosell pushed Smith further by asking if he was "proud
to be an American." Smith evasively answered, "I'm proud to be a black
American." Despite his elusiveness, Smith made it clear that he believed
his actions increased "black dignity."[69]

There were many hostile responses to Smith's and Carlos's gestures. Jim
Murray thought that the protest was misplaced. He sarcastically noted
that "our secret is out: we got race problems in our country. This will
come as a great astonishment to the reading public of the world, I am
sure." John Hall, a fellow *Los Angeles Times* columnist, was hostile: "I'm
sick of Tommie Smith and John Carlos. I'm sick of their whining, mealy-
mouth, shallow view of the world. I'm sick of apologizing and saying they
are trying to improve things." Perhaps the most offensive critique came
from Brent Musburger. "Smith and Carlos," wrote Musburger, "looked
like a couple of black-skinned storm troopers. . . . Carlos ran looking
like a trinket shop, beads and badges and the medallions bouncing as he
dashed toward the finish line."[70]

Jesse Owens, who was a guest of the Mexican government, a radio
commentator for the Mutual Broadcasting Company, and a consultant
for the USOC at the Mexico City Games, was sent by the USOC to talk
with Smith, Carlos, and other black athletes. The meeting between Owens,
twenty-five African American athletes, and a smattering of white athletes
degenerated into hostile accusations, exposing the cultural divide between
the two generations. Owens left the meeting saddened and frustrated. As
the Smith-Carlos incident continued to be front-page news, Jesse Owens
feared that most Americans would think that Smith and Carlos spoke for
the majority of African Americans. After the Games, Owens, along with
ghostwriter Paul Neimark, started work on a book, *Blackthink,* to assert
that most black Americans did not support the "racial anger and disre-
spect of the flag" exemplified by the two track stars. He described Black
Power advocates as "pro-Negro bigots," "professional haters," and "soapbox
blackthinkers." Owens affirmed his belief in the justice and legitimacy
of the American racial order, arguing that "if the Negro doesn't succeed
in today's America, it is because he has chosen to fail." Although Owens
would retreat from his strong statements a few years later in his follow-

up book, *I Have Changed* (1972), white reviewers, with virtual unanimity, praised *Blackthink*.[71]

The International Olympic Committee held the United States Olympic Committee responsible for the actions of Smith and Carlos, claiming that their gestures violated a basic principle of the Olympic Games that "politics play no part whatsoever." After a five-hour emergency session, the USOC issued a formal apology to the IOC for the "discourtesy" displayed by Smith and Carlos. The USOC decided not to take action against Smith and Carlos, but warned that a "repetition of such an incident will be viewed as a willful disregard of Olympic principles." Unsatisfied, the IOC was concerned that the USOC did not have control of its team and threatened to disqualify the entire U.S. team if stronger action was not taken. The IOC overreacted and multiplied the impact of the protest by forcing their suspension. Nonetheless, the international body was determined to ensure that the protest did not lead to a broader demonstration.[72]

Intense pressure from the IOC forced the USOC to revoke Smith's and Carlos's Olympic credentials and expel them from the Olympic Village. Had the IOC not demanded such harsh action, the impact of the protest probably would have been forgotten in a few days. The expulsion of the medalists placed the protest at the forefront of the international media, alongside coverage of the possibility of Russian intervention in Vietnam, George Wallace, Apollo 7, and Jacqueline Kennedy's wedding to Aristotle Onassis.

One month before the Games, a group of twenty-one African American athletes had signed a petition asking for the resignation of Avery Brundage because the athletes thought that Brundage specifically threatened African American athletes with expulsion from the Olympic Village if they protested. Brundage clarified his point: "I made a general statement that demonstrations are not permitted at the Games and that the word boycott is not used in Olympic circles and that demonstrators of any nationality would be sent home. This is permanent Olympic policy." By insisting upon upholding this policy, Brundage's actions granted the two athletes "instant martyrdom."[73]

Despite Brundage's claims that the Olympics were apolitical, America had touted the success of African American athletes as emblematic of democracy and testaments to the virtues of American equality. However, as Doug Hartmann has argued, Olympic symbolism did not allow participants to represent nonnational identities, including race, religion, gender, ethnicity, and sexual orientation. The racial concerns that Smith and Car-

los introduced could not effectively be expressed in accepted individual
and national Olympic identities. Traditionally, African American athletes
were expected to be patriotic, to suppress their grievances in order to but-
tress America's international prestige and honor. By injecting race into
the Olympic dialogue, Smith and Carlos co-opted the traditional symbolism associated with the "black athlete" and inserted a new definition for
themselves and the world. The "Black Power salute" denounced America
before a world audience and offered a new "lasting racial consciousness"
that historian and former NAACP executive office Julian Bond claims
united black America.[74]

Smith's and Carlos's defiance and subsequent suspensions led to speculation regarding further protest gestures. After their suspension, Lee
Evans, whom one reporter referred to as "the number three militant" and
who had been one of the most vocal and active supporters of the OPHR,
became the center of attention. Evans heard about the expulsion on his
way to breakfast on October 18. Evans had considered not running the
final of the men's 400-meter dash when he heard about the suspensions.
However, one of the last things that John Carlos did before he left the
Olympic Village was to remind Evans of the team's pledge: "You run, win,
and then do your thing, man." After sweeping the race, when the three
African American medalists, Lee Evans, Larry James, and Ron Freeman,
took the victory stand, wearing black berets on their heads, and raised
bare black fists into the air, an act of defiance seemed imminent. However, the three smiling athletes lowered their fists and took their berets
off as "The Star-Spangled Banner" began to play. The actions of the trio
did not draw the wrath of the USOC. The *New York Times* ran a photo
of Evans, James, and Freeman on the victory dais with the caption "Not
Quite the Same Thing."[75]

After the victory ceremony, Evans said that they donned black berets
simply because it had rained. He explained away the clenched fist as "just
a salute. Some do it like this, some do it like that. This is our way of salut-
ing." The gold medalist said, "I won it for all the black people in America."
When asked if he had won it for some white people, he acquiescingly
acknowledged, "I have a lot of white friends at San Jose State and a lot all
over the world. This was for them too." However, to questions regarding
the suspension of Smith and Carlos, Evans answered, "No comment." The
USOC was appeased by Evans's explanation. Douglas Roby described the
ceremony as "perfectly all right."[76] Evans's behavior helped further isolate
Smith and Carlos's protest as gestures by two individuals rather than a
statement representative of a larger community.

Harry Edwards contemptuously condemned Evans for taking the victory stand, "waving and smiling. There was no sign of protest. Evans had disappointed his people." Even after winning a second gold medal as a member of the men's 1,600-meter relay team, Lee Evans did not make a bold statement against racial oppression. "Evans tried to do the impossible," Edwards maintained. "He attempted to stand up and be counted on both sides of the fence at once. Because this is a struggle for black survival in which there is no middle ground, he failed on both accounts."[77]

Harry Edwards did not attend the Games in Mexico City. On different occasions, Edwards has claimed that he was turned away at the border and that death threats kept him away. His critics maintain that he made only a token attempt to get to the Games. Others have offered different speculative possibilities: he was threatened with imprisonment in Mexico, he accepted a bribe from the CIA, he opted to concentrate on his studies, he was fearful of violence, or he realized that his boycott movement was dead. Notwithstanding his criticism of Lee Evans, where was Harry Edwards? At the critical juncture when the African American athletes in Mexico City could have benefited from his guidance and perspective, Edwards remained in the United States.[78]

Smith's and Carlos's raised fists became the "high-water mark in the liberation efforts of black youth during the 1960s." Their defiant actions became the defining moment of the XIXth Olympiad. "Smith and Carlos were banished for having committed the ultimate black transgression in a white supremacist's society," argued Harry Edwards. "They dared to become visible, to stand up for the dignity of Black people, to protest from an international platform the racist inhumanity of American society."[79] Young African Americans loved the duo for their courage; they returned home heroes.

Stateside, Tommie Smith and John Carlos immediately began a national speaking tour that began at Howard University, a historically black university. At the rally, Stokely Carmichael noted, "We are letting white America and everybody else know we will pick our own heroes. Our heroes are not those who will bow down to white America, but those who will stand up for our people."[80] Thousands of telegrams and acknowledgments from African Americans, including black leaders Adam Clayton Powell Jr., Elijah Muhammad, and H. Rap Brown, were sent. Receptions in their honor were hosted by black African nations. The defiance of the two American Olympic champions signaled the end of the "accommodating," soft-spoken athlete as heroic in the African American community. Edwards likened the "New Black Athlete" to the generation to which

Malcolm X had alluded—"a generation to which black dignity meant more than individual Negro 'gains.'"[81]

Gauging the Response to Mexico City

International attention placed on U.S. race relations had been instrumental in previous instances of civil rights reform. The drive to desegregate the military, the 1954 *Brown v. Board of Education* decision, the 1964 Civil Rights Act, and the 1965 Voting Rights Act were all implemented because of the geopolitical implications of continued racial oppression upon the United States' effort to win the Cold War. However, by the 1968 Olympic protest, the impetus to reform the U.S. system waned within government circles. There are several reasons for this: most important, government officials began to realize that U.S. racial policies were no longer as severe a hindrance to U.S. foreign policy as had been the case since the beginning of the Cold War. The international response to the violence at Selma in 1965 had marked a significant shift for State Department officials.

Early in the morning on Sunday, March 7, 1965, six hundred Africans American gathered outside Brown Chapel African Methodist Episcopal Church to prepare for a march through Selma, leading to the state capitol in Montgomery. King had favored delaying this march until Tuesday, hoping that federal judge Frank Johnson would overturn the ban that Alabama's governor, George Wallace, had ordered against the march. Nonetheless, with grassroots organizer Hosea Williams and the Student Nonviolent Coordinating Committee's John Lewis at the helm, the marchers approached the Edmund Pettus Bridge, where sheriff's officers on horseback and state troopers wearing gas masks waited on the other side. Major John Cloud, the spokesman for the state troopers, warned the approaching marchers: "Turn around and go back to your church." The assembled masses refused, and the troopers charged. John Lewis and others stood their ground. Struck by a fierce blow, Lewis's skull was fractured in the same place where he had been assaulted during the Freedom Rides. Vicious billy-club swings sent other innocent citizens to the ground, while some white onlookers cheered. Notwithstanding the bravery of John Lewis, most ran as the baton-swinging officers approached. However, numerous marchers were unable to outrun the brutish law enforcement agents. By the end of the savage beating, seventy African Americans were hospitalized, including five women who were found unconscious at the initial site of the attack. Other bloody, bruised, and limping marchers sought relief in the black community surrounding Brown Chapel.[82]

The violence at Selma moved President Johnson to address a joint session of Congress. On Monday evening, March 15, the president entered the House of Representatives to make his case for a powerful civil rights bill focusing on voting rights. If the United States did not resolve its civil rights issue, he said, "then we will have failed as a people and as a nation." He likened Selma to other turning points in American history: Lexington, Concord, and Appomattox. Johnson told the members of Congress and the national television audience that "the effort of American Negroes to secure themselves the full blessings of American life . . . must be our cause, too. Because it is not just Negroes, but really all of us who must overcome the crippling legacy of bigotry and injustice." In a speech punctuated with nearly forty ovations from the floor of Congress, President Johnson concluded with a pledge and battle cry that brought tears to the eyes of Martin Luther King: "We shall . . . overcome."[83]

The United States Information Agency tracked press coverage of the Selma incident; despite its brutality, Selma was not front-page news. One foreign newspaper argued that President Johnson's speech marked "the end of official United States indifference, hypocrisy and passivity toward the position of African Americans." The agency gleefully reported that the world recognized that in "one year the United States has moved rapidly toward a new phase of race relations based upon the Civil Rights Bill" of 1964. "The world," the report concluded, "is seeing that African Americans are winning their struggle with the support of the United States government and the support of most Americans." Editorials continued to be critical of the violence, but rather than condemning the United States for permitting the violence, foreign nations began to assert that the United States was doing its best to make sure all Americans could exercise their constitutional rights, the report suggested.[84]

Selma signaled a major shift: a sharp distinction was made between the actions of the American government and "racial bigots." Before the passage of the 1964 Civil Rights Act, that distinction had not been widely made. Worldwide, there was a general acceptance of the notion that the violence of Selma was part of the evolutionary process toward equality that the majority of Americans favored; the violence was interpreted as a "sign of the tension when integrating a national minority. The United States could be seen as good, even when racism was abhorrent." Therefore, racial discrimination was increasingly interpreted as a sectional issue that was moving toward eradication, according to the State Department report. Editorials in Tunisia, Nigeria, and Kenya expressed confidence that the American federal government would take the necessary course of action to ensure that African Americans were afforded the rights guaranteed by the Constitution.[85] This notion was strengthened when Congress moved swiftly by passing the Voting Rights Act of 1965, which outlawed a variety of measures that were used by local and state governments to disenfranchise African American voters.[86]

A widely circulated 1966 USIA report, "Racial Issues in the U.S.: Some Policy and Program Indications of Research," revealed that international condemnation of American race relations had been replaced by criticism of U.S. policy in Vietnam as the principal threat to U.S. influence in the world. Nonetheless, nations around the world continued to harbor "unrelieved disapproval" of U.S. race relations. The report noted that reaction to U.S. racial problems continued to be an aspect of American society where international opinion was "universally adverse . . . [and] strongly negative." The report argued that the "unfavorable view is widespread, strong, and persistent." Yet it also made the vitally important observation that instances of racial justice appeared "to be more conspicuous as a blot on our image . . . than as a problem for our influence." This was a crucial recognition. Rather than a mounting obstacle, "Racial Issues in the U.S." suggested that confronting international condemnation of U.S. racism occupied government officials more "than the facts warrant." Therefore, while nations were critical of the treatment and living conditions of African Americans, it did not mean that racial discrimination was still a hindrance to U.S. foreign policy objectives.[87]

State Department officials had worked hard to portray the African American struggle as a story of progress. "Racial Issues in the U.S." suggested that their goal had been achieved because there was a new "general belief that things have changed, will continue to change, and that the change is for the better."[88] The report maintained that the 1964 Civil Rights Act and 1965 Voting Rights Act had caused foreign audiences to view U.S. race relations through different philosophical lenses. Increasingly, the U.S. government was perceived as being in full support of the extension of political and social rights for African Americans.

Terming the new foreign attitudes about U.S. race relations a "watershed" moment, the report suggested a change in policy. Instead of intensive programming directed at counteracting potential hostile attitudes after public incidents like the 1968 Mexico Olympic protest, "Racial Issues in the U.S.," suggested that the government should allow the issues to play out in the public media. Rather than responding "dramatically to drama," it was suggested that the best action that the U.S. State Department could take was to allow the public to draw their own conclusions about U.S.

racial injustice. Because foreign audiences were now more willing to see instances of racial confrontation as representative of progress, and no longer as "shameful exposures of a static and evil situation," the report effectively minimized the importance of foreign condemnation of U.S. racism as a consideration that should preoccupy the State Department. A consequence of the new policy was that the leverage that civil rights activists and Black Power proponents had successfully used to force the United States to work toward solving America's domestic civil rights problems dwindled.[89]

The Bureau of Educational and Cultural Affairs' budget cuts seem to support the conclusions of "Racial Issues in the U.S." The bureau's reduced appropriations after 1964 were in part because the government did not believe that the programs were as essential to U.S. efforts to win the Cold War in Africa, Asia, and Latin America, areas where the racial issue had caused the most damage. The bureau was allocated $2,869,241 for fiscal year 1964. Then the budget fell to $2,000,000 for 1965 and 1966. Because of budgetary reductions by the administration and then by Congress in 1967, the Bureau of Educational and Cultural Affairs was forced to cancel approximately one-third of the musical, athletic, and other cultural tours proposed. Because of fixed commitments to some phases of the bureau's program, such as the academic and leadership exchanges, the cuts fell heaviest upon the smallest but one of the most successful aspects of the program—the presentation abroad of American cultural and athletic achievements. The available funds dropped to around $1,000,000 at the close of the Johnson administration. Given the declining significance of race as a foreign policy concern, the areas of concentration shrank to just the Soviet Union and Eastern Europe. With a few exceptions, the State Department completely sponsored tours that were sent to the Soviet sphere of influence. In order to reach other parts of the world, the department increasingly relied upon the practice of extending and supplementing privately sponsored trips arranged for Africa, Asia, Latin America, and other regions.[90]

The legacy of the 1968 Mexico City Olympic protest is that it helped spotlight American racial abuses. Decades later Tommie Smith maintained that "what hurt—an agonizing hurt—for old heart of America was everybody saw it—the entire world saw it."[91] The editorial comments that the protest engendered bespeak the ways in which Americans who supported Smith and Carlos and those who opposed them both saw the protest gesture as potentially harmful for the United States' world image. However, there is no evidence that the USIA or the State Department tried to assess the international implications of the Smith and Carlos actions, as it had in other high-profile instances prior to the 1966 publication of "Racial Issues in the U.S." Given the lack of State Department records regarding Mexico City, it appears that the protest gestures of Smith and Carlos did not spark the concern of the federal government. The speculative claims that the State Department may have been instrumental in the forced suspension of Smith and Carlos cannot be substantiated with declassified State Department records.

Certainly, the image of Smith and Carlos on the dais is one of the most iconic moments in sports history. Their bravery and commitment to social justice continue to serve as a model for past athletes and contemporary sports figures. By no means am I suggesting that their protest was unfruitful or counterproductive. However, it must be acknowledged that Smith and Carlos achieved only a partial victory. Indeed, their protest served to highlight U.S. race relations abroad. However, their actions did not lead the U.S. government to aggressively work to solve civil rights problems.

Conclusion

The raised fists of Tommie Smith and John Carlos are the enduring symbols of the co-optation of the symbolic meaning of African American athletes. The notion that docility and acquiescence in the face of racial discrimination would be a benefit to the struggle for equal rights became associated with "Uncle Tomism." Coupled with political protests by Muhammad Ali, economic ventures by Jim Brown and the Negro Economic Industrial Union, and the massive protests on college campuses involving African American athletes, the Mexico City Games were the high point of the struggle to place the athletic world at the center of efforts to fight racial oppression, under terms set by African Americans.

Epilogue

The use of sport as a tool of U.S. foreign policy did not end after the Mexico City Olympic protests. The United States as well as other global powers continued to utilize sport as a means to solidify friendships, antagonize rivals, and advance claims about the viability of their political, social, and economic systems. Two of the most widely used tactics to express displeasure with other nations were boycotts and the denial of visas for potential competitors. Conversely, sport continued to be viewed as a means to initiate and foster positive relationships. In this regard, some of the most widely employed strategies included sports exchanges, training assistance, and facility construction. Hence, sport remained a venue through which nations articulated political alliances, battleground issues, and counternarratives that frequently went unnoticed by the general public when expressed through traditional diplomatic channels.[1]

Arguably, the two most high-profile Cold War–related incidents that involved the United States after the Mexico City protests were the visit of the United States Table Tennis Team to Beijing, China, to participate in a series of matches dubbed "Ping-Pong Diplomacy" and the U.S.-led boycott of the 1980 Summer Olympic Games held in the Soviet Union. Diplomatic relations between the United States and the People's Republic of China had been virtually nonexistent since a Communist government rose to power in China in 1949. However, both President Nixon and Chairman Mao had made public pronouncements that signaled their desire to improve Sino-U.S. relations in the late 1960s.

Table tennis provided an opening through which both nations could interact with each other in a public yet nonthreatening environment. At the 1971 World Table Tennis Championship in Japan, the Chinese extended post-tournament invitations to the several national teams but not the U.S. team because of the hostility between the two countries. As a good-will gesture, the U.S. team requested an invitation. After consulting with Chairman Mao, the Chinese extended an invitation to a surprised U.S. team. This was a significant gesture because table tennis was the national sport and held in the highest esteem in China.[2] Hence, the table tennis exhibition matches provided an opening that both nations realized was a safe yet highly visible space filled with symbolic importance.

On April 14, 1971, Chinese premier Zhou Enlai greeted the visiting athletes and acknowledged the tour as an important step toward thaw-ing relations between the two nations. "You have opened a new chapter in the relations of the American and Chinese people. I am confident that this new beginning of our friendship will certainly meet with majority support of our two peoples," Premier Zhou asserted. "We welcome you." Three months after the sporting exhibition, the U.S. national security adviser, Henry Kissinger, secretly traveled to China to meet with Zhou to prepare the way for President Nixon's historic 1972 visit. Certainly, "Ping-Pong Diplomacy" was not essential for the United States and China to move toward normalization, but its importance cannot be dismissed as inconsequential. For both nations, the symbolic gesture, which was powerfully expressed by the warm and cordial words and gestures that the competitors from both nations lavished upon each other, suggested that China and the United States could exist harmoniously.[3]

The 1979 Soviet invasion of Afghanistan drew widespread condem-nation from the international community. The United Nations General Assembly overwhelmingly passed a resolution that denounced Soviet aggression. As a display of U.S. disapproval, President Carter pressured the U.S. Olympic Committee to boycott the 1980 Olympic Games that were in Moscow, and he asked allied nations to forego sending teams. Thirty nations boycotted, and another thirty-three did not respond to their invitations.

One of the peculiarities of Carter's effort to reach out to African na-tions was his decision to send Muhammad Ali abroad to meet with Af-rican diplomats to garner their support for the boycott. While African American athletes had been sent abroad as goodwill ambassadors since the beginning of the Cold War, the position Ali occupied was far more significant: as an emissary of the president. On February 2, 1980, Ali began his five-nation trip that included stops in Tanzania, Kenya, Nigeria, Libe-ria, and Senegal. Typically, diplomatic overtures were handled between similarly classified government representatives. Ali's African hosts were not seduced by his credentials as a boxer or his status as an anticolonial icon because of his anti–Vietnam War stance. Rather, the diplomats were insulted. From their perspective, the Carter administration did not respect them enough to send someone who was in a position to negotiate an arrangement between the United States and its African allies. Hence, Ali's trip was viewed as a patronizing gesture rather than as a negotiation between sovereign nations.[4]

Muhammad Ali was unprepared to deal with the negative reactions that his tour engendered throughout parts of Africa. After Ali arrived in Tanzania, Tanzanian president Jules Nyerere refused his request for a meeting. Furthermore, Ali was unprepared to answer questions from reporters who asked why African nations should boycott the 1980 Games after the United States refused to join the African-led boycott of the 1976 Games because New Zealand had not been suspended from the Games for competing in a rugby match in South Africa. When reporters informed Ali that it had been Russian support rather that American support that funded several African liberation movements, Ali responded, "They didn't tell me in America that Russia supports these countries. Maybe I'm being used to do something that ain't right." By the time Ali arrived in Nigeria on February 4, he began to accuse President Carter of attempting to capitalize upon his fame to harm African nations. More specifically, the former heavyweight champ accused Carter of "sending me around the world to take the whipping from Black Africans opposed to the U.S. dealings with South Africa."[5] Ali's trip produced limited results; of the five countries he visited, three decided to send athletes to compete in Moscow: Senegal, Tanzania, and Nigeria. Liberia tried to assume a middle position by allowing its Olympic team to travel to Moscow but not compete, while Kenya did not send a delegation.

Despite the continued enlistment of sport as an aspect of U.S. foreign policy, domestically the United States continued publicly asserting that sport was best handled by private enterprise rather than the federal government. Certainly, the United States' desire to employ sport to contrast its free-market system with the Soviet state–sponsored model limited the role that government could play. Nonetheless, the poor performance of the U.S. team at the 1972 Munich Olympic Games led U.S. officials to question whether the government should become more involved in organizing and supporting the development of U.S. amateur sports teams. The decline of the U.S. team's performance at the 1972 Summer Olympic Games was the impetus for the Senate's passage of the 1974 Amateur Athletic Act. Had the

House of Representatives followed suit, the act would have nationalized elite amateur athletics in the United States and reversed long-standing beliefs in the superiority of privately funded and organized elite teams for international sports competitions. After the performance of the U.S. Olympic team improved in 1976, both houses of Congress passed the Amateur Sports Act of 1978. This was the first federal legislative bill that regulated the organization of amateur athletics in the United States. Rather than authorizing a government takeover of Olympic sport administration, the bill placed the authority for organizing the team within the power of a private organization. This act solidified the limited role that government would play in the selection of the U.S. Olympic teams.[6]

Just as the United States continued to be invested in sport as a political weapon, African Americans continued to use sport as an arena to advocate for social transformation. One of the most notable examples is this regard is Arthur Ashe's controversial visit to South Africa in 1973. At the time, the South African Open was the sixth-most-prestigious tennis tournament in the world, and Ashe had been denied a visa to compete in the open several times before. Once the South African government agreed to grant him a visa, Ashe sought to utilize his trip to demonstrate his solidarity with the black South Africans who were waging a campaign against the Nationalist government's racist apartheid laws.[7] Ashe's trip helped galvanize U.S. support for the antiapartheid movement that was beginning to intensify during the early 1970s.

The continued use of sport as a foreign policy tool reflected the same rationale that propelled the State Department to send African American athletes abroad to counteract anti-American hostility: sport was valuable when it could be linked to pressing foreign policy needs.[8] Hence, sport continued to be imbued with a host of political agendas throughout the Cold War.

Notes

Introduction

1. Montville, "Bill Russell," 124.

2. Russell and Branch, *Second Wind*, 99.

3. Ibid., 100.

4. Ibid.

5. Russell, *Go Up for Glory*, 152–54.

6. Lauren, *Power and Prejudice*, 190, 192–93, 228; Borstelmann, *Apartheid's Reluctant Uncle*, 142.

7. Krenn, *Black Diplomacy*, 76; Hixson, *Parting the Curtain*, 121; Southern, *Gunnar Myrdal and Black-White Relations*, 102.

8. Lauren, *Power and Prejudice*, 187–88; Shepherd, *Racial Influences*, 4.

9. Lauren, *Power and Prejudice*, 188; Dudziak, *Cold War Civil Rights*, 77, 80; Krenn, *Black Diplomacy*, 30–31, 33.

10. "Negro Slaying Spurs Inquiry in Georgia," *New York Times*, November 25, 1948; "Widow Held in Killing: Arrested at Funeral of Negro Victim in Georgia," *New York Times*, November 28, 1948; "Slain Negro's Widow Released in Georgia," *New York Times*, November 29, 1948.

11. Anderson, *Eyes Off the Prize*, 125.

12. Ibid., 190.

13. Krenn, *Black Diplomacy*, 30–31, 33; Dudziak, *Cold War Civil Rights*, 80.

14. Letter from Mr. Rusk to the Secretary of State, National Archives (NA), Record Group (RG) 59, 800/432.213.

15. Von Eschen, *Race against Empire*, 126, 3.

16. Singh, *Black Is a Country*, 178.

17. Luce, *The American Century*, 33–34; Herzstein, *Henry R. Luce*, 180.

18. U.S. Information Agency, "USIA Basic Guidance Paper," October 22, 1957, File on Agency History, RG 306, USIA.

19. "The President's Committee on Information Activities Abroad: Africa, PCIAA no. 31," Dwight D. Eisenhower Presidential Library (DDEL), U.S. President's Committee on Information Activities Abroad (Sprague Committee), Box 21, folder PCIAA #31.

20. For a detailed examination of the athletic revolution, see Scott, *The Athletic Revolution.*

Chapter 1. The Showcase African American

1. Lanctot, *Negro League Baseball,* 214–16.

2. "How New York Sportswriters Viewed Big League Attitude on Admitting Colored Baseball Aces," reprinted from the *Newspaper PM* article by Joe Cumminskey, *New York Amsterdam News,* December 11, 1943; Wendell Smith, "Publishers Place Case of Negro Players before Big League Owners," *Pittsburgh Courier,* December 11, 1943; "Publishers' Assoc. Cashes in Heavily on Big League Baseball Talk with Landis," *Atlanta Daily World,* December 5, 1943.

3. "How New York Sportswriters Viewed Big League Attitude," reprinted from the *Newspaper PM* article by Cumminskey; "Judge Landis, Leagues, Hear Negro Publishers' Plea," *New York Amsterdam News,* December 11, 1943; W. Smith, "Publishers Place Case of Negro Players before Big League Owners."

4. Ronald Smith, "Paul Robeson," 10.

5. Duberman, *Paul Robeson,* xii.

6. W. Smith, "Publishers Place Case of Negro Players before Big League Owners"; Stanley Frank, "How New York Sportswriters Viewed Big League Attitude on Admitting Colored Baseball Aces," reprinted from the *New York Post* article, *New York Amsterdam News,* December 11, 1943; "How New York Sportswriters Viewed Big League Attitude," reprinted from the *Newspaper PM* article by Cumminskey; "Judge Landis, Leagues, Hear Negro Publishers' Plea."

7. W. Smith, "Publishers Place Case of Negro Players before Big League Owners."

8. Ibid.; Alvin Moses, "Beating the Gun," *Atlanta Daily World,* December 19, 1943; Bob Williams, "Demand House Probe of Jim Crow Baseball," *Cleveland Call and Post,* May 5, 1945; Joel W. Smith, "Surveying the Sports Front," *Atlanta Daily World,* December 12, 1943.

9. W. Smith, "Publishers Place Case of Negro Players before Big League Owners."

10. Stout, "Tryout and Fallout," 11–15.

11. Dorinson and Warmund, *Jackie Robinson,* 5; Tygiel, *Baseball's Great Experiment,* 37.

12. Knee, "Jim Crow Strikes Out," 76.

13. Tygiel, *The Jackie Robinson Reader,* 147; Tygiel, *Baseball's Great Experiment,* 206.

14. Zirin, *What's My Name, Fool?,* 42–43; Van Deburg, *Black Camelot,* 100–101; Knee, "Jim Crow Strikes Out," 76.

15. Dan W. Dodson, "The Integration of Negroes in Baseball," in *The Jackie Robinson Reader,* ed. Tygiel, 162, 166; Tygiel, *Baseball's Great Experiment,* 55.

16. Prior to Robinson's first game as a member of the Brooklyn Dodgers, Bob Finch, Branch Rickey's secretary, had spoken to white groups about the "touchy subject of equality for all men." Finch argued that Robinson was "symbolic of what all Americans

want, an opportunity for everyone." He warned those who were opposed to integration that their efforts to hinder desegregation "would be a reflection on the democracy under which we live." Given the Cold War context of the integration of Major League Baseball, Finch's words were prophetic. Red Barber with Robert Creamer, "He Did Far More for Me . . .," in *The Jackie Robinson Reader,* ed. Tygiel, 53, 57, 63; Tygiel, *Baseball's Great Experiment,* 200, 105, 200, 333.

17. Tygiel, *Baseball's Great Experiment,* viii; Wendell Smith, "Dodgers Have Drawn 95,000 Fans in Four Exhibition Contests," *Pittsburgh Courier,* April 26, 1947.

18. Southern, *Gunnar Myrdal and Black-White Relations,* 1–7; Singh, *Black Is a Country,* 25.

19. Southern, *Gunnar Myrdal and Black-White Relations,* 1–7.

20. Ibid., xiii, 94, 187, 226.

21. Singh, *Black Is a Country,* 38–39, 134.

22. Fousek, *To Lead the Free World,* 86; Dudziak, *Cold War Civil Rights,* 7–8, 39.

23. Southern, *Gunnar Myrdal and Black-White Relations,* 55, 68–69.

24. Cox, *Caste, Class, and Race,* 509–11, 521–22, 538.

25. Duberman, *Paul Robeson,* xiii; Balaji, *Professor and the Pupil,* 25–27; Beeching, "Paul Robeson and the Black Press," 339.

26. Duberman, *Paul Robeson,* 314, 342; Len Graves Jr., "Leaders Question Cause of Loyalty Probe within Race," *Pittsburgh Courier,* July 23, 1949; Ronald Smith, "Paul Robeson," 15–19; "Robeson Denies Story Quoting Him on War," *Cleveland Call and Post,* March 7, 1949; "Robeson Tells What He Said," *Baltimore Afro-American,* June 25, 1949.

27. Lauren, *Power and Prejudice,* 187; Dudziak, *Cold War Civil Rights,* 27; Belmonte, "Defending a Way of Life," 270; Fousek, *To Lead the Free World,* 126–29.

28. Woods, *Black Struggle, Red Scare,* 27; Horne, *Fire This Time,* 62.

29. Von Eschen, *Race against Empire,* 97, 109, 112; Borstelmann, *Apartheid's Reluctant Uncle,* 56; Horne, *Fire This Time,* 92.

30. Lewis, *W. E. B. Du Bois,* 550–51, 556; Beeching, "Paul Robeson and the Black Press," 352.

31. Borstelmann, *Apartheid's Reluctant Uncle,* 66; Gardner, *Harry Truman and Civil Rights,* 61; Layton, *International Politics and Civil Rights Policies,* 3, 79.

32. Lauren, *Power and Prejudice,* 187; Pauley, *Modern Presidency and Civil Rights,* 32.

33. Pauley, *Modern Presidency and Civil Rights,* 56; Plummer, *Rising Wind,* 56.

34. Pauley, *Modern Presidency and Civil Rights,* 36, 43, 54.

35. Anderson, *Eyes Off the Prize,* 213.

36. Mary McLeod Bethune, "DAR Stands on Aid to Education Shocks; Robeson Missed His Cue," *Chicago Defender,* April 30, 1949; George Schuyler, "Views and Reviews," *Pittsburgh Courier,* May 7, 1949.

37. "Robeson Criticism Stirs Controversy among NAACP Folk," *Philadelphia Tribune,* July 5, 1949.

38. Graves, "Leaders Question Cause of Loyalty Probe within Race."

39. Woods, *Black Struggle, Red Scare,* 26–32.

40. Graves, "Leaders Question Cause of Loyalty Probe within Race"; "Hearings Regarding Communist Infiltration of Minority Groups—Part 1," in *Hearings before the*

Committee on Un-American Activities: House of Representatives, Eighty-first Congress, 1st sess., July 13, 14, and 18 (Washington, D.C.: Government Printing Office, 1949), 426–27. Hereafter referred to as HUAC Hearings.

41. HUAC Hearings, 472, 452–54, 465–67.

42. Herb Heft, "Jackie Robinson Chides Robeson," *Washington Post,* July 19, 1949; Jack Hand, "Jackie Tells Congress He Wants Raise in '50," *Atlanta Constitution,* July 19, 1949; Ronald Smith, "Paul Robeson," 19.

43. Peter Golenbock, "Men of Conscience," in *Jackie Robinson,* ed. Dorinson and Warmund, 20; Tygiel, *Baseball's Great Experiment,* 196–97; Simons, "Jackie Robinson and the American Mind," 40.

44. Tygiel, *Baseball's Great Experiment,* 4, 75; Biondi, *To Stand and Fight,* 33; Tygiel, *The Jackie Robinson Reader,* 6, 9.

45. Golenbeck, "Men of Conscience," in *Jackie Robinson,* ed. Dorinson and Warmund, 20; Peter Levine, "Father and Son at Ebbets Field," in ibid., 64.

46. Ronald Smith, "Paul Robeson," 7; Duberman, *Paul Robeson,* 342–43; Von Eschen, *Race against Empire,* 124–26.

47. Kahn, *Era, 1947–1957,* 201–2.

48. "Robinson versus Robeson," *Philadelphia Tribune,* July 16, 1949.

49. "Drop That Gun, Jackie," *Baltimore Afro-American,* July 16, 1949.

50. Heft, "Jackie Robinson Chides Robeson"; HUAC Hearings, 480–82.

51. "Jackie Robinson Brands Robeson's Talk Plain 'Silly,'" *Boston Globe,* July 7, 1949; "Jackie Robinson, American," *St. Louis Post-Dispatch,* July 19, 1949; "Robinson Hits U.S. Bigots," *Baltimore Afro-American,* July 23, 1949; "Jackie Robinson Hits Homer," *Philadelphia Tribune,* July 23, 1949.

52. "Solon Would Print Jackie's Testimony," *Pittsburgh Courier,* August 8, 1949; "Jackie Hits Homer at Red Probe," *Chicago Defender,* July 23, 1949; "Jackie Robinson Brands Robeson's Talk Plain 'Silly'"; "Jackie Robinson, American"; Ronald Smith, "Paul Robeson," 20; "Robinson Hits U.S. Bigots."

53. Duberman, *Paul Robeson,* 307–8.

54. Rampersad, *Jackie Robinson: A Biography,* 215; "Robeson Hails Jackie for Racial Contribution," *Baltimore Afro-American,* July 30, 1949; Balaji, *Professor and the Pupil,* 270; "Robeson Gives Views on Talk by Robinson," *New York Amsterdam News,* July 23, 1949.

55. "Holding Our Lines," *Pittsburgh Courier,* July 39, 1949.

56. Singh, *Black Is a Country,* 156.

57. Von Eschen, *Race against Empire,* 1, 107; Krenn, *Black Diplomacy,* 67; Marable, *Race, Reform, and Rebellion,* 22–23.

58. Beeching, "Paul Robeson and the Black Press," 346.

59. Balaji, *Professor and the Pupil,* 283; Duberman, *Paul Robeson,* 342–43, 389–90; Von Eschen, *Race against Empire,* 124–26.

60. Dudziak, *Cold War Civil Rights,* 49; Hixson, *Parting the Curtain,* 129–30.

61. Southern, *Gunnar Myrdal and Black-White Relations,* xiii; *The Negro in American Life,* NA, RG 59, Lot 52D235.

62. *The Negro in American Life.*

63. John D. Silvera, "Color—a Factor in U.S. Psychological Warfare: An Appraisal and Approach to the Use of the Negro as PsyWar Themes," DDEL, Central Files, Official File (OF) 133-L-6, Box 673, OF 133-M 1952–53 (3).

64. Ibid.

65. Letter from Lester Granger to C. D. Jackson, July 22, 1953, DDEL, Central Files, OF 133-L-6, Box 673, Folder 133-M Psychological Warfare, 1952–53 (1).

Chapter 2. "Spreading the Gospel of Basketball"

1. Michener, *Sports in America,* 144; Klein, *Cold War Orientalism,* 119–22.

2. Letter from Dean Acheson to Walter F. O'Malley, May 15, 1952, NA, 811.4553/5-1552; "Telephone Conversation between Mr. Walter F. O'Malley and M. C. Jones," September 3, 1952, NA, 811.4533/9-452.

3. "Telephone Conversation between O'Malley and Jones."

4. Saperstein named the Chicago-based team the "Harlem" Globetrotters because he wanted potential opponents to know that the team was composed of African American players. "Visit to Santiago of U.S. Basketball Stars," June 7, 1951, NA, 811.4553/6-751; *New York Times,* May 30, 1950.

5. "Visit of American Basketball Teams to Oporto," May 22, 1950, NA, 840.4533/5-1050.

6. Zinkoff with Williams, *Around the World,* 109–10.

7. Green, *Spinning the Globe,* 235–40.

8. Throughout the 1950s, Abe Saperstein periodically employed Jesse Owens as a master of ceremonies, sports commentator, and halftime performer: Owens performed the demeaning task of running hurdles that were set up around the basketball court.

9. Green, *Spinning the Globe,* 191–92.

10. Letter from Dean Acheson to American Legation—Damascus, July 28, 1952, NA, 811.453/7-2852 (emphasis added).

11. Watkins, *On the Real Side,* 94; Wolf, *Foul!,* 126.

12. Letter from Dean Acheson to American Legation—Damascus, July 28, 1952, NA, 811.453/7-2852.

13. Wetterhahn, "Saperstein's Sambos," 12–18.

14. Thomas, "Around the World," 780–86; *Abe Saperstein's Fabulous Harlem Globetrotters Official Souvenir Program.*

15. Green, *Spinning the Globe,* 64.

16. *Abe Saperstein's Fabulous Harlem Globetrotters Official Souvenir Program;* Zinkoff with Williams, *Around the World,* 15; *Chicago Defender,* July 7, 1951.

17. *Abe Saperstein's Fabulous Harlem Globetrotters Official Souvenir Program;* Zinkoff with Williams, *Around the World,* 15; Lombardo, "Harlem Globetrotters," 62; *Chicago Defender,* July 7, 1951.

18. *Abe Saperstein's Fabulous Harlem Globetrotters Official Souvenir Program;* Thomas, "Around the World," 784–89.

19. Given the nature of Zinkoff's text, it is quite possible that this tale has been embellished or greatly exaggerated. Nonetheless, how Zinkoff recounts this narrative

suggests how the Globetrotter officials sought to represent the team. Zinkoff with Williams, *Around the World*, 11, 32, 35, 85, 88, 96–98, 130, 143, 154–55.

20. Ibid., 85, 88, 96–98, 130, 143, 154–55.

21. The official history of the team is still chronicled on its website, although many of the claims have been made by Saperstein and others since, at least, the mid-1950s. Zinkoff with Williams, *Around the World*, 22–25; Green, *Spinning the Globe*, 64.

22. George, *Elevating the Game*, 43–44.

23. Until approximately 1947, *Globe Trotters* was typically spelled as two words. I use *Globetrotter* throughout for consistency. Green, *Spinning the Globe*, 3.

24. Ibid., 39–52, 77.

25. The 1927 date that Saperstein frequently quoted as the "beginning" of the Harlem Globetrotters has been challenged. For a discussion of this issue, see Ben Green's history of the team, *Spinning the Globe*. Zinkoff with Williams, *Around the World*, 28, 32; George, *Elevating the Game*, 48–49; http://www.harlemglobetrotters.com/history/timeline/ (accessed September 20, 2008).

26. Zinkoff with Williams, *Around the World*, 22, 38–39; M. Smith, "Basketball's Court Jester," 8; Cohane, "Harlem Globetrotters," 69.

27. Christgau, *Tricksters in the Madhouse*, 9–10; *Rochester (Minn.) Post-Bulletin*, December 17, 1935.

28. *Northwest Monitor* (Minneapolis), January 31, 1933.

29. *Chicago Defender*, March 22, 1944.

30. J. Michael Kenyon, letter to the author, April 12, 2004.

31. Chamberlain and Shaw, *Wilt*, 98; Menville, *Harlem Globetrotters*, 69–70.

32. George, *Elevating the Game*, 48; Zinkoff with Williams, *Around the World*, 28–29, 32.

33. *Kelowna (B.C.) Courier*, March 2, 1935; *Spokesman-Review* (Spokane, Wash.), February 11, 1935.

34. *Chicago Defender*, February 22, 1936; Rayl, "New York Renaissance Professional Black Basketball Team," 232, 159; Green, *Spinning the Globe*, 53.

35. Rogosin, *Invisible Men*, 119–20, 145.

36. Ibid., 144.

37. Ibid.; Green, *Spinning the Globe*, 162.

38. Geist and Nelson, "From Plantation to Bel-Air," 267; Ely, *Adventures of "Amos 'n' Andy,"* 29; Watkins, *On the Real Side*, 29.

39. Coleman, *African American Viewers*, 39; Watkins, *On the Real Side*, 66; Bogle, *Toms, Coons, Mulattoes, Mammies, and Bucks*, 8.

40. Geist and Nelson, "From Plantation to Bel-Air," 267; Watkins, *On the Real Side*, 28–29.

41. Savage, *Broadcasting Freedom*, 6, 256–57; George, *Elevating the Game*, 49.

42. Bogle, *Toms, Coons, Mulattoes, Mammies, and Bucks*, 4, 41; Watkins, *On the Real Side*, 255.

43. Green, *Spinning the Globe*, 164.

44. Marshall Smith, "Basketball's Court Jester"; Zinkoff with Williams, *Around the World*, 73; Green, *Spinning the Globe*, 161.

45. M. Smith, "Basketball's Court Jester," 51; Zinkoff with Williams, *Around the World*, 71; George, *Elevating the Game*, 52.

46. Wetterhahn, "Saperstein's Sambos," 42; Wolf, *Foul!*, 141.

47. Zinkoff with Williams, *Around the World*, 71; Ronald Smith, "Paul Robeson," 42–44; Bogle, *Toms, Coons, Mulattoes, Mammies, and Bucks*, 39–41.

48. Christgau, *Tricksters in the Madhouse*, 38–40; Lombardo, "Harlem Globetrotters," 60–63.

49. Christgau, *Tricksters in the Madhouse*, 82–86.

50. Boskin, *Sambo*, 13–14.

51. Ibid., 60.

52. Acham, *Revolution Televised*, 6–7; Kelley, *Race Rebels*, 6–10.

53. Roberts, *From Trickster to Badman*, 34; Watkins, *On the Real Side*, 50.

54. Ibid.

55. Coleman, *African American Viewers*, 35; Watkins, *On the Real Side*, 38, 52.

56. *Chicago Defender*, December 25, 1954.

57. Roberts, *From Trickster to Badman*, 18, 23, 35–36.

58. Green, *Spinning the Globe*, 6, 233; *Chicago Defender*, March 4, 1950; *New York Times*, January 3, 1952.

59. Zinkoff with Williams, *Around the World*, 13; Menville, *Harlem Globetrotters*, 103–5; *Boston Post*, March 3, 1950.

60. Green, *Spinning the Globe*, 228–29.

61. Ibid., 230–33; *Chicago Defender*, August 12, 1950.

62. *New York Daily Compass*, February 17, 1952; *New York Times*, October 1, 1953.

63. *New York Times*, April 2, 1954.

64. *New York Times*, March 30, 1953; *Daily Compass*, February 7, 1951.

65. *Abe Saperstein's Fabulous Harlem Globetrotters Official Souvenir Program*.

66. Menville, *Harlem Globetrotters*, 103.

67. "Commercially Distributed Film Advances USIS Objectives," October 2, 1953, NA, 811.452/10-253.

68. Ibid.; Wetterhahn, "Saperstein's Sambos," 26–27.

69. "Commercially Distributed Film Advances USIS Objectives"; Wetterhahn, "Saperstein's Sambos," 26–27.

70. "Commercially Distributed Film Advances USIS Objectives."

71. Wolf, *Foul!*, 125.

72. Lemon, *Meadowlark*, 152, 156.

73. Green, *Spinning the Globe*, 147–48; Lemon, *Meadowlark*, 152, 156.

74. Lemon, *Meadowlark*, 152–56.

75. Wolf, *Foul!*, 125.

76. "Globetrotting Globetrotters," 42–43; Wolf, *Foul!*, 125, 142–43; Green, *Spinning the Globe*, 254, 258, 269.

77. Wetterhahn, "Saperstein's Sambos," 33; Zinkoff with Williams, *Around the World*, 48, 72; Green, *Spinning the Globe*, 254, 258, 269; Krzemienski, "On the Initial Sack," 65.

78. *Chicago Defender*, March 5, 1955.

79. Undated newspaper clipping, J. Michael Kenyon personal collection.

Chapter 3. Playing Politics

1. "Irate Fans Toss Rubbish," Avery Brundage Papers, Box 290, Folder "Basketball, 1960–1970."

2. Having accomplished its goal, the Soviets forfeited their first-place standing in the tournament when they chose to make a political statement by refusing to play the team representing China. Since the Soviets had not recognized China as a nation, Soviet team officials argued that the Chinese team did not represent a nation. Juan de Oniss, "Loss to Russia Costs U.S. Basketball Prestige," *New York Times,* January 30, 1959.

3. Juan de Oniss, "Russia Halts U.S. to Stay Unbeaten in World Basketball Tourney," *New York Times,* January 29, 1959; "Brazil Nears Title," *New York Times,* January 31, 1959.

4. *Washington Post,* January 31, 1959; Oniss, "Loss to Russia."

5. Edward Warnecke to Christian Herter, March 12, 1959, NA, 800.453/3-1259.

6. Domer, "Sports and Cold War America," 139–40.

7. "Observations of the Third World Basketball Tournament in Santiago, Chile," NA, 800.453/2-1359.

8. "Soviet Victory over U.S. Basketball Team in Santiago," NA, 800.453/1-3059.

9. "U.S.S.R. Defeat of U.S. in Basketball Impairs U.S. Prestige in Brazil," NA, 800.453/2-559.

10. Ibid.; William Macomber to Senator Lyndon B. Johnson, March 2, 1958, NA, 800.453/2-1859; "Psychological Aspects of U.S. Participation in III World Basketball Championship," NA, 800.453/2-359; "Third World Basketball Tournament," NA, 800.453/1-2259.

11. "Soviet Victory over U.S. Basketball Team at Santiago."

12. Macomber to Johnson, March 2, 1958.

13. "Soviet Victory over U.S. Basketball Team at Santiago."

14. Dudziak, *Cold War Civil Rights,* 60.

15. Belmonte, "Defending a Way of Life," 287, 301; Davenport, *Jazz Diplomacy,* 61; Robert Bendiner, "The Diplomacy of Culture," *Show,* April 1962, in Bureau of Educational and Cultural Affairs Historical Collection (CU), Box 48, Folder 15; "Annual Report on Education Exchange Program," American Embassy, Leopoldville, November 25, 1961, CU, Box 316, Folder 28.

16. Bendiner, "The Diplomacy of Culture," 51–53.

17. "Report on Visit to Lagos of Dr. Max Yergan," American Consulate, Lagos, Nigeria, July 30, 1952, NA, 811.411/7-3952; Dudziak, *Cold War Civil Rights,* 56; Anderson, *Eyes Off the Prize,* 163.

18. "Report on Visit to Lagos of Dr. Max Yergan"; Dudziak, *Cold War Civil Rights,* 56.

19. Dudziak, *Cold War Civil Rights,* 58–59.

20. "Visit of Leader Grantee Mr. Carl T. Rowan," American Consulate, Calcutta, August 16, 1954, NA, 511.913/8-1654; "Ryoulla YMCA, Bombay, Plays Host to Visiting American Journalist, Carl Rowan, with R. K. Karanjia, Editor of *Blitz,* in the Chair," USIS in Bombay, September 8, 1954, NA, 511.913/9-854; "American Leader Specialist—Mr. Carl T. Rowan," American Consulate, Madras, India, September 30, 1954, NA, 511.913/9-3054.

21. "Annual Report on the Educational and Cultural Exchange Program for the Period July 1964–June 1965," American Embassy, Algiers, August 5, 1965, CU, Box 316, Folder 3; "Educational and Cultural Exchange: American Specialist Lecturer Dr. Raleigh Morgan," American Embassy, Fort Lamy, July 22, 1964, NA, 811.412/7-5013.

22. Dudziak, *Cold War Civil Rights,* 104–5; "United States Policy toward Africa South of the Sahara—Comments on Department's Study Paper," American Consul General in Leopoldville, December 28, 1955, NA, 611.70/12-2855.

23. "Why a People-to-People Sports Committee?," Central Files, People-to-People, Box 933, Folder 325 "People-to-People"; *New York Times,* December 15, 1951; J. R. Newson to Earl Newson, "International Sports," C. D. Jackson Papers, Box 62, Folder "International Sports," DDEL; Belmonte, "Defending a Way of Life," 148; Clumpner, "American Federal Government Involvement in Sport," 316–17.

24. Domer, "Sports and Cold War America," 20, 4.

25. Dyreson, *Making the American Team,* 32–33, 51, 71.

26. Pope, *Sporting Traditions,* 46–48; Dyreson, *Making the American Team,* 136.

27. Osgood, "Total Cold War," 22–24; Vaughn, *Failure of American and British Propaganda,* 115.

28. "International Athletics: Cold War Battleground," Jackson Papers, Box 62, Folder "International Sports," DDEL; Arthur Daley, "Sports of the Times: Seeing Red," *New York Times,* February 3, 1959.

29. "The Campaign of Truth," CU, Box 303, Folder 36; Peppard and Riordan, *Playing Politics,* 68, 72; Domer, "Sports and Cold War America," 22.

30. Peppard and Riordan, *Playing Politics,* 107–8; Riordan, "Role of Sport."

31. Riordan, "Role of Sport," 581–82; Peppard and Riordan, *Playing Politics,* 107–12.

32. John T. McGovern, "We'll Lose the Next Olympics," Brundage Papers, Box 277, Folder "Russia Amateurism Controversy, 1945–1959"; "Russian Athletes Getting Tough," Brundage Papers, Box 245, Folder "What I Saw during 3 Weeks behind the Iron Curtain"; Domer, "Sports and Cold War America," 162, 164; Kennedy, "The Soft American."

33. "Russian Athletes Getting Tough"; Domer, "Sports and Cold War America," 162, 164; Kennedy, "The Soft American"; "Reds Hope to Rule Sports Too: 12 Million Athletes in Training to Beat the West," *U.S. News and World Report,* August 20, 1954, 35–37.

34. "Brundage Says: Russians Take Big Sport Stride, U.S. 'Too Soft,'" Brundage Papers, Box 245, Folder "What I Saw during 3 Weeks behind the Iron Curtain"; Avery Brundage, "I Must Admit—Russian Athletes Are Great!"; Canham, "Russia Will Win the 1956 Olympics."

35. "What I Saw during Three Weeks behind the Iron Curtain," speech by Avery Brundage in Brundage Papers, Box 245, Folder "What I Saw during 3 Weeks behind the Iron Curtain."

36. Ibid.

37. Harry Schwartz, "Stalin Trains His Olympic Teams," Brundage Papers, Box 277, Folder "Russia Amateurism Controversy, 1945–1959"; "I Must Admit—Russian Athletes Are Great!"; John J. Karch, "How the Soviet Union Exploits Sports"; Avery Brundage, "Reports Ruthless Extermination of Kremlin Foes—Few Old People," address, Brundage Papers, Box 245, Folder "Commonwealth Club of California."

38. McGovern, "We'll Lose the Next Olympics," 7, 16; "Brundage Says Russ[ia] Observe[s] All Edicts of Amateurism," in Brundage Papers, Box 245, Folder "Avery Brundage Book—Russia Sports—1954"; "I Must Admit—Russian Athletes Are Great!"

39. "Brundage Says Russ[ia] Observe[s] All Edicts of Amateurism."

40. "International Athletics: Cold War Battleground," Jackson Papers, Box 62, Folder "International Sports," DDEL.

41. Abbott Washburn to C. D. Jackson, January 11, 1955, Jackson Papers, Box 62, Folder "International Sports," DDEL.

42. Domer, "Sports and Cold War America," 159.

43. "International Athletics—Cold War Battleground."

44. "U.S. Acts to Expose Red 'Colonialism,'" New York Times, August 30, 1954.

45. Domer, "Sports and Cold War America," 140–41.

46. Ibid., 142.

47. Ibid., 117–18; Osgood, "Total Cold War," 191.

48. Domer, "Sports and Cold War America," 56.

49. "U.S. Cultural Presentations: A World of Promise," CU, Box 47, Folder 15; "Cultural Presentations: Objectives and Issues," CU, Box 47, Folder 8.

50. "USIS Libya Country Plan for Fiscal Year 1961," USIS in Tripoli, June 30, 1960, NA, 611.72/9-0543.

51. Bendiner, "The Diplomacy of Culture," 56; Hawthorn, Propaganda, Persuasion, and Polemic, vii–ix, 4; "USIA Basic Guidance Paper."

52. "A Study of the Impact of Sports on the Achievement of U.S. Foreign Policy Objectives," CU, Box 89, Folder 17.

53. "Basketball Tour to Africa," October 2–November 26, 1963, CU, Box 89, Folder 21; "U.S. Track Team in Hungary," American Embassy, Budapest, August 8, 1958, NA, 032 Amateur Athletic Union/8-858; "Report of the Interagency Committee on International Athletics to the President and the Secretary of State," April 1965, NA, Edx 32; "Racist Articles in the Local Newssheets," American Embassy, Lomé, Togo, July 5, 1961, NA, 811.411/7-561.

54. "Africa: The President's Committee on Information Activities Abroad," July 11, 1960, DDEL, Sprague Committee, Box 4.

55. Domer, "Sports and Cold War America," 18; Lipsky, How We Play the Game, 43.

56. Domer, "Sports and Cold War America," 268.

57. "Report of the Interagency Committee on International Athletics to the President and the Secretary of State," NA, appendix, D3.

58. Ibid.; "U.S. Specialists Program Memo," NA, 511.203/2-154.

59. "U.S. Specialist Program: American Track Coaches William J. Bowerman and Jack Mashin," NA, 511.90D3/2-1056.

60. Professor Robert Singer, "Multidisciplinary Symposium on Sport," CU, Box 88, Folder 23; "Successful Results of American Competition in International Badminton Championship Match," NA, 897.4537/6-452.

61. "Successful Results of American Competition in International Badminton Championship Match."

62. The number of tours to Africa might seem small by comparison, but it is impor-

tant to remember that colonization still existed in many parts of Africa, and most of the African nations at the beginning of 1962 had been free fewer than three full years.

63. "Report of the Interagency Committee on International Athletics to the President and the Secretary of State."

64. "New Dimension in Foreign Relations: A Report on Effectiveness of the Educational and Cultural Exchange Program," CU, Box 189, Folder 15; "Contribution of American Sports and Visiting Sportsmen to American Prestige," NA, 032 Tom Courtney; Domer, "Sports and Cold War America," 124.

65. "Report of the Interagency Committee on International Athletics to the President and the Secretary of State"; Domer, "Sports and Cold War America," 139; Alan Reich, "International Understanding and People-to-People Diplomacy through Sports," CU, Box 90, Folder 22.

66. The State Department did not have a committee or panel of sports experts to advise on athletic attractions for the program. It relied on the acknowledged national organization under whose jurisdiction a particular sport fell for advice and handling of tours for those groups. "Handbook for the Cultural Presentations Program," CU, Box 48, Folder 9; Abbott Washburn to C. D. Jackson, January 11, 1955, Jackson Papers, Box 62, Folder "International Sports," DDEL.

67. "U.S. Cultural Presentations: A World of Promise"; "Round-Table Conference on International Athletic Exchanges," CU, Box 87, Folder 16.

68. Domer, "Sports and Cold War America," 285; "Track and Field Sports Project," American Embassy, Djakarta, July 20, 1960, CU, Box 318, Folder 4; Bendiner, "The Diplomacy of Culture," 53–54.

69. "USIA Basic Guidance Paper."

70. Kertzer, *Ritual, Politics, and Power*, 96, 13; Joyce, *The Propaganda Gap*, 66–68, 78; Hawthorn, *Propaganda, Persuasion, and Polemic*, ix; Stephens, *Facts to a Candid World*, 23, 30.

71. Kertzer, *Ritual, Politics, and Power*, 99, 10; Hawthorn, *Propaganda, Persuasion, and Polemic*, ix.

72. Letter from Edward P. F. Eagan to People-to-People Sports Committee, December 25, 1957, DDEL, Central Files, People-to-People, Box 933, Folder 325 "People-to-People"; Bendiner, "The Diplomacy of Culture," 54–56; "Presentation of American Sports Equipment Abroad," American Consulate, Kuala Lumpur, July 11, 1952, NA, 897.4537/7-1152; Kertzer, *Ritual, Politics, and Power*, 1, 29, 119.

73. Hawthorn, *Propaganda, Persuasion, and Polemic*, viii; Barber, *Jihad vs. McWorld*, 66–67, 83; Edwards, *Sociology of Sport*, 166.

74. Don DeMicheal, "Jazz in Government"; "Annual Report on Educational and Cultural Exchange FY 1964," CU, Box 319, Folder 4; "American Athletes Win Friends for U.S.," *Department of State News Letter*, December 1966.

75. "Cultural Presentations: Suggestions for Further Programs," CU, Box 47, Folder 13.

76. "Sports Activities in the East Asian Programs of Educational and Cultural Exchange," CU, Box 92, Folder 7.

77. Wagnleitner, *Coca-Colonization and the Cold War*, xiii; "Main Conclusions of

U.S. Missions Abroad on U.S. Educational and Cultural Exchange Programs," date unknown in 1967, CU, Box 48, Folder 29; "Polishing U.S. Image Abroad," *Christian Science Monitor,* January 4, 1968.

78. "An American Specialist Program Directed to Youth," CU, Box 89, Folder 18.

79. "U.S. Cultural Presentations: A World of Promise."

80. Prevots, *Dance for Export,* 35.

Chapter 4. "The Good Negroes"

1. "U.S. Specialist Program," April 11, 1956, NA, 032 San Francisco Basketball Team/4-1156; Deford, "Ring Leader."

2. Russell and Branch, *Second Wind,* 79–80; Deford, "Ring Leader," 96.

3. "Visit of U.S. Specialists San Francisco Dons Basketball Team," American Embassy, Guatemala, July 26, 1956, NA, 032 San Francisco Basketball Team/7-2056.

4. "Appearance in Panama of San Francisco Dons Basketball Team," American Embassy, Panama, August 16, 1956, NA, 032 San Francisco Basketball Team/8-1656; "U.S. Specialists Program: President's Emergency Fund for San Francisco Basketball Team Project."

5. "U.S. Specialists: Report on Visit of San Francisco Dons to Asuncion [*sic*]," American Embassy, Asunción, August 28, 1956, NA, 032 San Francisco Basketball Team/8-2856.

6. "U.S. Specialist Program: Visit of the University of San Francisco 'Dons' Basketball Team," American Embassy, Caracas, July 26, 1956, NA, 032 San Francisco Basketball Team/7-2696; "U.S. Specialist Program Visit of San Francisco Basketball Team—President's Emergency Fund," USIS São Paulo, August 13, 1956, CU, Box 92, Folder 14; "Visit of the San Francisco 'Dons' to Guayaquil," USIS Guayaquil, August 22, 1956, NA, 032 San Francisco "Dons"/8-2256; "U.S. Specialists Program: President's Emergency Fund for San Francisco Basketball Team Project," American Embassy, San Salvador, June 25, 1956, 032 San Francisco Basketball Team/6-2556."

7. M. Whitfield, *Beyond the Finish Line,* viii.

8. "American Specialist Program: Report on Mal Whitfield's Visit to East Africa," American Consulate, Nairobi, January 30, 1958, NA, 032 Whitfield, Mal/1-3058; Fimrite, "Call to Arms"; "American Specialist Program—Mal Whitfield," March 1, 1957, NA, 032 Whitfield, Mal/3-157; "Visit of Mal Whitfield to Liberia and Sierra Leone," American Embassy, Monrovia, October 4, 1957, NA, 032 Whitfield, Mal/10-457.

9. "U.S. Specialists Program—Mal Whitfield," American Embassy, Karachi, January 5, 1955, NA, 511.90D3/1-555; "U.S. Specialist Program," American Embassy, Rangoon, January 14, 1955, CU, Box 93, Folder 8.

10. Riley, *Presidency and Politics of Racial Inequality,* 180–82; Borstelmann, *Cold War and Color Line,* 89, 93; Burk, *Eisenhower Administration and Black Civil Rights,* 93; Rowley, *Richard Wright,* 440.

11. Hamilton, *Adam Clayton Powell Jr.,* 210; Burk, *Eisenhower Administration and Black Civil Rights,* 192; Borstelmann, *Cold War and Color Line,* 86–87, 90–92; Singh, *Black Is a Country,* 168; Anderson, *Eyes Off the Prize,* 211, 227, 230; Gardner, *Harry Truman and Civil Rights,* 74.

12. Borstelmann, *Cold War and Color Line,* 97.

13. Rowley, *Richard Wright,* 440; "Local Reaction to Decision of the United States Supreme Court Outlawing Segregation in Schools," American Consulate, Dakar, May 26, 1954, NA, 811.411/5-2654; Borstelmann, *Cold War and Color Line,* 93; Gerstle, *American Crucible,* 250.

14. "Local Reaction to Decision of the United States Supreme Court Outlawing Segregation in Schools"; Dudziak, *Cold War Civil Rights,* 106.

15. M. Whitfield, *Beyond the Finish Line,* 24.

16. "U.S. Specialist Program—Mal Whitfield," American Embassy, Accra, October 29, 1954, CU, Box 93, Folder 8; "Report on the Visit of Mal Whitfield to Kenya on the 18th of January, 1955," American Embassy, Nairobi, undated, CU, Box 93, Folder 8.

17. Although it was customary for the New York Athletic Club to give memberships to medalists in the Olympic track and field events, Whitfield was repeatedly denied membership. "U.S. Specialist Program—Mal Whitfield," American Embassy, Accra, October 29, 1954, CU, Box 93, Folder 8; "Report on the Visit of Mal Whitfield to Kenya on the 18th of January, 1955"; "Visit of Mal Whitfield," American Embassy, Athens, January 2, 1955, CU, Box 93, Folder 8; M. Whitfield, *Beyond the Finish Line,* 47.

18. "U.S. Specialists' Program—Mr. Mal Whitfield," USIS Belgrade, January 18, 1955, CU, Box 93, Folder 8.

19. "Visit of Mal Whitfield," American Embassy, Athens, January 2, 1955, CU, Box 93, Folder 8; "Visit of U.S. Specialist—Mal Whitfield," USIS Dacca, January 13, 1955, NA, 511.003/1-1355.

20. Burk, *Eisenhower Administration and Black Civil Rights,* 23–24.

21. Krenn, *Black Diplomacy,* 93–94; Burk, *Eisenhower Administration and Black Civil Rights,* 16, 44.

22. The public service of E. Frederic Morrow exemplifies how the administration, publicly committed to racial equality, did not place its African American members in positions to make sound policy recommendations. Morrow had impressive credentials before he became a member of the Eisenhower administration: a degree from Bowdoin College, experience as a Works Progress Administration social worker, employment as a branch coordinator for the NAACP, and a law degree from Rutgers University. After receiving an appointment in the White House near the end of Eisenhower's first term, Morrow's duties—arranging for security, securing office space for special projects, and allotting parking spaces—clearly did not match his qualifications. In addition to serving as "window dressing," Murrow's most important task was defending the Eisenhower administration's record before black audiences: he gave more than three hundred speeches before largely hostile crowds. Initially, Morrow had conceived of his presence in the White House as an important advancement for African Americans. However, by the end of the Eisenhower presidency, with its lack of commitment to racial justice, Morrow was led to wonder whether his appointment had been used by the administration to try to pacify African Americans and the international community. Burk, *Eisenhower Administration and Black Civil Rights,* 69–70, 79, 83; Borstelmann, *Cold War and Color Line,* 88–89.

23. Kimche, *Afro-Asian Movement,* 1; Lauren, *Power and Prejudice,* 220; Von Eschen, *Race against Empire,* 3, 5.

24. Hamilton, *Adam Clayton Powell Jr.,* 187, 238–39; letter from Nelson A. Rockefeller to Sherman Adams, April 6, 1955, DDEL, White House Central Files.

25. Rockefeller to Sherman Adams, April 6, 1955 (emphasis added).

26. Ibid.

27. LaFeber, *Michael Jordan,* 140; Borstelmann, *Cold War and Color Line,* 40–41, 112, 178; Kimche, *Afro-Asian Movement,* 23.

28. Ibid.

29. Letter from William Gowen to C. D. Jackson, August 19, 1955, DDEL, Jackson Papers, Box 56, William Gowen (2); Hamilton, *Adam Clayton Powell Jr.,* 239–45; Singh, *Black Is a Country,* 178.

30. "American Specialist Program—Mal Whitfield," March 1, 1957, NA, 032 Whitfield, Mal/3-157; "Visit of American Specialist, Mal Whitfield," American Embassy, Tripoli, July 27, 1957, NA, 032 Whitfield, Mal/7-2757; "Visit of Mal Whitfield to Liberia and Sierra Leone," American Embassy, Monrovia, October 4, 1957, NA, 032 Whitfield, Mal/10-457.

31. "Visit of American Specialist, Mal Whitfield," American Embassy, Tripoli.

32. "US Specialist Mal Whitfield's Program in Uganda," USIS Kampala, October 9, 1957, NA, 032 Whitfield, Mal/2-1342.

33. "American Specialist Program—Report on Mal Whitfield's Visit to East Africa," American Consulate, Nairobi, January 30, 1958, 032 Whitfield, Mal/1-3058; "American Specialist Program—Report on Mal Whitfield's Visit to East Africa," American Consulate, Nairobi, October 29, 1957, NA, 032 Whitfield, Mal/10-2957.

34. Review of *The Best That I Can Be,* by Rafer Johnson, *Booklist,* July 1998; Wes Lukowsky, "*The Best That I Can Be* Book Review," *Booklist,* July 1998, 1826; Ned Cronin, "Cronin's Corner," *Los Angeles Times,* April 24, 1958; Frank Waldman, "Frankly Speaking: Rafer," *Christian Science Monitor,* August 30, 1958.

35. Paul Zimmerman, "Rafer to Carry U.S. Colors in Olympic March," *Los Angeles Times,* August 23, 1960; "Choice of Rafer Hailed by U.S. Teammates," *Christian Science Monitor,* August 25, 1960.

36. Burk, *Eisenhower Administration and Black Civil Rights,* 176; Sitkoff, *Struggle for Black Equality,* 29–31.

37. Ibid.; Branch, *Parting the Waters,* 223.

38. Burk, *Eisenhower Administration and Black Civil Rights,* 184–85.

39. Ibid., 174–76; Sitkoff, *Struggle for Black Equality,* 32; Krenn, *Black Diplomacy,* 88; Riley, *Presidency and Politics of Racial Inequality,* 196; Borstelmann, *Cold War and Color Line,* 104; Dudziak, *Cold War Civil Rights,* 121.

40. Memo from Bern to Secretary of State, September 12, 1957, NA, 811.411/9-1257; "World Reaction to US Racial Integration Incidents," September 12, 1957, DDEL, Ann Whitman File, Dwight D. Eisenhower (DDE) Diary Series, Box 27, Sept. 1957 Toner Notes; "Telephone Call to Attorney General Brownell," September 24, 1957, DDEL, John Foster Dulles Papers, Telephone Calls Series, Box 7, Memo Tel. Conv.—Gen., Sept. 2, 1957 to Oct. 31, 1957 (3); "Overcoming Adverse Reaction to the Little Rock Incident," October 10, 1957, NA, 811.411/10-1057.

41. "American Specialists Program—Rafer Johnson," American Consul General,

Leopoldville, March 27, 1958, NA 032 Johnson, Rafer/3-2753; "Rafer Johnson Visit," American Embassy, Colombo, September 26, 1957, 032 Johnson, Rafer/9-2657.

42. Johnson, *Best That I Can Be,* 131, 180, 188–89, 261; Bill Becker, "Rafer Johnson: A Goodwill Ambassador," *New York Times,* May 3, 1964.

43. Office of Research and Intelligence, United States Information Agency, "Post–Little Rock Opinion on the Treatment of Negroes in the U.S.," January 1958, DDEL, Central Files, Subject Series, Box 99, USIA (2); Office of Research and Intelligence, United States Information Agency, "Public Reactions to Little Rock in Major World Capitals," October 29, 1957, DDEL, Central Files, Subject Series, Box 99, USIA (1); "Editorial Reaction on Desegregation," American Embassy, Djakarta, October 7, 1957, NA, 811.411/10-757; Krenn, *Black Diplomacy,* 77–78; Borstelmann, *Cold War and Color Line,* 103.

44. "Local Reaction to Racial Disturbances in the United States," American Consulate, Paramaribo, September 18, 1957, NA, 811.411/9-1857; "Little Rock, Arkansas," American Consulate, Amsterdam, September 16, 1957, NA, 811.411/9-1657; "Canadian Editorial Comment on Racial Tensions in the United States," American Embassy, Ottawa, November 6, 1957, NA, 811.411/11-657.

45. Borstelmann, *Cold War and Color Line,* 107; letter from Marta Castillon Giffard to General Eisenhower, September 16, 1957, NA, 811.411/10-957.

46. "Overcoming Adverse Reaction to the Little Rock Incident."

47. Krenn, *Black Diplomacy,* 104, 110; "Post–Little Rock Opinion on the Treatment of Negroes in the U.S."

48. "Rafer Johnson Visit," American Embassy, Colombo; Klein, *Cold War Orientalism,* 139.

49. Layton, *International Politics,* 95; "Treatment of Minorities in the United States—Impact on Our Foreign Relations," NA, 811.411/12-458 (emphasis added).

50. Layton, *International Politics,* 95; "Treatment of Minorities in the United States."

51. Remnick, *King of the World,* 103–4, xi–xiii.

52. Hartmann, "'Golden Ghettos,'" 2, 9–10.

53. Matusow, *Unraveling of America,* 20; Hamilton, *Adam Clayton Powell Jr.,* 50; Van Deburg, *Black Camelot,* 13–15.

54. Matusow, *Unraveling of America,* 63; Pauley, *Modern Presidency and Civil Rights,* 105; Borstelmann, *Cold War and Color Line,* 140.

55. Borstelmann, *Cold War and Color Line,* 158; "Racial Strife: The Overseas Impact," address by Donald M. Wilson, deputy director, USIA, June 10, 1963, NA, RG 306; Krenn, *Black Diplomacy,* 135; Dudziak, *Cold War Civil Rights,* 175.

56. Borstelmann, *Cold War and Color Line,* 158; "Racial Strife"; Krenn, *Black Diplomacy,* 135; Dudziak, *Cold War Civil Rights,* 175.

57. Sitkoff, *Struggle for Black Equality,* 129–30; Matusow, *Unraveling of America,* 86; Fairclough, *Better Day Coming,* 274.

58. Matusow, *Unraveling of America,* 87; Pauley, *Modern Presidency and Civil Rights,* 124; Dudziak, *Cold War Civil Rights,* 187.

59. Pauley, *Modern Presidency and Civil Rights,* 124; Dudziak, *Cold War Civil Rights,* 187; letter from G. Mennen Williams to the Secretary of State, undated, NA; Borstelmann, *Cold War and Color Line,* 160–62.

60. "Civil Rights—for Our Own Sake," *New York Times,* July 12, 1963; "Rusk Declares Race Issue Hits U.S. Overseas," *Washington Post,* May 28, 1963.

61. "Racial Strife."

62. Ibid.

63. Gerstle, *American Crucible,* 280; Riley, *Presidency and Politics of Racial Inequality,* 220–21; Pauley, *Modern Presidency and Civil Rights,* 108; Borstelmann, *Cold War and Color Line,* 160–61.

64. "Memo for the President on Civil Rights."

65. As originally conceived by the 1948 Smith-Mundt Act, cultural presentations were employed as a strategy in the East-West ideological competition and as an answer to questions about American values and lifestyles. However, the 1961 Fulbright-Hays Act signaled a shift in emphasis. Thereafter, the program stressed cultural presentations' role in enhancing mutual understanding and strengthening communications ties between the United States and other nations. The State Department's new emphasis claimed that sports competitions and exhibitions were important because they "demonstrate the cultural interests, developments and achievements of the people of the United States and the (U.S.) contributions . . . made toward . . . a more fruitful life . . . and to promote international cooperation for . . . cultural advancement." Mark Lewis, "Remarks Prepared for Meeting of U.S. Advisory Commission on Education and Cultural Affairs," CU, Box 47, Folder 15; Domer, "Sports and Cold War America," 260; Cobbs, "Decolonization," 86.

66. The archives of the Interagency Committee on International Athletics are currently unavailable.

67. "Report of the Interagency Committee on International Athletics to the President and the Secretary of State," NA, appendix, D2.

68. Latham, *Modernization as Ideology,* 109–10, 119–20.

69. Ibid., 110, 117–20; Cobbs, "Decolonization," 80–81.

70. Domer, "Sports and Cold War America," 283–86; Clumpner, "American Federal Government Involvement in Sport," 342–44.

71. Zimmerman, "Beyond Double Consciousness," 1000, 1004–5, 1010–11; Cobbs, "Decolonization," 86–88.

72. Zimmerman, "Beyond Double Consciousness," 1004–10; Latham, *Modernization as Ideology,* 110–13; Cobbs, "Decolonization," 87–88.

73. Riley, *Presidency and Politics of Racial Inequality,* 220–24; Fairclough, *Better Day Coming,* 282–83.

Chapter 5. Black Power

1. M. Whitfield, "'Let's Boycott the Olympics.'"

2. Ibid., 96–97.

3. Edwards, *Revolt of the Black Athlete,* 41–42.

4. Edwards, *Struggle That Must Be,* 174; Edwards, *Revolt of the Black Athlete,* 49.

5. Lomax, "Bedazzle Them with Brilliance," 55–65.

6. Bass, "Flag on the Field," 123, 290; Van Deburg, *Black Camelot,* 31; Plummer, *Rising Wind,* 218.

7. Edwards, *Struggle That Must Be*, 217–21; Hartmann, "'Golden Ghettos,'" 251.

8. Edwards, *Struggle That Must Be*, 241; Edwards, *Revolt of the Black Athlete*, 34; Bass, "Flag on the Field," 44; Hartmann, "'Golden Ghettos,'" 171.

9. Maureen Smith, "Identity and Citizenship," 1; Hartmann, "'Golden Ghettos,'" 135–37; Edwards, "Why Negroes Should Boycott Whitey's Olympics"; Van Deburg, *Black Camelot*, 66.

10. Scott, *The Athletic Revolution*, 63–66.

11. Along with other African American collegiate All-Americans Elvin Hayes, Neal Walk, Bob Lanier, Wes Unseld, Larry Miller, and Don May, Jabbar's withdrawal from the Olympic basketball trials caused an uproar. At an appearance on *Today* shortly after he announced his decision not to attend the 1968 Games, Jabbar told Joe Garagiola that the United States was "not really my country." Responding to the resentment and bewilderment that his comment unleashed, he tried to explain his stance: "What I was trying to get across was that until things are in an equitable basis this is not my country. We have been a racist nation with first-class citizens and my decision not to go to the Olympics is my way of getting the message across." A myriad of events had caused Jabbar to withdraw from white America: the bombing of an African American church in Birmingham resulting in the death of four little girls had a chilling effect on him, the "Whites Only" signs that he saw on a trip to North Carolina were difficult for him to handle, the white media's preoccupation with property damage rather than racial injustice during the Harlem riots in 1964 bothered him, and the publication of Malcolm X's autobiography helped shape his view of race relations and his role as an African American athlete. Frustrated with "the silly, routine questions" reporters asked him, Jabbar developed a reputation as being ill-mannered and inconsiderate because he wanted to talk about racism and injustice instead of basketball strategy and defensive rebounding. Edwards, *Struggle That Must Be*, 177–80; *Santa Barbara News-Press*, November 24, 1967; Edwards, *Revolt of the Black Athlete*, 52–53; Bass, "Flag on the Field," 256; Jabbar, *Giant Steps*, 46, 60–63, 72, 157.

12. Van Deburg, *Black Camelot*, 87; "Negro Group in Boycott," *San Jose Mercury News*, November 23, 1968; Bass, "Flag on the Field," 137.

13. Carmichael and Hamilton, *Black Power*, viii–ix; Carmichael, "Power and Racism," 63–64.

14. Van Deburg, *Black Camelot*, 9; Weisbrot, *Freedom Bound*, 173–75; Wright, "Crisis Which Bred Black Power," 119; Gerstle, *American Crucible*, 298.

15. Dudziak, *Cold War Civil Rights*, 57.

16. Carmichael and Hamilton, *Black Power*, 5, 77–78, 51; Carmichael, "Power and Racism," 64.

17. *Los Angeles Times*, November 25, 1967; Charles Maher, "Boycott Would Bring More Grief than Good," Brundage Papers, Scrapbook 91.

18. *Chicago Tribune*, November 29, 1967.

19. Weisbrot, *Freedom Bound*, xiii; Hartmann, "'Golden Ghettos,'" 73.

20. Arrow, *Bearing the Cross*, 439–40; Weisbrot, *Freedom Bound*, 189; "What Must Be Done," 39.

21. Hamilton, "Riots, Revolt, and Relevant Response," 204.

22. Van Deburg, *Black Camelot*, 18–19.

23. Ibid., 22–23.

24. Horne, *Fire This Time,* 186.

25. Edwards, *Struggle That Must Be,* 168–69; Bass, *Not the Triumph but the Struggle,* 228–29; Southern, *Gunnar Myrdal and Black-White Relations,* 262.

26. *Track and Field News,* December 1967; Rodgers, "Step to an Olympic Boycott."

27. Rodgers, "Step to an Olympic Boycott"; *Chicago Tribune,* July 4, 1968.

28. Edwards, *Revolt of the Black Athlete,* 58–59.

29. Remnick, *King of the World,* 103–4, xi–xiii; Zirin, *What's My Name, Fool?,* 63.

30. Remnick, *King of the World,* 207.

31. Sammons, *Beyond the Ring,* 195–96.

32. Remnick, *King of the World,* 285–88; Frank Litsky, "Negro Olympic Boycott Group Demands Brundage Resign," *New York Times,* December 15, 1967.

33. *Chicago American,* November 25, 1967; Red Smith, "The Art of Thinking," Brundage Papers, Scrapbook 91; Frank Litsky, "Negro Olympic Boycott Group Demands Brundage Resign," *New York Times,* December 15, 1967.

34. Remnick, *King of the World,* 289–90.

35. Maureen Smith, "Identity and Citizenship," 156–57.

36. Gray, "Prelude to the Protest," 77–78; Hartmann, "'Golden Ghettos,'" 107.

37. "Should Negroes Boycott the Olympics?"; Edwards, *Revolt of the Black Athlete,* 55–56; Hartmann, "'Golden Ghettos,'" 123.

38. Hartmann, "'Golden Ghettos,'" 117, 120, 146; Edwards, *Revolt of the Black Athlete,* 183–92.

39. "Negro Ex-Olympians Rap Proposed Boycott," *Los Angeles Daily News,* November 25, 1967; *Santa Barbara News-Press,* November 30, 1967; "Olympic Boycott?," 59; *Chicago Defender,* May 18, 1968.

40. Edwards, *Struggle That Must Be,* 181–83; Baker, *Jesse Owens,* 168, 174; Moore, "Courageous Stand," 60.

41. Baker, *Jesse Owens,* 207–9; "Games Boycott Condemned by Mal Whitfield," Brundage Papers, Scrapbook 91.

42. Edwards, *Struggle That Must Be,* 181.

43. Baker, *Jesse Owens,* 141–43; *Los Angeles Sentinel,* October 17, 1968; Van Deburg, *Black Camelot,* 99.

44. Hano, "Black Rebel," 32; Bass, *Not the Triumph but the Struggle,* 265.

45. Cleaver, *Soul on Ice,* 84–85; Edwards, "Why Negroes Should Boycott Whitey's Olympics."

46. Gray, "Prelude to the Protest," 69.

47. Edwards, *Struggle That Must Be,* 217.

48. Maureen Smith, "Identity and Citizenship," 84; Edwards, *Black Students,* 48.

49. Bass, *Not the Triumph but the Struggle,* 196–97.

50. Clarke, *Malcolm X,* 318; Malcolm X, *Autobiography of Malcolm X,* 399.

51. Clarke, *Malcolm X,* 253, 289–92.

52. Malcolm X, *Autobiography of Malcolm X,* 394–419.

53. *Los Angeles Times,* November 24, 1967; Rodgers, "Step to an Olympic Boycott"; Edwards, *Struggle That Must Be,* 189 (emphasis in the original); Bass, *Not the Triumph but the Struggle,* 236.

54. Edwards, *Revolt of the Black Athlete,* 115–16.

55. "American Specialist Program—Report on Joe Yancey's Visit to Lima," American Consulate, Lima, January 23, 1966, NA, Yancey, Joe/1-3058.

56. Edwards, *Struggle That Must Be,* 242; Edwards, *Revolt of the Black Athlete,* appendix E, 190; Bass, "Flag on the Field," 277.

57. Bass, "Flag on the Field," 378.

58. Edwards, *Revolt of the Black Athlete,* 65.

59. Edwards, *Struggle That Must Be,* 184–85; Bass, "Flag on the Field," 207–12.

60. Hoffer, *Something in the Air,* 59–60; Bose, *Sporting Colours,* 66.

61. Hartmann, "'Golden Ghettos,'" 107–8; Witherspoon, *Before the Eyes of the World,* 65–70; Bose, *Sporting Colours,* 75.

62. "The Angry Black Athlete"; *Chicago Tribune,* July 1, 1968.

63. Gray, "Prelude to the Protest," 114; Edwards, *Struggle That Must Be,* 195; Maureen Smith, "Identity and Citizenship," 229.

64. Edwards, *Struggle That Must Be,* 195–96.

65. *Chicago Tribune,* July 2, 1968; *Santa Barbara News-Press,* August 1, 1968.

66. Bass, "Flag on the Field," 319; Edwards, *Revolt of the Black Athlete,* 103; Gray, "Prelude to the Protest," 123; "Amid Gold Medals, Raised Black Fists," 64.

67. Bass, "Flag on the Field," 321.

68. Baker, *Jesse Owens,* 211; Bass, "Flag on the Field," 323–24.

69. Bass, "Flag on the Field," 324–25.

70. Jim Murray, "Excuse My Glove," *Los Angeles Times,* October 18, 1968; John Hall, "It Takes All Kinds," *Los Angeles Times,* October 18, 1968; Brent Musburger, "Bizarre Protest by Smith, Carlos Tarnishes Medals," *Chicago American,* October 17, 1968.

71. Baker, *Jesse Owens,* 212–13.

72. Bass, "Flag on the Field," 345–47.

73. *Chicago American,* September 24, 1968; *Chicago Daily News,* September 25, 1968; *Chicago Tribune,* September 25, 1968; "The Olympics"; "The Olympics' Extra Heat."

74. "Amid Gold Medals, Raised Black Fists," 18, 67; Bass, "Flag on the Field," 385–86.

75. *Chicago Daily News,* October 19, 1968; Red Smith, "The Black Berets," in *The Red Smith Reader,* 38–39; Moore, "Eye of the Storm"; Charles Maher, "U.S. Duo Banned," *Los Angeles Times,* October 19, 1968; Bass, "Flag on the Field," 350–51.

76. Bass, "Flag on the Field," 359–61; *Chicago Daily News,* October 19, 1968.

77. Edwards, *Revolt of the Black Athlete,* 105.

78. Lipsyte, *Sportsworld: An American Dreamland,* 137–39.

79. Edwards, *Struggle That Must Be,* 203–4.

80. Maureen Smith, "Identity and Citizenship," 255.

81. Edwards, *Revolt of the Black Athlete,* 100–103.

82. Garrow, *Bearing the Cross,* 387–88; Branch, *Parting the Waters,* 561–62; Weisbrot, *Freedom Bound,* 137–38.

83. *Public Papers of the Presidents of the United States: Lyndon B. Johnson, 1964,* 281–85.

84. "World Press Reaction to Selma," RG 306, Research "R" Reports of the Office of Research, 1964–82, Box 7, NA.

85. Dudziak, *Cold War Civil Rights,* 241, 232–34; "World Press Reaction to Selma."

86. Cairo to Department of State, July 18, 1964, RG 59, Central Foreign Policy Files, 1964–66, SOC 14-1 US, NA; Dudziak, *Cold War Civil Rights,* 236–38.

87. "Racial Issues in the U.S.: Some Policy and Program Indications of Research," Special "S" Reports, 1953–1983, RG 306, Box 22, NA.

88. Ibid.

89. Ibid.

90. Mark Lewis, "Remarks Prepared for Meeting of U.S. Advisory Commission on Educational and Cultural Affairs," CU, Box 47, Folder 15; Memo to Music Panel, CU, Box 47, Folder 14; John W. Finney, "Budget Cuts Bar Arts Trips Abroad," *New York Times,* December 28, 1966; "Handbook for the Cultural Presentations Program," CU, Box 48, Folder 9, 12; "Exchanges in Sports," CU, Box 91, Folder 25; "Exchanges in Sports," CU, Box 91, Folder 25; "Minutes from the Advisory for International Athletics Meeting," CU, Box 87, Folder 17; "Main Conclusions of U.S. Missions Abroad on U.S. Educational and Cultural Exchange Programs," CU, Box 48, Folder 29.

91. Bass, *Not the Triumph but the Struggle,* 287.

Epilogue

1. Riordan, "Role of Sport in Soviet Foreign Policy"; Clumpner, "American Federal Government Involvement in Sport," 316, 335–40.

2. Xia, "China's Elite Politics," 10–17.

3. Goldberg, "Sporting Diplomacy," 65–67; Xia, "China's Elite Politics," 12–15.

4. Wenn and Wenn, "Muhammad Ali," 44–66.

5. Slater, "Muhammad Ali"; Wenn and Wenn, "Muhammad Ali," 45–56.

6. Chalip, *National Sports Policies,* 408–10, 425–27; T. Hunt, "Countering the Soviet Threat," 801–7.

7. Thomas, "Quiet Militant."

8. Chalip, *National Sports Policies,* 427.

Bibliography

Abe Saperstein's Fabulous Harlem Globetrotters Official Souvenir Program, 26th Season, 1952–53. Chicago: Harlem Globetrotters, 1952.

Acham, Christine. *Revolution Televised: Prime Time and the Struggle for Black Power*. Minneapolis: University of Minnesota Press, 2005.

Anderson, Carol. *Eyes Off the Prize: The United Nations and the African American Struggle for Human Rights, 1944–1955*. New York: Cambridge University Press, 2004.

Appy, Christian G., ed. *Cold War Constructions: The Political Culture of United States Imperialism, 1945–1966*. Amherst: University of Massachusetts Press, 2000.

Arrow, David J. *Bearing the Cross: Martin Luther King, Jr., and the Southern Christian Leadership Conference*. New York: Quill, 1986.

Baker, William. *Jesse Owens: An American Life*. New York: Free Press, 1988.

Balaji, Murali. *The Professor and the Pupil: The Politics of W. E. B. Du Bois and Paul Robeson*. New York: Nation Books, 2007.

Barber, Benjamin. *Jihad vs. McWorld*. New York: Ballantine Books, 1996.

Bass, Amy. "Flag on the Field: The Popular Construction of the Black Athlete." Ph.D. diss., State University of New York at Stony Brook, 1999.

———. *Not the Triumph but the Struggle: 1968 Olympics and the Making of the Black Athlete*. Minneapolis: University of Minnesota Press, 2003.

Beeching, Barbara J. "Paul Robeson and the Black Press: The 1950 Passport Controversy." *Journal of African American History* 87 (Summer 2002): 339–54.

Belmonte, Laura A. "Defending a Way of Life: American Propaganda and the Cold War, 1945–1959." Ph.D. diss., University of Virginia, 1996.

———. *Selling the American Way: U.S. Propaganda and the Cold War*. Philadelphia: University of Pennsylvania Press, 2010.

Biondi, Martha. *To Stand and Fight: The Struggle for Civil Rights in Postwar New York City*. Cambridge, Mass.: Harvard University Press, 2003.

Bogle, Donald. *Toms, Coons, Mulattoes, Mammies, and Bucks: An Interpretive History of Blacks in American Films*. New York: Bantam Books, 1974.

Borstelmann, Thomas. *Apartheid's Reluctant Uncle: The United States and Southern Africa in the Early Cold War*. New York: Oxford University Press, 1993.

———. *The Cold War and the Color Line: American Race Relations in the Global Arena*. Cambridge, Mass.: Harvard University Press, 2001.

Bose, Mihir. *Sporting Colours: Sport and Politics in South Africa*. London: Robson Books, 1994.

Boskin, Joseph. *Sambo: The Rise and Demise of an American Jester*. New York: Oxford University Press, 1986.

Boyer, Paul. *By the Bomb's Early Light: American Thought and Culture at the Dawn of the Atomic Age*. Chapel Hill: University of North Carolina Press, 1994.

Branch, Taylor. *Parting the Waters: America in the King Years, 1954–1963*. New York: Touchstone Books, 1988.

Brundage, Avery. "I Must Admit—Russian Athletes Are Great!" *Saturday Evening Post*, April 30, 1955, 28–29, 111–12, 114.

Burk, Robert Fredrick. *The Eisenhower Administration and Black Civil Rights*. Knoxville: University of Tennessee Press, 1984.

Canham, Don. "Russia Will Win the 1956 Olympics." *Sports Illustrated*, October 25, 1954, 11–12, 60, 65.

Carmichael, Stokely. "Power and Racism." In *The Black Power Revolt: A Collection of Essays*, ed. Floyd Barbour. New York: Collier Books, 1968.

Carmichael, Stokely, and Charles V. Hamilton. *Black Power: The Politics of Liberation in America*. New York: Vintage Books, 1967.

Caute, David. *The Dancer Defects: The Struggle for Cultural Supremacy during the Cold War*. Oxford: Oxford University Press, 2003.

Chalip, Laurence. *National Sports Policies: An International Handbook*. New York: Greenwood Press, 1996.

Chamberlain, Wilt, and David Shaw. *Wilt: Just Like Any Other 7-Foot Black Millionaire Who Lives Next Door*. New York: Macmillan, 1973.

Christgau, John. *Tricksters in the Madhouse: Lakers vs. Globetrotters, 1948*. Lincoln: University of Nebraska Press, 2004.

Clarke, John Henrik. *Malcolm X: The Man and His Times*. New York: Africa World Press, 1991.

Cleaver, Eldridge. *Soul on Ice*. New York: Delta Books, 1968.

Clumpner, Roy A. "American Federal Government Involvement in Sport, 1888–1973." Ph.D. diss., University of Alberta, 1976.

Cobbs, Elizabeth A. "Decolonization, the Cold War, and the Policy of the Peace Corps." *Diplomatic History* 20, no. 1 (1996).

Cohane, Tim. "The Harlem Globetrotters: Basketball's Good-Will Ambassadors." *Look*, November 1, 1952.

Coleman, R. Means. *African American Viewers and the Black Situation Comedy: Situating Racial Humor*. London: Routledge Books, 2000.

Cox, Oliver. *Caste, Class, and Race: A Study in Social Dynamics*. New York: Monthly Review Press, 1959.

Crawford, Russ. *The Use of Sports to Promote the American Way of Life during the Cold War: Cultural Propaganda, 1945–1963*. Lewiston, N.Y.: Edwin Mellen Press, 2008.

Davenport, Lisa. *Jazz Diplomacy: Promoting America in the Cold War Era.* Oxford: University of Mississippi Press, 2009.

Deford, Frank. "The Ring Leader: The Greatest Team Player of All Time, Bill Russell, Was the Hub of a Celtics Dynasty That Ruled Its Sport as No Other Team Ever Has (the 20th Century)." *Sports Illustrated,* May 10, 1999, 96–97.

DeMicheal, Don. "Jazz in Government." *Down Beat,* January 17, 1963, 15–18.

Domer, Thomas. "Sports and Cold War America, 1953–1963: The Diplomatic and Political Use of Sport in the Eisenhower and Kennedy Administrations." Ph.D. diss., Marquette University, 1976.

Dorinson, Joseph, and Joram Warmund, eds. *Jackie Robinson: Race, Sports, and the American Dream.* New York: M. E. Sharpe, 1998.

Duberman, Martin. *Paul Robeson.* New York: Ballantine Books, 1990.

Dudziak, Mary. "Birmingham, Addis Ababa, and the Image of America: International Influence on U.S. Civil Rights Policy during the Kennedy Years." In *Window on Freedom: Race, Civil Rights, and Foreign Affairs, 1945–1988,* ed. Brenda Gayle Plummer. Chapel Hill: University of North Carolina Press, 2003.

———. "Brown as a Cold War Case." *Journal of American History* 32 (June 2004): 32–42.

———. *Cold War Civil Rights: Race and the Image of American Democracy.* Princeton, N.J.: Princeton University Press, 2000.

———. "Desegregation as a Cold War Imperative." In *Race and U.S. Foreign Policy during the Cold War,* ed. Michael L. Krenn. New York: Garland Press, 1998.

———. *Exporting American Dreams: Thurgood Marshall's African Journey.* Oxford: Oxford University Press, 2008.

———. "Josephine Baker, Racial Protest, and the Cold War." In *The African American Voice in U.S. Foreign Policy since World War II,* ed. Michael L. Krenn. New York: Garland Press, 1998.

———. "The Little Rock Crisis and Foreign Affairs: Race, Resistance, and the Image of American Democracy." *Southern California Law Review* 70 (1997): 1641–1716.

Dyreson, Mark. *Making the American Team: Sport, Culture, and the Olympic Experience.* Urbana: University of Illinois Press, 1998.

Edelman, Robert. *Serious Fun: A History of Spectator Sports in the USSR.* Oxford: Oxford University Press, 1993.

Edwards, Harry. *Black Students.* New York: Free Press, 1970.

———. "The Olympic Project for Human Rights: An Assessment Ten Years Later." *Black Scholar* 10 (March 1979): 2–7.

———. *The Revolt of the Black Athlete.* New York: Free Press, 1969.

———. *Sociology of Sport.* Homewood, Ill.: Dorsey Press, 1973.

———. *The Struggle That Must Be.* New York: Macmillan, 1980.

Ely, Melvin. *The Adventures of "Amos 'n' Andy": A Social History of an American Phenomenon.* New York: Free Press, 1991.

Fairclough, Adam. *Better Day Coming: Blacks and Equality, 1890–2000.* New York: Viking, 2001.

Fimrite, Ron. "A Call to Arms: Athletes in World War II." *Sports Illustrated,* October 16, 1991, 98–103.

Fousek, John. *To Lead the Free World: American Nationalism and the Cultural Roots of the Cold War.* Chapel Hill: University of North Carolina Press, 2000.

Fraser, Cary. "Crossing the Color Line in Little Rock: The Eisenhower Administration and the Dilemma of Race for American Foreign Policy." *Diplomatic History* 24 (Spring 2000): 233–64.

Fried, Richard. *The Russians Are Coming, the Russians Are Coming: Pageantry and Patriotism in Cold War America.* Oxford: Oxford University Press, 1999.

Gaines, Kevin K. *American Africans in Ghana: Black Expatriates and the Civil Rights Era.* Chapel Hill: University of North Carolina Press, 2006.

Gardner, Michael R. *Harry Truman and Civil Rights: Moral Courage and Political Risks.* Carbondale: Southern Illinois University Press, 2002.

Garrow, David J. *Bearing the Cross: Martin Luther King Jr. and the Southern Christian Leadership Conference.* New York: W. Morrow, 1986.

Geist, Christopher D., and Angela M. S. Nelson. "From Plantation to Bel-Air: A Brief History of Black Stereotypes." In *Popular Culture: An Introductory Text,* ed. Jack Nachbar and Kevin Lause. Bowling Green, Ohio: Bowling Green University Popular Press, 1992.

George, Nelson. *Elevating the Game: The History and Aesthetics of Black Men in Basketball.* New York: Simon and Schuster, 1992.

Gerstle, Gary. *American Crucible: Race and Nation in the Twentieth Century.* Princeton, N.J.: Princeton University Press, 2001.

Gienow-Hecht, Jessica. *Transmission Impossible: Journalism as Cultural Diplomacy in Postwar Germany, 1945–1955.* Baton Rouge: Louisiana State University Press, 1999.

"Globetrotting Globetrotters: After 25 Years Famous Magicians of the Hardwood Courts Travel around the World." *Ebony,* February 1954.

Goldberg, Jeremy. "Sporting Diplomacy: Boosting the Size of the Diplomatic Corps." *Washington Quarterly* 23 (Autumn 2000): 63–70.

Gorn, Elliott J., ed. *Muhammad Ali: The People's Champ.* Urbana: University of Illinois Press, 1995.

Goudsouzian, Aram. *King of the Court: Bill Russell and the Basketball Revolution.* Berkeley and Los Angeles: University of California Press, 2011.

Gray, David. "A Prelude to the Protest at the 1968 Mexico City Olympics." M.A. thesis, San Jose State University, 1997.

Green, Ben. *Spinning the Globe: The Rise, Fall, and Return to Greatness of the Harlem Globetrotters.* New York: Amistad Press, 2005.

Guttmann, Allen. "The Cold War and the Olympics." *International Journal* 43 (Autumn 1988): 19–25.

——. *A Whole New Ball Game: An Interpretation of American Sports.* Chapel Hill: University of North Carolina Press, 1988.

Hamilton, Charles V. *Adam Clayton Powell Jr.: The Political Biography of an American Dilemma.* New York: Atheneum, 1991.

——. "Riots, Revolt, and Relevant Response." In *The Black Power Revolt: A Collection of Essays,* ed. Floyd Barbour. New York: Collier Books, 1968.

Hartmann, Douglas. "'Golden Ghettos': The Cultural Politics of Race, Sport, and Civil

Rights in the United States, 1968 and Beyond." Ph.D. diss., University of California, San Diego, 1997.

———. "The Politics of Race and Sport: Resistance and Domination in the 1968 African American Olympic Protest Movement." *Ethnic and Racial Studies* 19 (Summer 1996): 548–66.

———. *Race, Culture, and the Revolt of the Black Athlete: The 1968 Olympic Protests and Their Aftermath.* Chicago: University of Chicago Press, 2003.

Hawthorn, Jeremy, ed. *Propaganda, Persuasion, and Polemic.* London: Edward Arnold, 1987.

Henriksen, Margot A. *Dr. Strangelove's America: Society and Culture in the Atomic Age.* Berkeley and Los Angeles: University of California Press, 1997.

Herzstein, Robert E. *Henry R. Luce: A Political Portrait of the Man Who Created the American Century.* New York: Macmillan, 1994.

Hill, Christopher. *Olympic Politics: Athens to Atlanta, 1896–1996.* New York: Manchester University Press, 1996.

Hixson, Walter L. *Parting the Curtain: Propaganda, Culture, and the Cold War, 1945–1961.* New York: St. Martin's Press, 1997.

Hoberman, John. *Sport and Political Ideology.* Austin: University of Texas Press, 1984.

Hoffer, Richard. *Something in the Air: American Passion and Defiance in the 1968 Mexico City Olympics.* New York: 1st Free Press, 2009.

Horne, Gerald. *Black and Red: W. E. B. DuBois and the Afro-American Response to the Cold War, 1944–1963.* Albany: State University of New York Press, 1986.

———. *Communist Front? The Civil Rights Congress, 1946–1956.* Rutherford, N.J.: Fairleigh Dickinson University Press, 1988.

———. *The Fire This Time: The Watts Uprising and the 1960s.* Charlottesville: University Press of Virginia, 1995.

Houlihan, Barrie. *Sport and International Politics.* New York: Harvester Wheatsheaf, 1994.

Hunt, Michael. *Ideology and U.S. Foreign Policy.* New Haven, Conn.: Yale University Press, 2009.

Hunt, Thomas. "American Sport Policy and the Cultural Cold War: The Lyndon B. Johnson Presidential Years." *Journal of Sport History* 33 (Fall 2006): 273–97.

———. "Countering the Soviet Threat in the Olympic Medals Race." *International Journal of the History of Sport* 24 (June 2007): 796–818.

Jabbar, Kareem Abdul. *Giant Steps.* New York: Bantam Books, 1985.

Johnson, Rafer. *The Best That I Can Be: An Autobiography.* New York: Doubleday, 1998.

Joyce, Walter. *The Propaganda Gap.* New York: Harper and Row, 1963.

Kahn, Roger. *The Era, 1947–1957: When the Yankees, Giants, and Dodgers Ruled the World.* New York: Bison Books, 2002.

Kaplan, Amy, and Donald E. Pease. *Cultures of United States Imperialism.* Durham, N.C.: Duke University Press, 1994.

Karch, John J. "How the Soviet Union Exploits Sports." *American Legion Magazine,* February 1962, 22–23, 47–48.

Kelley, Robin D. G. "'But a Local Phase of a World Problem': Black History's Global Vision, 1883–1950." *Journal of American History* (December 1999): 1045–77.

———. *Race Rebels: Culture, Politics, and the Black Working Class.* New York: Free Press, 1996.

Kennedy, John F. "The Soft American." *Sports Illustrated,* December 20, 1960, 15–17.

Kertzer, David I. *Ritual, Politics, and Power.* New Haven, Conn.: Yale University Press, 1989.

Keys, Barbara J. *Globalizing Sport: National Rivalry and International Community in the 1930s.* Cambridge, Mass.: Harvard University Press, 2006.

Kimche, David. *The Afro-Asian Movement: Ideology and Foreign Policy of the Third World.* Jerusalem: Israel Universities Press, 1973.

Klein, Christina. *Cold War Orientalism: Asia in the Middlebrow Imagination, 1945–1961.* Berkeley and Los Angeles: University of California Press, 2003.

Knee, Stuart. "Jim Crow Strikes Out: Branch Rickey and the Struggle for Integration in American Baseball." *Culture, Sport, Society* 6 (Summer–Autumn 2003): 71–87.

Krenn, Michael L. *Black Diplomacy: African Americans and the State Department, 1945–1969.* New York: M. E. Sharpe, 1999.

———, ed. *Race and U.S. Foreign Policy from the Colonial Period to the Present: A Collection of Essays.* New York: Garland Press, 1998.

Krzemienski, Ed. "On the Initial Sack: Goose Tatum—Two-Sport Star." *Nine: A Journal of Baseball History and Culture* 14 (Spring 2006): 59–67.

Kuisel, Richard. *Seducing the French: The Dilemma of Americanization.* Berkeley and Los Angeles: University of California Press, 1997.

LaFeber, Walter. *Michael Jordan and the New Global Capitalism.* New York: W. W. Norton, 2002.

Lanctot, Neil. *Negro League Baseball: The Rise and Ruin of a Black Institution.* Philadelphia: University of Pennsylvania Press, 2004.

Latham, Michael. *Modernization as Ideology: American Social Science and "Nation Building" in the Kennedy Era.* Chapel Hill: University of North Carolina Press, 2000.

Lauren, Paul Gordon. *Power and Prejudice: The Politics and Diplomacy of Racial Discrimination.* Boulder, Colo.: Westview Press, 1988.

Layton, Azza Salama. *International Politics and Civil Rights Policies in the United States, 1941–1960.* New York: Cambridge University Press, 2000.

Lemon, Meadowlark. *Meadowlark.* Nashville: Thomas Nelson, 1987.

Lewis, David Levering. *W. E. B. DuBois: The Fight for Equality and the American Century, 1919–1963.* New York: Macmillan, 2000.

Lipsky, Richard. *How We Play the Game: Why Sports Dominate American Life.* Boston: Beacon Press, 1981.

Lipsyte, Robert. *Sportsworld: An American Dreamland.* New York: Quadrangle Books, 1975.

Lomax, Michael. "Bedazzle Them with Brilliance, Bamboozle Them with Bull: Harry Edwards, Black Power, and the Revolt of the Black Athlete Revisited." In *Sports and the Racial Divide: African American and Latino Experience in an Era of Change,* ed. Michael Lomax. Jackson: University Press of Mississippi, 2008.

Lombardo, Ben. "The Harlem Globetrotters and the Perpetuation of the Black Stereotype." *Physical Educator* 35 (May 1978): 60–63.

Luce, Henry R. *The American Century.* New York: Farrar and Rinehart, 1941.

Malcolm X, with Alex Haley. *The Autobiography of Malcolm X*. New York: African American Images, 1987.

Mandell, Richard D. *The Nazi Olympics*. New York: Macmillan, 1971.

Marable, Manning. *Race, Reform, and Rebellion: The Second Reconstruction in Black America, 1945–1990*. 2nd ed. Jackson: University Press of Mississippi, 1991.

Matusow, Allen. *The Unraveling of America: A History of Liberalism in the 1960s*. New York: Harper Torchbooks, 1984.

May, Elaine Tyler. *Homeward Bound: American Families in the Cold War Era*. New York: Basic Books, 1988.

Menville, Chuck. *The Harlem Globetrotters: Fifty Years of Fun and Games*. New York: D. McKay, 1978.

Meriwether, James H. *Proudly We Can Be Africans: Black Americans and Africa, 1935–1961*. Chapel Hill: University of North Carolina Press, 2002.

Michener, James. *Sports in America*. New York: Random House, 1976.

Montville, Leigh. "Bill Russell." *Sports Illustrated*, September 19, 1994.

Ninkovich, Frank A. *The Diplomacy of Ideas: U.S. Foreign Policy and Cultural Relations, 1938–1950*. Cambridge: Cambridge University Press, 1981.

Osgood, Kenneth. *Total Cold War: Eisenhower's Secret Propaganda Battle at Home and Abroad*. Lawrence: University Press of Kansas, 2008.

———. "Total Cold War: U.S. Propaganda in the Free World, 1953–1960." Ph.D. diss., University of California, Santa Barbara, 2001.

Pauley, Garth. *The Modern Presidency and Civil Rights: Rhetoric on Race from Roosevelt to Nixon*. College Station: Texas A&M University Press, 2001.

Pells, Richard. *Not Like Us: How Europeans Have Loved, Hated, and Transformed American Culture since World War II*. New York: Basic Books, 1998.

Peppard, Victor, and James Riordan. *Playing Politics: Soviet Sport Diplomacy to 1992*. Greenwich, Conn.: JAI Press, 1993.

Plummer, Brenda Gayle. *Rising Wind: Black Americans and U.S. Foreign Affairs, 1935–1960*. Chapel Hill: University of North Carolina Press, 1996.

———, ed. *Window on Freedom: Race, Civil Rights, and Foreign Affairs, 1945–1988*. Chapel Hill: University of North Carolina Press, 2003.

Poiger, Uta G. *Jazz, Rock, and Rebels: Cold War Politics and American Culture in a Divided Germany*. Berkeley and Los Angeles: University of California Press, 2000.

Pope, S. W. *Sporting Traditions in the American Imagination, 1876–1926*. New York: Oxford University Press, 1997.

Prevots, Naima. *Dance for Export: Cultural Diplomacy and the Cold War*. Middletown, Conn.: Wesleyan University Press, 2001.

Rampersad, Arnold. *Jackie Robinson: A Biography*. New York: Alfred A. Knopf, 1997.

Rayl, Susan. "The New York Renaissance Professional Black Basketball Team." Ph.D. diss., Pennsylvania State University, 1996.

Remnick, David. *King of the World: Muhammad Ali and the Rise of an American Hero*. New York: Vintage Books, 1998.

Richmond, Yale. *Cultural Exchange and the Cold War: Raising the Iron Curtain*. University Park: Pennsylvania State University Press, 2003.

Riley, Russell. *The Presidency and the Politics of Racial Inequality: Nation-Keeping from 1831 to 1965*. New York: Columbia University Press, 1999.

Riordan, James. "The Role of Sport in Soviet Foreign Policy." *International Journal* 43 (Autumn 1988): 570–79.

———. *Soviet Sport: Background to the Olympics*. New York: New York University Press, 1980.

———. *Sport, Politics, and Communism*. Manchester: Manchester University Press / St. Martin's Press, 1991.

———. *Sport in Soviet Society: Development of Sport and Physical Education in Russia and the USSR*. Cambridge: Cambridge University Press, 1977.

———. *Sport under Communism: The USSR, Czechoslovakia, the GDR, China, Cuba*. Montreal: McGill-Queen's University Press, 1978.

Riordan, James, and Arnd Krüger. *The International Politics of Sport in the 20th Century*. New York: Routledge, 1999

Roberts, John W. *From Trickster to Badman: The Black Folk Hero in Slavery and Freedom*. Philadelphia: University of Pennsylvania Press, 1990.

Rogosin, Donn. *Invisible Men: Life in Baseball's Negro Leagues*. New York: Atheneum, 1983.

Romano, Renee. "No Diplomatic Immunity: African Diplomats, the State Department, and Civil Rights, 1961–1964." *Journal of American History* 87 (September 2000): 546–79.

Rosenberg, Emily S. *Spreading the American Dream: American Economic and Cultural Expansion, 1890–1945*. New York: Hill and Wang, 1982.

Rowley, Hazel. *Richard Wright: The Life and Times*. New York: Macrae Books, 2001.

Russell, Bill. *Go Up for Glory*. New York: Berkley Medallion Books, 1966.

Russell, Bill, and Taylor Branch. *Second Wind*. New York: Basic Books, 1976.

Sammons, Jeffrey. *Beyond the Ring: The Role of Boxing in American Society*. Urbana: University of Illinois Press, 1990.

Saunders, Frances Stonor. *The Cultural Cold War: The CIA and the World of Arts and Letters*. New York: New Press, 1999.

Savage, Barbara. *Broadcasting Freedom: Radio, War, and the Politics of Race, 1938–1948*. Chapel Hill: University of North Carolina Press, 1999.

Scott, Jack. *The Athletic Revolution*. New York: Free Press, 1971.

Senn, Alfred E. *Power, Politics, and the Olympic Games*. Champaign, Ill.: Human Kinetics, 1999.

Shepherd, George Jr., ed. *Racial Influences on American Foreign Policy*. New York: Basic Books, 1970.

Simons, William. "Jackie Robinson and the American Mind: Journalistic Impressions of the Reintegration of Baseball." *Journal of Sport History* 12 (Spring 1985): 39–64.

Singh, Nikhil Pal. *Black Is a Country: Race and the Unfinished Struggle for Democracy*. Cambridge, Mass.: Harvard University Press, 2004.

Sitkoff, Harvard. *The Struggle for Black Equality, 1954–1992*. New York: Hill and Wang, 1993.

Smith, Marshall. "Basketball's Court Jester." *Life,* March 1953.

Smith, Maureen. "Identity and Citizenship: African American Athletes, Sport, and the Freedom Struggles of the 1960s." Ph.D. diss., Ohio State University, 1998.

Smith, Red. *The Red Smith Reader.* New York: Random House, 1982.

Smith, Ronald. "The Paul Robeson: Jackie Robinson Saga and a Political Collision." *Journal of Sport History* 6 (Summer 1979): 5–27.

Smith, Tommie, and David Steele. *Silent Gesture: The Autobiography of Tommie Smith.* Philadelphia: Temple University Press, 2008.

Southern, David. *Gunnar Myrdal and Black-White Relations: The Use and Abuse of "An American Dilemma," 1944–1969.* Baton Rouge: Louisiana State University Press, 1987.

Stephens, Oren. *Facts to a Candid World.* Stanford, Calif.: Stanford University Press, 1955.

Stout, Glenn. "Tryout and Fallout: Race, Jackie Robinson, and the Red Sox." *Massachusetts Historical Review* 6 (2004): 11–37.

Thomas, Damion. "Around the World: Problematizing the Harlem Globetrotters as Cold War Warriors." *Sport in Society* 14 (June 2011): 778–91.

———. "'The Good Negroes': African-American Athletes and the Cultural Cold War." Ph.D. diss., University of California, Los Angeles, 2002.

———. "'Is It Really Ever Just a Game?'" *Journal of Sport and Social Issues* 29 (August 2005): 358–63.

———. "Let the Games Begin: Sport, U.S. Race Relations, and Cold War Politics." In *America's Game(s): A Critical Anthropology of Sport,* ed. Benjamin Eastman et al. London: Routledge Press, 2007.

———. "Playing the 'Race Card': U.S. Foreign Policy and the Integration of Sports." In *East Plays West: Sport and the Cold War,* ed. Stephen Wagg and David Andrews. London: Routledge Press, 2006.

———. "The Quiet Militant: Arthur Ashe and Black Athletic Activism." In *Outside the Shadows: A Biographical History of the Black Athlete,* ed. D. Wiggins, 275–90. Fayetteville: University of Arkansas Press, 2006.

———. "Touring for the Nation? African-American Athletes and the Cultural Cold War." In *The Physical Cultural Studies Reader: A Constitutive Anthology,* ed. Michael Silk and David Andrews. Philadelphia: Temple University Press, 2009.

Tygiel, Jules. *Baseball's Great Experiment: Jackie Robinson and His Legacy.* New York: Vintage Books, 1984.

———, ed. *The Jackie Robinson Reader.* New York: Dutton Books, 1997.

Van Deburg, William. *Black Camelot: African-American Culture Heroes in Their Times, 1960–1980.* Chicago: University of Chicago Press, 1997.

Vaughn, James. *The Failure of American and British Propaganda in the Middle East, 1945–1957: Unconquerable Minds.* New York: Palgrave Macmillan, 2005.

Von Eschen, Penny. *Race against Empire: Black Americans and Anti-Colonialism, 1937–1957.* Ithaca, N.Y.: Cornell University Press, 1997.

———. *Satchmo Blows Up the World: Jazz Ambassadors Play the Cold War.* Cambridge, Mass.: Harvard University Press, 2006.

Wagnleitner, Reinhold. *Coca-Colonization and the Cold War: The Cultural Mission of the United States in Austria after the Second World War.* Chapel Hill: University of North Carolina Press, 1994.

Wagnleitner, Reinhold, and Elaine Tyler May. *Here, There, and Everywhere: The Foreign Politics of American Popular Culture.* Hanover: University of New Hampshire Press, 2000.

Wang, Jessica. *American Science in an Age of Anxiety: Scientists, Anticommunism, and the Cold War.* Chapel Hill: University of North Carolina Press, 1998.

Watkins, Mel. *On the Real Side: A History of African American Comedy.* New York: Lawrence Hill Books, 1999.

Weisbrot, Robert. *Freedom Bound: A History of America's Civil Rights Movement.* New York: Plume Books, 1991.

Westad, Odd Arne. *The Global Cold War: Third World Interventions and the Making of Our Times.* Cambridge: Cambridge University Press, 2005.

Wetterhahn, Joshua. "Saperstein's Sambos: Examining the Harlem Globetrotters' Paradox during the 1950s." Senior honors thesis, Northwestern University, 2000.

Whitfield, Mal. *Beyond the Finish Line.* Washington, D.C.: Whitfield Foundation, 2002.

Whitfield, Stephen J. *The Culture of the Cold War.* Baltimore: Johns Hopkins University Press, 1996.

Wiggins, David K. *Glory Bound: Black Athletes in a White America.* Syracuse, N.Y.: Syracuse University Press, 1997.

———. "'The Year of Awakening': Black Athletes, Racial Unrest, and the Civil Rights Movement of 1968." *International Journal of the History of Sport* 9 (August 1992): 188–208.

Witherspoon, Kevin. *Before the Eyes of the World: Mexico and the 1968 Olympic Game.* DeKalb: Northern Illinois University Press, 2008.

———. "Protest at the Pyramid: The 1968 Mexico City Olympics and the Politicization of the Olympic Games." Ph.D. diss., Florida State University, 2003.

Wofford, Harris. *Of Kennedys and Kings: Making Sense of the Sixties.* Pittsburgh: University of Pittsburgh Press, 1992.

Wolf, David. *Foul! The Connie Hawkins Story.* New York: Holt, Rinehart, and Winston, 1972.

Woods, Jeff. *Black Struggle, Red Scare: Segregation and Anti-Communism in the South, 1948–1968.* Baton Rouge: Louisiana State University Press, 2004.

Wright, Nathan, Jr. "The Crisis Which Bred Black Power." In *The Black Power Revolt: A Collection of Essays,* ed. Floyd Barbour. New York: Collier Books, 1968.

Xia, Yafend. "China's Elite Politics and Sino-American Rapprochement, January 1969–February 1972." *Journal of Cold War Studies* 8 (Fall 2006): 3–28.

Zimmerman, Jonathan. "Beyond Double Consciousness: Black Peace Corps Volunteers in Africa, 1961–1971." *Journal of American History* 82 (December 1995): 999–1028.

Zinkoff, David, with Edgar Williams. *Around the World with the Harlem Globetrotters.* Philadelphia: MacRae Smith, 1953.

Zirin, David. *What's My Name, Fool? Sports and Resistance in the United States.* New York: Haymarket, 2005.

Index

Damion L. Thomas is Museum Curator of Sports at the Smithsonian National Museum of African American History and Culture.

Sport and Society

A Sporting Time: New York City and the Rise of Modern Athletics, 1820–70
  Melvin L. Adelman
Sandlot Seasons: Sport in Black Pittsburgh   *Rob Ruck*
West Ham United: The Making of a Football Club   *Charles Korr*
Beyond the Ring: The Role of Boxing in American Society   *Jeffrey T. Sammons*
John L. Sullivan and His America   *Michael T. Isenberg*
Television and National Sport: The United States and Britain   *Joan M. Chandler*
The Creation of American Team Sports: Baseball and Cricket, 1838–72
  George B. Kirsch
City Games: The Evolution of American Urban Society and the Rise of Sports
  Steven A. Riess
The Brawn Drain: Foreign Student-Athletes in American Universities   *John Bale*
The Business of Professional Sports   *Edited by Paul D. Staudohar and*
  James A. Mangan
Fritz Pollard: Pioneer in Racial Advancement   *John M. Carroll*
A View from the Bench: The Story of an Ordinary Player on a Big-Time Football
  Team (*formerly* Go Big Red! The Story of a Nebraska Football Player)
  George Mills
Sport and Exercise Science: Essays in the History of Sports Medicine
  Edited by Jack W. Berryman and Roberta J. Park
Minor League Baseball and Local Economic Development   *Arthur T. Johnson*
Harry Hooper: An American Baseball Life   *Paul J. Zingg*
Cowgirls of the Rodeo: Pioneer Professional Athletes   *Mary Lou LeCompte*
Sandow the Magnificent: Eugen Sandow and the Beginnings of Bodybuilding
  David Chapman
Big-Time Football at Harvard, 1905: The Diary of Coach Bill Reid
  Edited by Ronald A. Smith
Leftist Theories of Sport: A Critique and Reconstruction   *William J. Morgan*
Babe: The Life and Legend of Babe Didrikson Zaharias   *Susan E. Cayleff*
Stagg's University: The Rise, Decline, and Fall of Big-Time Football at Chicago
  Robin Lester
Muhammad Ali, the People's Champ   *Edited by Elliott J. Gorn*
People of Prowess: Sport, Leisure, and Labor in Early Anglo-America
  Nancy L. Struna
The New American Sport History: Recent Approaches and Perspectives
  Edited by S. W. Pope
Making the Team: The Cultural Work of Baseball Fiction   *Timothy Morris*
Making the American Team: Sport, Culture, and the Olympic Experience
  Mark Dyreson
Viva Baseball! Latin Major Leaguers and Their Special Hunger
  Samuel O. Regalado
Touching Base: Professional Baseball and American Culture in the
  Progressive Era (rev. ed.)   *Steven A. Riess*

Red Grange and the Rise of Modern Football   *John M. Carroll*
Golf and the American Country Club   *Richard J. Moss*
Extra Innings: Writing on Baseball   *Richard Peterson*
Global Games   *Maarten Van Bottenburg*
The Sporting World of the Modern South   *Edited by Patrick B. Miller*
The End of Baseball As We Knew It: The Players Union, 1960–81   *Charles P. Korr*
Rocky Marciano: The Rock of His Times   *Russell Sullivan*
Saying It's So: A Cultural History of the Black Sox Scandal   *Daniel A. Nathan*
The Nazi Olympics: Sport, Politics, and Appeasement in the 1930s
    Edited by Arnd Krüger and William Murray
The Unlevel Playing Field: A Documentary History of the African American
    Experience in Sport   *David K. Wiggins and Patrick B. Miller*
Sports in Zion: Mormon Recreation, 1890–1940   *Richard Ian Kimball*
Sweet William: The Life of Billy Conn   *Andrew O'Toole*
Sports in Chicago   *Edited by Elliot J. Gorn*
The Chicago Sports Reader   *Edited by Steven A. Riess and Gerald R. Gems*
College Football and American Culture in the Cold War Era   *Kurt Edward Kemper*
The End of Amateurism in American Track and Field   *Joseph M. Turrini*
Benching Jim Crow: The Rise and Fall of the Color Line in Southern
    College Sports, 1890–1980   *Charles H. Martin*
Pay for Play: A History of Big-Time College Athletic Reform   *Ronald A. Smith*
Globetrotting: African American Athletes and Cold War Politics
    Damion L. Thomas

Reprint Editions

The Nazi Olympics   *Richard D. Mandell*
Sports in the Western World (2d ed.)   *William J. Baker*
Jesse Owens: An American Life   *William J. Baker*

The University of Illinois Press
is a founding member of the
Association of American University Presses.

———————————————————————————

University of Illinois Press
1325 South Oak Street
Champaign, IL 61820-6903
www.press.uillinois.edu